THE COME'ERE
FROM WALES TO
CHINCOTEAGUE ISLAND

WRITTEN AND ILLUSTRATED BY
DANIEL P.T. THOMAS

TABLE OF CONTENTS

DEDICATION

My grandmother was called "May Spain." Her husband was a director of MacAndrews and Company based in Seville whose major export was oranges. At the beginning of the Second World War, the British government asked my grandfather if he would help smuggle British agents on the ships from neutral Spain. Grannie would be told when and where to meet someone who needed to be transported home. Escapees knew to look for the woman in the silk scarf and they consequently named her "May Spain". During the war, she smuggled over 600 government agents, military personnel, and the Rumanian royal family back to Britain from Seville. Her story was never told, as no one ever wrote a book about her amazing life, despite being asked to do so by many of us in her family. This book is, therefore, dedicated to my maternal grandmother, Anne May Evans, who was an amazing unsung war hero. She never did receive the OBE that she earned, because the plane carrying the recommendation letter was shot down over Spain. She subsequently lived to age 100. When the centenarian birthday card arrived from the queen, my brother opened it. He remarked how nice it was of the queen to write to her. She commented back, "She never signed that; it was printed." Sharp as a tack until her final days.

Grannie always supported and encouraged me in whatever I pursued so she was very special to me. She noticed my love of art early and complimented me every time I created a painting. Her favourite was a pen and ink drawing of Berlin. It reminded her of a lovely visit and it made her think of me. Throughout my life, Grannie was always there as someone I could go to when I needed support and love.

She was honest and the only one who expressed her love when I was young, more so than anyone else. She never judged me, would often refer to me as Dan "bach," a term of endearment in Welsh, and many times was the one person who believed in me.

PREFACE

On Chincoteague Island, a person who is not born and raised here is called a Come'ere. I am the ultimate "Come'ere".

This book shares how I found myself—a journey that (for now) ends on Chincoteague. I have had to summon courage as I faced numerous challenges that derailed my life plans. My journey has involved picking up jigsaw pieces along the way to see which fits into my goals. You might be on a similar journey, seeking your own sense of belonging and meaning in your life, or the desire to escape the daily humdrum and stress of crowded cities. I invite you to join me in my search for confidence, recognition, and a place where I feel I belong.

When I was eight, I couldn't wait to read my weekly Victor comic extoling army life and then play with my little soldiers, laying out great armies on the bedroom floor. I was brought up in a military life with its attending discipline. Boarding school taught me to conform and accept without objection the expectations and the way I was treated.

I was not born with a silver spoon in my mouth, but I was raised in a privileged environment as the son of a British army clergyman whose career was on an exalted trajectory. I received an excellent education, and I hobnobbed with the social elite. I even brushed shoulders with the Royal Family.

Naturally, I dreamed of being a leader someday. When that dream exploded, I had to regroup. I had to step into the void in search of a new career and life path. I was shell-shocked; would other depth charges laid in my earlier life detonate later?

I have also had two fathers, one I never knew and one who didn't provide the love I so needed. Consequently, I have had a 'dadless' upbringing. For those readers who have had a similar experience of an absent Dad, my story provides encouragement and the need to persevere with one's own self-belief.

The difficult relationship with my stepfather and a tough schooling away from home are experiences I still struggle with. Such emotional pains never go away. They lie in our subconscious to shape who we are. The collective sum of these experiences either knock us back or allow us to learn and grow. Some journeys are smooth and others not. I have lived with and learned from both sides of the class divide.

I have lived on two continents. I emigrated to the USA where I learned the UK and USA are two countries separated by a common language.

"Humblebrag" is a word in the English urban dictionary that means to subtly let others know how fantastic your life is while undercutting it with a bit of self-effacing humour or "woe is me" gloss. Since I am Welsh and used to writing in a self-deprecating way, the reader will notice this style earlier in my book, but as I transition to the USA, I have strived to write with a much bolder, direct approach.

I hope you enjoy my journey and find encouragement from the way I dealt with my struggles that may speak to your own life's experiences.

1

JUST FOLLOW THE RULES

My Tuckbox

I was eight years old in early January 1967 when I returned to Haileybury Junior School after the Christmas break. The weather was overcast and just above freezing, so it was no wonder we boys didn't want to go outside for gym.

We entered the changing rooms where Mr. Sampson, a tall imposing gym teacher, shouted at us.

"Get undressed quickly, wrap your towels around your waists, and form a line by the door. The swimming pool isn't that far, so you won't freeze."

When I heard Mr. Sampson's orders, giant alarm bells rang in my head, and my hands shook uncontrollably. I looked around the room at the other boys' faces for some reassurance. Was I the only one who couldn't swim? Surely not. I was too shy to ask anyone as I didn't know them, having only joined the school in the fall. Weirdly enough, no one else seemed concerned, so we all peeled off our school uniforms to reveal our pale milky selves.

Out we marched single file. The pavement slabs beneath my bare feet were slippery and ice cold. Ordered to form a neat line at the far end of the pool, we wrapped our arms around our chests in a vain effort to preserve warmth, while our teeth chattered away above our trembling jaws. I noticed the depth marker on the edge of the pool read eight feet, and a silky mist rose from its dark green surface. Surely they weren't going to ask us to jump in? I was wrong. In a terrifying moment, Mr. Sampson yelled: "Throw your towels on the fence and everyone jump in and swim to the edge."

Ordered to leap into a freezing swimming pool when I couldn't even swim was petrifying. I will never forget the shock of sinking below the surface and paddling furiously in a panic trying to make it to the top. When I did, I saw my fellow students breaking the surface with ashen faces looking just like Edvard Munch's painting, *The Scream*: a sea of eight and nine-year-olds struggling for air and trying to make sense of the madness. Luckily I came up, kicking and spluttering, near the pool's steel handrails. I could see now I wasn't the only boy who didn't know how to swim. Most of us clung to the sides for dear life. It might have been a slight comfort had I not been so terrified—and so very cold.

Someone yelled that one tiny boy was going under again, so the teacher stretched out a long pole for him to grab onto.

Then he tossed some white foam flotation devices into the pool.

"Grab a float and swim into the middle of the pool!" he yelled.

My float was so paltry it hardly kept my head above water, so I stayed as close to the edge as I could. So did everyone else, eyes wide open in terror. One hand clung to a float while the other stayed glued to the slippery wall.

2

The teacher calmly strutted along the edge, stepping on the kids' hands while he shouted, "Do as I say. Swim out into the middle."

Every week from that day on we were marched out by the gym teacher and lined up at the edge of the pool. Typical of privately supported English "public" schools of that day, this was a rite of passage we had to endure. It was the start of many I would experience until I was eighteen, an entire upbringing, not just a one-off.

The terror of that incident remains crystal clear in my memory, as I expect it does for many others as well. Haileybury's so-called "character building" was the norm in the 1960s, as thousands of boys around Britain experienced similar treatment in public schools.

It might interest the reader to know that British private schools are known as "public" schools because they were the first schools to be open to anyone who could pay, not just the upper class. Nevertheless, the cost of the education delivers a significant snob appeal. (What Americans call "public" schools are known as "state" schools in England.)

Joy Schaverien, a well-respected psychotherapist in the UK, in 2015 published *Boarding School Syndrome*. Based on extensive research with ex-boarders, she discusses the enduring psychological effects of this trauma. Numerous therapists, she writes, fail to recognise the significance of boarding school in their patients' problems because such an education is still regarded as a character-forming privilege.

When I first arrived at Haileybury, I was struck by the school's grand setting. A long pebbled driveway wound its way up through the grounds and then through a walled entrance with statues on each side. The drive led to the main giant schoolhouse, a vast, gothic edifice set in well-manicured grounds with numerous aged cedar trees whose branches splayed out, and hardly hovered above the ground.

Despite its grandeur, the school had an air of foreboding so that even Count Dracula would have immediately felt at home. I am sure its location was intentionally set far enough away from the public that no one could hear you scream. It would also take quite a while until you reached the real world if you chose to run away.

My father was a military chaplain, and in his opinion, sending me off to Haileybury, where many army officers sent their children, was the perfect way to build my "character," and get a well-rounded English education while he was stationed in Germany. In fact, it was more like privileged abandonment to an eight-year-old whose parents were pricey airplane rides and phone calls away.

I had a very strict upbringing, and I suppose this should have prepared me for the discipline of boarding school. My father was modest in stature, but his voice was loud, and what he said my brothers and I had to follow. Instruction rained down on us constantly. He had definite table manner rules such as not holding our knives like a pencil and keeping elbows off the table. We had to wear slippers at all times in the house.

While his parents were warm and affectionate with us boys, I could tell that my father had been heavily disciplined by the way they spoke to him. Being an only child must have been tough for him. The rigid environment my father grew up in affected and moulded how he fathered us.

I can now see that his situation was rather like that of Prince Charles. Charles' childhood was lonely, too. His formal, remote mother had been prone to such unmaternal moves as leaving her toddler son at home while she travelled on an extended business trip around the world. It was well documented that the Duke of Edinburgh despised his son's softness as a sniveling weakness. He was from the "no crying" school of parenting. His method of shouting at Charles in front of company reminded me of how my father spoke to me. Maybe it was a generational thing from times gone by. Viewers of the television series *The Crown* will know that Charles had a rough time at Gordonstoun School, a very severe institution in northeast Scotland.

My mother, on the other hand, was much softer and would often argue with my father about his discipline and the consequences he used. She was a well-dressed and stylish mum who had a passion for music, especially opera, and played the piano. She understood my creative side early on.

Mum had seen more of the world, having spent her youth in Seville. But she didn't know at the time what she was sending us off to. Before I left for Haileybury, she had spent weeks sewing my nametags into every article of clothing, a school requirement. Even recently I came across a school sock with the initials 'DPT Thomas' in blue ink. It made me think of all the piles of neatly folded clothing she once laid out on my bed. A specific number of each item was required by the school.

My parents found a black antique trunk with a lock on it so I could store my belongings below my bed in the dorm; it was just like those you see in the Harry Potter movies. Now that I look back, I think I lived through my own version of Hogwarts back in the late 60s and early 70s—but without the magic.

My brother Steve also went to Haileybury. Steve is three years younger than I, much stockier and not as tall. He was born with his esophagus going into his lungs and a few other complications. This meant he had to undergo some serious surgery when he was a baby and spent many months in the hospital. As a result, he grew up as a rather detached, tough, and resilient kid. He was often a pest and rather ornery with me, so we used to fight regularly, as brothers do. I once tried to poke him in the eye with a pencil but fortunately missed, leaving only a dark blue gash below his eye.

Steve and I both took back to school what was called a tuck box. Mine had 'DPT Thomas' stencilled in heavy black letters on the top. Most boys came to school with one of these to keep all our prized possessions in a safe place. We each had our own locks for them. There was an unspoken law that no one had the right to open your tuck box except you: no teacher, matron, or even the headmaster. I stuffed my box with my own favourite supplies, including copies of my best Victor comics and some of my soldiers and model kits. We kept our tuck boxes below our desks in the study room.

At Haileybury, I was called Thomas One; Steve was called Thomas Two. My youngest brother Matthew hadn't been thought of yet and would later have to suffer being called Thomas Three. A long tradition in public schools, some unfortunate students were referred to as Williams Four or Five as they had multiple brothers. Consequently, it all got a little ridiculous some days hearing the masters' call after boys and trying to distinguish which was which.

Because my father was stationed in Germany, half terms or (short holidays) I spent at the homes of other classmates' families. This should have been exciting, but it was upsetting for me as my parents didn't want to fly me home. I felt very alone.

At least I didn't have to go through the upheaval of saying goodbye several times during the term like the England-based boarders did. When they returned to school on Sunday nights after short exeats[1], teachers herded students into the enormous television room. The lights were turned out so that all the homesick students could cry their eyes out without being seen. Often I couldn't hear the film because of the constant whimpering.

When one was homesick, the only option was to call home from the one call box on the ground floor in the main corridor. On Sunday nights, I got to call home. Since my parents were in Germany, I couldn't call for long. I had to feed so many coins into the slot that I could barely keep up with the voice on the phone asking for more.

I would shove a handful of coins into the phone and wait for Mum to answer. The minute I heard her voice, it was everything I could do to keep from crying. Most calls were about a recent ailment. One could never show emotions at Haileybury, so I sought comfort from my parents convincing them that I was

---

[1]   A period of absence from a boarding school.

coming down with a potential health problem and provoking concern to get their attention. No doubt, my father was rolling his eyes as he heard my voice crack as I tried to hold back the tears. I, of course, was oblivious to my desperate strategy to get their attention.

Having my parents worry about me made me feel better in a strange way. I would call my mother to tell her how horrible Mr. Backhouse was. He was my math teacher who put the fear of God into me. Mr. Backhouse wasn't physically imposing but looked like Heinrich Himmler, one of Hitler's generals from my history textbook. He didn't have much hair and wore small rimless glasses that covered his piercing, beady eyes. Thankfully, he didn't have Himmler's tiny moustache below his nose. There was no kindness in his look.

In his classroom, we had to place our arms straight out in front of us on the desk with our fingers folded downwards into a fist with our knuckles exposed. Mr. Backhouse asked questions while gently slapping a steel ruler into his palm as he paced around the classroom. We shook nervously, waiting for his temper to boil over. One never knew when Mr. Backhouse would strike a boy's knuckles with his ruler if he got an answer wrong.

When he struck me, a throbbing pain jolted through my hand and flooded up my arm. I let out a great gushing gasp. The pain reverberated every few seconds like waves up my arm. I wanted to put my hand in my mouth to soothe the pain, as my knuckles felt like they were on fire. It was everything I could do to keep from crying out. But one took his punishment quietly; cries were discouraged as this made it worse for us.

Stars were issued for behaving well and stripes for unacceptable. If one got too many stripes it was a visit for a caning, which was still permitted in schools in the early 1970s. Luckily I wasn't caned much, but I will never forget the stinging sensation and the red welts that stayed for days after, even though we rubbed Vaseline on our backsides after the event. One time I got away with sticking part of my Victor comic down my pants to lessen the pain. It was one of several survival skills I had to think of in school.

My mother never believed what I told her on the phone about Mr. Backhouse and the corporal punishments. Maybe she was in denial, or maybe she knew there was nothing she could do about it.

I wrote home practically every week. I always looked for some praise, but my parents weren't around to give it. I received only the odd letter from my mother. My father always thought Mum was too soft on me, so this dissuaded her from writing. Every letter I have today from that period sings my own praises about my grades so that my parents knew how well I was doing. No letter could contain emotions or complaints. The teachers would inspect our letters home, and if we complained, we were punished.

Our matron could have been a front row forward on most rugby teams—full, round like an apple and capable of holding you down with one arm. A middle-aged and a rather plain woman with dark hair and huge breasts, she had a German-helmet-shaped hairstyle and wore a dark blue nurse's outfit with a small, clear-faced watch fastened above the pocket over her huge right breast. Her loud voice boomed around the building so you heard her well before she appeared. Her bosom was so huge I was sure she couldn't see her toes when she stood up. We couldn't see her face if we stood directly below her—which was very unsettling. She was responsible for our general well-being at school, basic medical needs, and maintaining order in the dorms. She was very unsympathetic if we ever had a cut; she would slam the drenched antiseptic cotton wool on to our wounds while giving us an awful icy stare while we screamed out in pain.

Matron had the power to send you to Mr. Kemp, our housemaster, for anything you did wrong. Traipsing down to him in your pyjamas in the evening never ended in a good way and often resulted in a caning. His creepy approach in spongy shoes earned him the nickname 'Bungee'. His wispy white warlock hair and very big red lips gave you quite a surprise if you ran into him in the corridor.

The long stone bathroom building was unheated and freezing cold as if one were outside. Because there were no doors on the boy's toilets, you watched someone else do their business while you waited. I can't fathom this today, but back then it was part of what we were used to. The only plus point was at least the seat was warm when it was your turn.

Bath time every other night was exciting because the assistant matrons washed our backs as we sat in individual bathtubs in an enormous room. The assistants were in their early twenties and often pretty in their white nurse uniforms. They were the total opposite of Matron: they always smiled and took pity on us, so we looked forward to our time with them. Boys would ask them to keep rubbing their backs in the hope the nurses lost the soap and had to delve into the murky water to find it. We never got a deep bath as they filled them only halfway, so our top halves were always shivering. I was too tall to lower myself down into the hot water, but some of the shorter boys managed it.

The fun ended back in the dormitory when Matron would appear seemingly from nowhere to watch us brush our teeth in cold water in the wash sinks at the far end of the dormitory. She then hovered menacingly over us while we got settled for bed.

Before lights-out, we had to kneel by our beds and relieve ourselves into an enamel chamber pot. For the twelve boys in the dormitory, there were only four chamber pots. We got into trouble many times because it was fun for us to use one chamber pot so it was full to the brim. The chamber lady would then get soaked when she pulled it out from underneath the bed in the morning. By this time the urine was putrid, musty, and stale, giving off a foul stench. I can't imagine a worse job for those poor chamber ladies.

When the door closed, the antics started in our dormitories. Matron roamed the halls, listening quietly outside for any sounds and bursting in to turn the lights on if she heard anything.

On one occasion when Matron surprised us, she found two boys in the same bed. We were at the age when we were exploring and experimenting with our sexuality. A lot of what happened was not appropriate. Playing "Kiss, Dare, Truth or Promise" was a risky prospect after lights-out if someone suggested it. One person had to kiss another boys' you-know-what, or their butt, and it had to be witnessed... ugh! The forfeits (such as being made to do extra chores) were grim, so one felt compelled to do it. It was again a rite of passage at Haileybury.

One night a boy announced to our dorm that he had a huge erection. Of course, everyone wanted to see it, so he used a torch to show a shadow of his achievement on the wall. We all giggled—it was huge and made us wonder why we couldn't achieve anything like that. He said it was because he was dreaming about one of the younger matrons who had washed his back earlier in the bath. The following morning someone discovered a giant carrot lying on the floor beside his bed, so he never tried that trick again.

One kindness we were allowed was to have our own teddy bears. I retrieved "Bongo" and "Bengo" from under my bed and tucked them in with me. When everyone had settled down and fallen to sleep I read my Victor comic with a torch[2] under my sheets. Only then was it safe to escape into my own world.

As time passed by we heard that some boys touched a few of the young matrons inappropriately. Consequently, the administrative staff began to add bromide to the tea urns we so enjoyed drinking from. This was so we didn't get too sexually active. I could only surmise that bromide was a sedative. We were only ten years old, for heaven's sakes!

When I first arrived at Haileybury, our milk came in glass bottles; I remember savouring the delicious cream off the top.

---

[2]   A flashlight

Then the bottles with cream disappeared, and we received miniature cartons with straws, which was a huge disappointment.

We ate a lot of stews with stringy meat that tasted rather sweet. I could have sworn it was horsemeat but it tasted okay with vegetables and potatoes mixed up. I became used to liver and onions with gravy and mash, which I can't believe I still miss today. The school food wasn't as lousy as gruel from Oliver Twist's days, so I survived.

I found it a joy to write with my first fountain pen with ink cartridges, rather than using a plastic ballpoint pen. Writing neatly with ink and the perfect nib was enjoyable, even if it was slower, and I created great cursive letters for my essays. Later I used a Parker pen I filled with ink from a glass bottle. As this presented some spillage problems, I switched back to cartridges.

When I played sport, I had no one to cheer me on. My father had been a great football player, but he never came to see me play. It would have boosted my self-confidence enormously had he even written to me to acknowledge my sport successes.

For me, daily life involved constant instruction with very few breaks. The one highlight each week was the opening of the tuck[3] shop when we would form an orderly line along the corridor to get our sweets. Our favourites were red and multi-coloured Gobstoppers and sherbet straws. After making our purchases we ran back to our sacred tuck boxes and stored away our stash, rationing ourselves to make it last another week.

One of my friends, Buxton, put a young starling in his tuck-box, and we all helped keep it alive. The starling would start squawking during quiet-time which occurred during "prep", which was study time. We all thought we would be found out and in trouble.

To survive the constant abuse by Mr. Backhouse in math and the weekly swimming trauma, I developed a protective

---

[3]   Candy or sweets

shell. I appeared confident on the outside, but I was very sensitive underneath. I longed to escape the corporal punishment and shouting. My Latin teacher, Mr. Collins, ran the Young Ornithologists Club, giving talks and conducting field trips to nature reserves. In it, I could let down my shell and connect with the real world. I also did some drawings of birds for the newsletter. I understand how author John Buxton found solace in studying the redstart when he was a prisoner in World War II and later wrote *The Redstart*, one of the finest natural history books of the twentieth century. Although I wasn't in prison at Haileybury, some days I sure felt like I was, and the club helped me devise my own mental escape if only for short times. I grew to enjoy birding, which I would pursue for the rest of my life.

Curiously, my escape from Haileybury came when Mr. Boddy, the headmaster, took me for an interview at Bloxham, a senior boarding school. Two months later, in March 1972, a letter came in the mail addressed to my father. It was from Mr. Seymour, the headmaster of Bloxham School who offered a place at the school in view of Mr. Boddy's support. Mr. Seymour noted that my test results showed just average ability and that I needed to put in a great deal of special effort to "plug some of the gaps," particularly in math.

Thankfully, Haileybury Junior School's emotional abuse of children ended when it closed in 1997. As a historically listed building, it was preserved and carved up into luxury flats, each worth a ton of money. Perhaps even today a couple sits on their sofa in one of those fine flats with no idea that once in that spot eight-year-old boys like me used to kneel and pee in a chamber pot before they went to bed.

2

GOING HOME

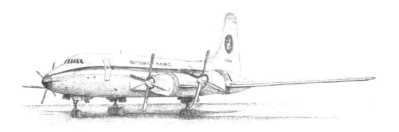

A Bristol 175 Britannia 102 Propeller Plane

The water always enchanted me—before my terrifying experiences in the swimming pool at Haileybury. When I was three, we lived in a beautiful home by the ocean in the secluded little seaside village of Borth-y-Gest. Overlooking the Black Rock Sands beach, our house was named *Cilan* (pronounced Kill-Ann), a Welsh word meaning *inlet*. Black Rock Sands can be dangerous at times. My grandfather told me about the treacherous quicksands, which could engulf you if you weren't careful.

The brightly coloured compact sailboats and workboats, some painted green and red like the Welsh flag, bobbed in the cove below. Golden teak trim on the wooden workboats shone in the sunshine. At low tide, they rested on their keels at forty-five degrees like tired men sleeping on deckchairs.

Borth-y-Gest, one mile west of Porthmadog, sits in a shallow bowl that sweeps down to a sheltered bay, with hidden sandy coves and cliffs. Organized rows of colourful Victorian houses lend the village much of its Victorian charm. Once a busy shipbuilding centre, Porthmadog was established as a slate-exporting port. Pilots could keep a watch for ships needing help from special houses, still known as "pilot houses", built at the mouth of the harbour. In years past, it was the departure point for crossings over the Glaslyn Estuary.

When I was just three, the story of the "Owl and the Pussy Cat" fascinated me. I would sit at my bedroom window reading my nursery rhyme book and watch the boats. My mother once told me that my first words were "Boat down there."

One picture in the book captivated me. As the owl and the pussycat sailed away, their pea green boat, with its enormous green sail, took me to places where I, too, could escape. I dreamed of finding a way out to the ocean in that pea green boat.

The boats bobbing up and down in the secluded bay below enthralled me. Coincidentally, a sailboat moored in the bay below our house had a green sail furled on its boom. I sometimes saw it beautifully unfurled in the afternoon sun out in the bay, but as the boat approached the cove again, whoever sailed it took the green sail down.

I imagined that such a boat would transport me to a place where the sea rules, with vast horizons dotted with tiny islands of wonder to explore. It would take me off my land-based feet to sense the movement of water, to a place where my world blurred as the sea blended with the vast sky. Perhaps this was prescient; today I own a boat that does just that for me on the water of the Eastern Shore of Virginia.

My father was a young vicar when we lived in Borth-y-Gest, but he wanted to pursue a career as an army chaplain, so we had to move away to a posting in Germany. It was a jolt to me to settle into an unfamiliar place far from the ocean. At the same time, I was diagnosed with scarlet fever, a serious disease in the 1960s. I remember my burning fever, a very sore red tongue, and being told I could die. Fortunately, I recovered.

As I tried to adjust to my new home in Germany, my parents decided to ship me off to Haileybury at just eight years old.

This separation caused a huge rupture in attachment to my parents. I had to live without love since I wasn't home much to get any. To survive the harsh environment of public school life, I became detached and a loner to shield myself. I needed that shield to survive emotionally. I am lucky I have been able to drop my shield over time so that I could begin to feel and be open to new experiences.

The discipline at Haileybury echoed at home but I can't blame my father for how he treated us. He was the only son in a strict Welsh family, which wasn't easy, and he followed the patterns of his own upbringing and how his parents had raised him. Hence he was very strict with us.

I remember most my father's loud voice. He ruled us with it. It wasn't a physical beating we got, but by God, if his voice got going, that was enough to send tremors through us all. My father told Mum that she spoiled us too much. He prevented her coming up to our rooms to console us when he was angry. Sometimes we would have to stay up there alone for hours after we had been chastised.

At times, my father made blatant fun of me. When I concentrated hard on something, I would stick out my tongue. I didn't even know I was doing it. He would point it out and say, "There he goes again." This embarrassment sometimes happened in public and continued for the rest of my father's life.

Once while disciplining Steve, my father said to him, "I will not have children in my house with no feet on their slippers," instead of "slippers on their feet." He was incensed when Steve snickered and sent him to his room for a long time. Eventually Mum called up to say Steve could come downstairs.

We boys had to conform to the dictum: "children should be seen but not heard." I remember this phrase so well. Years ago, children used to be viewed as a convenience and a nuisance. For the British upper class, a layer of nannies and nurses kept children from having much contact with their parents except on a formal basis until they were teenagers. It wasn't quite that extreme for us, but we had to behave.

We attended many formal army events where we had to be well mannered, especially at the post-church curry lunches held at the officer's mess[4]. Those I actually enjoyed. Being polite and saying the correct thing became second nature to me. I don't recall ever enjoying church because of the preparation; our shoes always had to be polished, and we had to look smart. It was such a chore simply getting ready for it.

Even though my parents were always on the move from post to post in Germany, and we never had a place I could identify as home, the hardships of being in a boarding school made coming home like heaven. When the holidays came, it was like leaving prison.

We boys who lived overseas left the school last and travelled on a coach to Luton Airport. I hated having to wear a badge labeling me as an "Unaccompanied Minor" so people at Britannia Airways knew who I was. An elegantly dressed "stewardess"—as we called them back then—escorted me to the propeller plane whose blades were already turning slowly. I asked her why the logo on the tail looked like a lady sitting in a wheelchair. She calmly explained it was a symbol of Roman Britain, the lady with a Trident spear and Corinthian helmet, with a Union Jack as her shield.

The stewardesses always wore makeup and looked very glamorous in their light blue, puffed-up silk scarfs tastefully tied around their necks with prim navy hats perched perfectly on their heads. Their kind and polite demeanour overwhelmed me compared to that of Matron, who had bid us farewell earlier.

I always sat near the front behind the cockpit, and immediately the stewardess handed me a coloring book, colored pencils, and some playing cards. There was no in-flight entertainment back then; we simply looked out the window. I occasionally smelt tobacco wafting up from the back of the plane where the smokers sat. Once during the flight, I could see the pilots

---

[4]   A place where military personnel socialize

eat some sandwiches for lunch through the open cockpit door. Heaven forbid that happened today! On the descent into Germany, I was given copious amounts of hard-boiled sweets and told to chew them. The stewardess always watched me intently to make sure I did, in case I was delivered to my parents with burst eardrums. The sweets lasted forever, and I always got a few extras to take with me.

It was such a joy to see Mum at the gate who welcomed me with her broad smile. Often Grannie would be home too. My father would say hello briefly, as he was always busy. He was never warm and attentive, as he simply wasn't the child-hugging type. My father only wanted to know that my grades were satisfactory and I was doing well in school.

Once I settled in after a day or two, I loved to lose myself in play. A combination of watching the Great War movies shown on TV at that time and the splendour of the military parades we attended fueled my imagination. I entertained myself for hours in my room with my miniature soldiers. I built military planes and ships with the Airfix model kits or created mock battles between my troops. I lined up hundreds of soldiers in giant battle scenes on my bedroom floor. Sometimes I attacked the Romans with the Foreign Legion or used the paratroopers and commandos as the rescue forces. I especially treasured the British infantry from the battle of Waterloo and the mounted French cavalry as my creative ideas flew wild. If I played outside on the pavement, I used German firecrackers to burn or explode tanks in a more realistic battle scene.

I wanted my father to take an interest and share in this fun, but he didn't. My father, however, did enjoy playing "Risk" with us, which became a favorite family board game and one thing we did as a family that brought us together for a few laughs.

Sometimes my parents sent Steve and me off to spend the summer with our grandparents at *Isyfoel* in Bethesda, North Wales. *Foel* means bare or bald hill in Welsh, and there were several bald hills behind their house. Here we could escape the monotony of army life, church, and school, to roam and dream in the mountains and paddle in the streams, catching Sticklebacks[5] at the back of our uncle's farm. We were sometimes gone for a few weeks, which suited us perfectly.

The only negative was the four-and-a-half hour car journeys, because my father wouldn't stop the car and instead handed us a milk bottle to pee in. On the drive north, we would pass a particular mountain, Tryfan, when we entered the Snowdonia National Park. The mountain looked very imposing with its grey slate igneous form rising steeply from the roadside. The sheer remoteness and jaggedness of the place impressed me with the timeless age-old mountains all around. Out on the wind-driven slopes of Tryfan, rock was everywhere on an enormous scale, chiselled and thrown about around its bulk.

"Tryfan held many stories," my father said. "There were wild mountain goats roaming its craggy pathways."

At the very top, we could see two tall pillars close together that looked like huge people standing side by side. "They are called Adam and Eve," my father told us. "Climbers ascend either one of the pillars and then jump from one to the other. The leap confers upon the jumper the *freedom of Tryfan*. It is a climbing tradition." I wanted to climb it myself one day when I had a chance.

Isyfoel still has vivid memories for me. From the main road, one took a winding road up that twisted and turned as it rose to the far side of the village. Nana and Taid's house was in a cul-de-sac with the back of the house facing the mountains. A long narrow garden led back to where Taid (Welsh name for *grandfather*) would grow his beloved new potatoes and other vegetables. I used to play for hours in a small clump of trees with massive rocks on an island at the end of the cul-de-sac, fighting imaginary Indians or other enemies in my head. I remember there were always jackdaws (small members of the

---

[5]   Small 'tiddler' fish

crow family) on the chimney pots around the house, and Taid told me they mated for life.

My grandparents kept a coal fire roaring in the sitting room with Taid's armchair close to it. Taid's chair had those old-fashioned, white ornate linen covers on the arms and the headrest as well. From his chair, Taid could see "Drosgl" out of the back window in the distance. Drosgl was a summit in the Carneddau mountain range in the Snowdonia National Park. I asked Taid why there were dark areas on the tops of the mountains. He said some were from bonfires built to celebrate the coronation of King George VI. Other dark spots were from where bombers crashed into the mountains in the Second World War. My father once told us that when he was a boy, up there he found a leather jackboot from a German pilot.

A scary-looking painting of the Lord's Last Supper hung behind the sofa. Taid also treasured a painting of the quarry where he used to work as an electrician. Nana kept her collection of brass candlesticks in the adjacent room. I have kept one brass ornament in particular: a brass lady wearing a traditional Welsh costume with a tiny bell concealed under her dress. When shaken, she makes quite a racket. That sound takes me back to when Nana used to ring it to call us for tea in Isyfoel.

Nana always served homemade Bara Brith, a traditional Welsh tea-soaked fruit bread, for afternoon tea on a table covered with a fancy lace tablecloth. As we walked across the front room's squeaky floorboards, the candlesticks and Gordy china bowls and teacups would clink on the huge dark oak Welsh dresser that stood proud against the wall.

At night, I could hear the haunting tick-tock of the grandfather clock down in the hall. When it chimed, the vibrations filled the house as the metal gears ground together with a metallic click. I slept upstairs in a compact front room with a giant, dark, floor-to-ceiling mahogany wardrobe that contained many drawers. It reminded me of the wardrobe in *The Chronicles of Narnia*. To turn the light on, I pulled the long chord with a tassel on the end attached to the ceiling by my bed. The solid horsehair mattress had no coil system at all. It was very firm and dense with an itchy sensation to it. A perfect u-shaped valley formed when I sank into it as if I was sleeping on a pile of hay.

Getting up out of a warm bed in the middle of the night for the bathroom was quite an ordeal. The bathroom faced the back of the house and the mountains, and the window was always left open. Each morning in the winter we would have to crack the ice in the toilet. The bathroom always smelt of disinfectant and fresh mountain air. My father's parents were hardy types and lived to a ripe old age breathing in all that healthy air.

In addition to Isyfoel, we also visited nearby Hirdir Farm, which was my Uncle Ben and Auntie Myre's farm, and which held special memories for us all. To get there we had to drive up twisting narrow lanes lined each side with high bluish purple slate walls into the mountains. Uncle Ben's house was a solid stone building built with the slate from the surrounding quarry. Thick slabs made the walls with thin slate on the roof. It felt totally impregnated with Welshness, set in a quiet, remote location at the end of a lane. A huge coal fire off the kitchen generated the only heat, but no hot water. Everyone would gather around the fire and speak in Welsh. We sat with the cats and Ben's sheepdogs drinking numerous cups of tea and eating homemade bread and butter with jam. I remember every so often a cat would fly across the room to catch a mouse, whereupon Auntie Myre would give a piercing look that could turn milk sour.

Slate waste piled up so high around the farm that it formed its own range of mini-mountains. To us boys, the piles looked like giant heaps of graphite pencils thrown up through the earth's crust.

Huge, elongated slate slabs—heavy, thick, and bluish purple in colour—bordered the fields. These tall, thin slabs served as fences, cut and dug into the soil on their ends and held in place with a thick wire that wrapped around each piece and then onto the next

Steve and I enjoyed many activities on the farm. It was a wonderful place to explore, with only the sound of bleating sheep in the background. We fought imaginary battles in the outbuildings where my aunt used to churn her butter, and we carved our names into the wall on the side of the house. We tried Uncle Ben's shotgun, but it never worked, unlike the prehistoric cast-iron mole traps he used that did a great job. We also used Ben's vintage wooden fishing poles, but we never caught anything in those crystal clear streams. On looking back, I know now we didn't have the correct approach or tackle, nor the understanding to know which fly we should use. But we sure had fun trying.

My parents used to speak to each other in Welsh when we were around so we didn't know what was going on. I remember being told I was a *bachgen drwg*, or "naughty boy", on occasions, but I didn't pick up a lot of the language growing up. I wish they had taught us boys to speak Welsh.

After an enjoyable summer in North Wales or at home, the time always came for our term grades to arrive in the mail from school. At that point, the family fun was always ruined. If my father was suddenly in more of a crappy mood, I knew it was because of that. He hid away and emerged later with never a compliment spoken. I dreaded the feedback, as he always said something along the lines that I could do better. It became a common occurrence throughout my school years.

I felt like I was never good enough. Dan "always had to show more effort in everything"—never "Wow, this is a great job, Dan." I didn't have a "poor me" attitude back then, but I sure could have used some praise.

I don't recall seeing my report cards as my parents kept them. It was only much later in my life—after my mother had died—that I was able to read the comments and grades. The common words were, "needs to make more of an effort", "always distracted", and "can do better."

I was left to "get on with it", as no one was pampered in those days—the "stiff upper lip" mentality and all that. After all, in the 1960s, Britain was still using rationing books, so we had to make do with what we had. It was "keep calm and carry on." Have a cup of tea and you'll be fine.

On one of my holidays in Germany when I was about nine, I had to have my tonsils and adenoids removed. I still think of the smell of gas anaesthesia and the surgeon holding me down on the table while they placed that mask over my mouth. The surgery must have gone fine, but it was such a horrible experience that I hate hospitals to this day.

After that trauma, on another occasion, I dashed through the kitchen and accidentally knocked a pot of boiling water off the stove onto my bare foot. My mother wrapped my foot in tinfoil with butter inside. Needless to say, with this treatment the pain was even worse than the burn—an old folklore remedy, but I guess she didn't know any better. Sometimes I turned up for school again even more battered than when I had left.

On the night before we flew back to school, I would ask for my favourite meal, like a prisoner's last meal before execution. I always requested chicken à la king,[6] and we would all sit a bit somberly around the dining table trying to keep the conversation light. We knew that my father inevitably would raise the subject of improving our grades again. Mum reassured us that things would be fine for another gruelling term. I do believe my mother cried when I left for school, but she never showed it. Undoubtedly, my father would tell her to stop being so soppy towards us.

---

[6]   A dish consisting of diced chicken in a cream sauce.

Here is a photo of Steve and me with my grandmother on the
steps at Dusseldorf Airport in Germany back in 1971.
Once again shipped off to school.

Dressed in our school uniforms, we were ready to go back
to school on the Britannia Airways prop plane. I wore black
lace-up shoes, grey knee-length woollen socks with blue turnovers[7], grey flannel trousers, a V-neck jumper[8], a grey shirt, my
bright red Alexander House tie, a navy flannel blazer with the
school crest on the breast pocket, and a navy school cap with
the same crest above the peak. I think my uniform would have
fit perfectly with one of the houses in Hogwarts. The only
splash of colour was our ties. My mother took the photo as
she was so proud of how we looked, all smart and turned out.
Little did she know that she was sending us off to experience
more hell back in England.

---

[7]   Socks folded over at the top.
[8]   Sweater

3

LEUKAEMIA

Carbolic Soap

I was having issues with my teeth. My wisdom teeth were uncomfortable and impacted, so before I returned to Bloxham I had them removed. This meant another unpleasant surgical procedure similar to the one I had experienced before, which didn't help my nervous disposition at all. I felt I was becoming prone to hospital visits and thought about the previous tonsils and adenoids experience, as well as the boiling water that had fallen onto my bare foot.

By the time I returned to school, my mouth still hurt from my wisdom teeth surgery, but I was on the mend. I was eleven years old now and placed in Crake House at Bloxham, where I began to settle into boarding school once again. My first impressions were that Bloxham was not that much better than Haileybury. My dorm was in the roof of what looked like a tall Victorian workhouse, built in the neo-Gothic style. A few scary gargoyles looming from the rooftops would have completed the sinister, gloomy facade. I was recently amused to read that in 1853 the "Gentleman's Magazine" referred to Bloxham as the "most beautiful modern Gothic buildings ever devoted in England to a scholastic purpose." Our bed frames were made of thick black steel piping with bedding of bright red blankets. Trunks that contained all our belongings had to fit under our beds.

At the end of the dormitory from where a strong odour emanated were the washbasins. The smell was the carbolic soap, a mild antiseptic, with a deep pinkish/red colour caused by the carbolic acid. It was the household soap of my childhood, with its nostalgic strong, tar-like scent. We didn't know it at the time, but it killed bacteria and also acted as a mild deodorant when used as a body soap. Hence, everyone smelled the same in school. Even today, I keep a bar of that stinky soap as a reminder of how far I have progressed since those unpleasant days. It's the smell of school for me and reminds me of being at one of the dormitory room sinks.

The 1970s was the era when vinyl records and record players were the rage. It was impressive to have one in your room, and the boys always compared the different makes and models. This was also the dawn of great bands like Yes, Jethro Tull, Black Sabbath, and Deep Purple, also the era of the synthesizer with great keyboarding tracks. Vinyl was fashionable, and album covers were collected and studied as much as the courses we took. I remember one album by the Rolling Stones, "Sticky Fingers", and how everyone raved about the zipper on the album cover.

Many boys' first introduction to beer was the fruity taste of Old Hooky, which was around 20 pence, a pint. We would leave school during prep (study time) when we were mostly left to our own devices and sneak out of school to the back entrance of the Elephant and Castle pub in the village. When we knocked three times on a tiny hatch, a man would open the doors and serve us. We felt all grown up accomplishing this as it was a special treat. I can remember this ritual and rite of passage, which continued for several years at Bloxham.

Around that time, girls from Tudor Hall School down the road joined sixth form classes at Bloxham for the first time. Naturally, the boys checked them all out! One girl, in particular, was Pippa, who developed a reputation for introducing boys to their first kiss, and later became known as "Pippa the Bike." One arranged a meeting with Pippa if you wanted a kiss. She would have to check you out first though, to make sure she was willing to kiss you. Recently I was amazed when I discovered a Facebook site for Old Bloxhamists. "Pippa the Bike" was still posting there, but somehow I felt a kiss from her today wouldn't have the same appeal as it used to!

Pursuing my studies at Bloxham was not easy, as I was always nervous and not quite at ease. My parents were once again a long way off in Germany and my self-confidence was lacking. There was a constant pressure to do well and fit in with the other boys. I started once again to express my anxiety and depression through imaginary or psychosomatic symptoms and had times when my world was a spiral of panic. Worrisome thoughts spun through my head stemming from a fear of dying ever since the Haileybury swimming pool incident and my earlier bout of scarlet fever. I had no one to talk to for reassurance, in another school where emotions were not acceptable, and no one knew how to deal with me. There was no cognitive behaviour therapy back in those days. My experiences embodied the grand old Victorian public school virtues or failings as I saw them. These were the suppression of emotions, devotion to the team, distrust of women, and minimal empathy for the weak and ordinary boys.

I longed for summer holidays when I could go to North Wales and visit my grandparents up in the mountains. In the summer of 1975 when I was seventeen, Mum and Dad told Steve and me that we were going for a week to North Wales to stay with her mother in Rhos-on-Sea. My grandmother was very special to me. She was warm-hearted, reassuring, and always generous when we visited her. Repeatedly to us boys Grannie would say "Cariad" which meant "darling" in Welsh. She had a penchant for doing things right, in a traditional old-fashioned way, such as loading up her squeaky wooden tea trolley with goodies from her kitchen and wheeling it into the lounge. She insisted we drink our tea from her delicate Minton china teacups. When it was time for us to leave, she always stood in the bay window of her flat waving to us. Grannie lived an amazing life in Seville, Spain, and was always willing to tell us one of her Second World War experiences from there. She was no pushover, mind you, and would stand up to my father on many occasions if he treated us unfairly. This stemmed from the determination, resilience, and unwavering courage Grannie developed in the Second World War.

Before embarking on our journey to North Wales, my parents told us how cramped Grannie's flat would be. I, therefore, knew Steve and I would be sleeping on the floor in the living room. North Wales brought fresh air, exploring the mountains and fishing, but I didn't like being there with my parents. My father's adherence to discipline meant that he often ended up in an argument with my mother about how spoilt we were.

One morning after we had arrived and settled in, I strolled into the kitchen, and my mother and grandmother were talking. I must have surprised them as I overheard my grandmother saying to my mother, "You have to tell the boy. It's time, and he's old enough to know now."

I asked, "Know what?"

My grandmother looked at my mother with a glare and then said, "Take him into the lounge and talk about it."

My mother said nothing at first and then turned to me. "Would you like a cup of tea as the kettle just boiled?"

"Sure." I was a little curious about what was going on. My grandmother went off to her bedroom. My father and Steve had gone down to the shops at the end of the road to get some more eggs for breakfast.

"Let's sit in the lounge as I have something to discuss with you." Mum's voice then became crackly and broke up as she stumbled to go on.

"I hardly know where to begin with this, but I want you to understand that what I am about to tell you is something I have thought about for some time. I didn't know when would be the appropriate time, and your father and I have argued a lot about it. He didn't want you to know until later, and for life to go along as usual."

By this point, I sat on the edge of my seat and begged her to stop rambling and tell me. "What's the big deal? Are you taking me out of Bloxham? You know how much I hate it there."

"No, it's more important than that." Mum paused, her mouth trembling as she looked at me nervously and said, "You see, your father is ...not your biological father."

I didn't reply as I was processing her words in shock.

"You may have noticed that you don't look like your father. He is much shorter than you."

Again, I was silent. I had noticed that we did have a huge height difference, which didn't help our relationship. The news was devastating, but it explained how my father had treated me up to this point. Now I felt even more like an outcast.

"Your real father was a Turner—I called him "Big Dan"— which is why you may have wondered why you have four names. I married him back in 1957 in a military church in Cyprus. Anyway, something awful happened. After our honeymoon, he served as an army officer in Cyprus, and I had to travel back to Wales. Then out of the blue, I received a telegram saying that he was taken seriously ill. It was so sudden; he had contracted leukaemia and moved to a military hospital on Malta where they had better facilities. Despite their best efforts, he died three days later and is buried in the military cemetery on the island. In those days it was too expensive to fly someone home to be buried, so that is why he is out there."

I was dumbfounded. "So when did you meet Neville, I mean my father?" It was the first time I used his given name. But with this shocking news, I couldn't imagine calling him "Dad".

"Well, he was training as a deacon during that time in Borth-y-Gest. He would come and look in on me while I was recovering from Dan's death and after I had you."

"Is Steve my blood brother?"

"I had Steve with your present father."

I was so stunned and grasping for solid ground that I asked, "You said my father died of leukaemia, correct?"

"Yes."

"Isn't that hereditary?" Once again, I reverted to my fear of disease and started thinking I was going to die.

"No, it's not in most cases. You don't need to worry. His leukaemia was probably caused by all the messing around he did with radios. He was a radio fanatic and spent hours working on them. In those days, no one knew about the damage that radio waves could do to the body."

"Where did you say he is buried?"

"In the Imtarfa Military Cemetery on the island of Malta."

"I must go there and visit him." I felt determined that I would.

Mum and I heard my father coming back into the flat. She asked me not to say a word, as she hadn't told my father she was telling me about Big Dan. Unfortunately, the following day my grandmother inadvertently let it slip out and said, "How good it was that the boy knows his background."

Afterwards I heard my father storm into the kitchen and confront my mother. "I thought we agreed that he would be told later."

I could hear them arguing, and it made me very upset, so much so, that I decided to take off. I took a long walk and climbed up an enormous hill that overlooked the town. From there I could look down on them all and think about what I heard at seventeen years old. Why would my father not want to talk to me about it? I eventually decided to head back to the flat and crept back in. Grannie was very comforting; she put her arms around me and said that if I ever needed to talk about Big Dan to come to her. I avoided my parents from that point on as much as I could and was just quiet, processing my thoughts. My father didn't bring up the subject in the coming days or later; it would have been an opportunity for us to build a better relationship, had he done so.

I don't know, and I never did know, from that moment on, what my father thought of me being his son. He took on the father role from the minute he married Mum. My father had difficulty acknowledging his own feelings and wasn't comfortable expressing himself.

4

THE FISHING TRIP

Mackerel

I think my father thought an attempt to connect with me was taking me out on a fishing trip. Maybe a welcome diversion from the shocking news I had received that week. What better a place to experience some peace and reflection than in the Welsh Mountains fishing for trout. My head was still spinning with questions about Big Dan, so I didn't know what to say to my present father. I had listened to him berating Mum for telling me, so I didn't think I could broach the subject with him and understand how he felt. Besides, I had never felt I could have a close, intimate discussion with him. Instead, there was a pit in my stomach. I felt insignificant, unwanted, and so cheated about the life-changing information withheld from me. What other dark secrets didn't I know of? Heck, if they waited until I was seventeen to tell me this, then what else was unsaid?

Uncle Toby, my mother's brother, was also up in North Wales at that time. Toby was rather strict, just like my father, but in a different way; his discipline centred on what he didn't say, rather than a raised voice like my father. Toby's stare was stern enough if you had done something wrong. He reminded me of Marlon Brando in the movie "The Godfather," with his distinguished moustache and hard-nosed scary faces. Toby and my father looked like two old men up to some mischief in their own way. They both shared a rather sordid type of humour, as I was about to find out.

The fishing trip provided the opportunity to clear the air, and maybe I could laugh somewhat with them both so some bonding could occur. I had been pestering my father to take me fishing for ages. As kids, whenever we visited North Wales, my father would regale us with his fishing exploits as a boy and how the huge Salmon would sit below the Ogwen falls waiting to travel up the river to spawn. Every time he told us the story, Steve and I couldn't wait to go fishing with him, but it never happened.

Instead, Steve and I had always enjoyed wandering off in the local streams around my grandparent's farm "Hirdir", but we hadn't done any real fishing. We had seen the beautifully marked wild trout lying cautious, tempting us below the surface in the local rivers but we had no idea how to catch them. I loved that clear, crisp water up in the mountains. It was refreshing to drink, so cold and pure. The wild North Wales Brown Trout are incredibly colourful, radiant, and beautifully marked. They have brassy brown sides fading to creamy white on the fish's belly, with medium-sized spots surrounded by lighter halos. Maybe I would catch one of the rare Arctic Char[9] that was up there as well. I was very excited since at last a promised fishing trip was happening despite the awkwardness that hung in the air in the preceding days.

We drove to Llyn Ogwen in the Snowdonia National Park, which is about forty minutes by car from Grannie's flat in

---

[9]   A cold-water fish in the family Salmonidae.

Rhos-on-Sea. As we approached the long glacial lake set in the Nant Ffrancon Pass, I immediately recognized Tryfan, whose vast rock face rose inexorably from the lakeside. Its distinctive rocky, blade-like shape dominated the view around Nant Francon, and from every direction, it showed off nothing but steep crags and striking ridges. I had always loved Tryfan since I was very young when my father drove Steve and me up to North Wales to spend the summers with our grandparents. Tryfan would suddenly appear on the horizon as we turned a corner on the A5.

From afar, it resembled a massive grey surfacing shark with three intimidating dorsal fins. I remember looking up out of the car window, straining my neck to locate the two rocks Adam and Eve on the top that my father had told us about when we were children. Whenever we passed it, there were always climbers dangling on ropes half way up on the slabs. Tryfan is so rocky that some say it is impossible to climb without using one's hands. All I know is that it is a magical place.

The lake below Tryfan, Llyn Ogwen, has a mythical story attached to it. In my school history books, I learned that the lake was one of two supposed locations for the final resting place of King Arthur's sword Excalibur. According to legend, Sir Bedivere, a loyal knight, returned Excalibur to the Lady of the Lake after the Battle of Camlann. Tryfan is his burial site. When he tossed the sword into the depths, the Lady of the Lake reached up from beneath the surface to catch it and disappeared. I always felt the gin-clear surface looked magical as if it held a whole history of secrets in its depths. I sure needed some magic to occur between my father and me that day.

We decided to head to the far end of the lake away from where it flows out to the River Ogwen. The water was so clear that I could see every detail on the huge brown boulders on the bottom that reached all the way out. The disadvantage to this clarity was the fish could spy you a mile away, so one had to be stealthy. My father told us that the best times to fish the lake were a dull day with a stiff breeze, which increased the odds of catching. No such luck for us, for it was a bright and sunny day with no wind.

We set up on opposite banks. My father and Uncle Toby stayed together; my father said he needed to help Toby with his gear since he hadn't fished for trout before. I headed over to a giant rock sticking out on the far bank from which I could cast and see all the action. I had no idea what lures to use, except I knew I had trout lures so I picked one out and started spinning. I thought I might be lucky and hook King Arthur's sword on the bottom instead of a trout. That would be one heck of a catch.

After fishing for half an hour, all of a sudden I heard my uncle shout, "We got one, Dan!"

I was excited, but also rather jealous, as we had all been there for some time without any luck. I reeled my line in and sprinted as fast as I could around to the other side to see the fish, which they laid on the grassy bank. I looked down and immediately thought to myself that it wasn't a trout or a salmon and started to think about what species it was.

"I know this fish," I said to myself, but could not remember from where. Maybe it was the infamous rare Arctic Char. Oh well.

"I am sure you'll get one soon," Toby said and encouraged me to go back to my rock and continue trying. "Hopefully we'll catch more for dinner tonight. Go back and try on your side."

I was now determined to catch one, so I changed my spinning gear to a larger spoon so I could cast further. Five minutes passed, and I heard my father shouting this time that he had one as well. I dropped my rod and shot over even more eagerly, making it in time to watch them reeling it in. I said, "It isn't moving much. Is it okay?"

Toby said, "Its fine. Sometimes they don't put up much of a fight in this cold mountain water."

They placed the fish on the grass bank, and I remember saying, "But it's not even breathing, the gills aren't moving, it looks dead." Just then, a light bulb flickered on in my head. I looked at both of them and stood up. In the meantime, they looked at each other with cheeky grins.

"Where's the first fish?" I asked. "Can you put it alongside the one you just caught?" They did so sheepishly and laid the two striped fish side by side on the bank. When both were beside each other, I recalled where I had seen this fish before. It was down at the waterfront in Conwy. The fishermen were unloading some buckets of them, which they had caught at sea.

"These are Mackerel," I shouted, "and there is no way a Mackerel would be up here in a Welsh mountain lake three thousand feet up from the ocean."

Toby quickly replied, "Mackerel aren't just saltwater fish, Dan, and regularly come up the rivers."

"Well, why was it not breathing then? You wouldn't be pulling in dead fish would you"? They knew how excited I had been about the prospect of catching a wonderful wild trout, so why had they done this? Why would they bring fish with them and spoil the day with such deception? I wouldn't have minded had none of us caught anything, and we'd had a few laughs trying, but to pretend they were having fun at my expense in a teasing way made my blood boil. It was as if I was back at Haileybury when I wanted the last piece of candy and two boys laughed at me as they took it. They both harped on for a while about the fish, still insisting they lived in the lake, but eventually when I stopped talking, they suggested that maybe we should go home, as I clearly wasn't enjoying myself anymore.

"This is supposed to be a fun day out, Dan. Don't take it so seriously," my uncle said. I wanted to say something rude back to him, but I bit my tongue and suffered in silence as I had done so many times before.

To this day, I still feel lousy about that devious plan. It also reminded me of how my father used to laugh and tease me when I stuck my tongue out when I concentrated. "There he goes again, Look," my father would say. I had had enough trickery at both of my schools and didn't need it at home as well.

5

SUMMERS AWAY

Park Hill, East Meon

Before I headed back to Bloxham, I had two weeks back at our house in East Meon in Hampshire. My parents had named the house "Highlands" and bought it when they were in Germany. Now we used it as a UK base. I was fortunate to have the time to regroup and mentally get myself psyched up for school again.

My black school trunk was in for repair at the time, so my mother had to find me a replacement suitcase to use for the upcoming term. We had all kinds around the house, some shabby ones from Nana and Taid in Isyfoel, and some that had come out of Uncle Ben's barn that were soiled and torn in the corners. Mum asked me to root around in the outside shed and pick one out. My parents had put luggage out there since there was no room for such items in the house. One suitcase, in particular, caught my eye: a heavy, weathered brown leather suitcase with reinforced corners that looked like it had travelled many places. It looked like Newt Scamander's magical suitcase in "Fantastic Beasts." The stickers on the outside named various exotic destinations in Europe. I also brought in a large soft-sided grey one that would expand when I filled it with my clothes. I showed them to my mother after dusting them off. She immediately said, "Oh you can't use the brown one. That one is special and too heavy for you anyway. Your father must have put it outside by mistake, so leave that in here, please."

"What's so special about it? It looks so neglected and beaten up."

"I'll tell you later, but not now."

"It also feels rather heavy. What's in it?"

"Just some special mementos of mine. Use the grey one as it will fit all your clothes, and I can put an extra strap around the middle to add more support for you."

"Okay, I'll put it in my room."

I then saw Mum take the brown suitcase into her bedroom. I was curious as to why she had taken it back in there. What was so special about that one, and what did it contain?

Fall came and it was time to go back to Bloxham. My mother had been busy sewing yet more school nametags into my clothing. When I returned to school this time, I was even more nervous and confused, having been told about my real father and how he died. The whole revelation really weighed on me and affected my schoolwork. Despite Mum telling me that I would not inherit leukaemia, I didn't believe her and thought it would claim me as well. I feared contracting the illness that robbed me of my father. As a result, I developed a number of nervous habits and phobias. When I noticed floaters in my eyes, they freaked me out since I didn't know what they were. I also became obsessed with cleanliness and hand washing. I became an even worse hypochondriac than at Haileybury and worried about everything.

All this anxiety caused me to fail math again. This time my math teacher was Mr. Fiori, a heavy smoker whom I wouldn't go near because I thought he would give me lung cancer. When he leaned over me to check my work, his colossal puffy yellow nicotine-stained hands would rest on my desk. The smell and look of them sent me into fits, so I would do anything to get him to move away. I never asked for his help, as I didn't want him wandering over to talk to me.

One teacher who saw my potential was Mr. Tideswell. He was the athletic teacher and encouraged me in the skill of javelin throwing, which was a huge boost to my self-confidence. I learned how to time my run-up to the throwing line to gain the most momentum and release the javelin at exactly the correct time so it flew in a perfect arc to make a mark on the field. Otherwise, it did not count. Athletics was the one activity I looked forward to each week.

To keep myself going and to remain positive, I channelled my nervous energy and fears into creative pursuits. I pursued my love of art and indulged in studying birds. It was quite amusing to read some of the statements my teachers used in their end-of-term summaries about me.

One read, "The boy is apt to be looking out of the window at birds."

My housemaster at that time was Mr. Kemp, who wrote in my end of term report. "Dan is always distracted and must stop worrying about unnecessary things."

I think my nervous unnecessary worrying was the side that my father didn't like about me. He didn't understand how sensitive I was, hence, he was always telling me to toughen up. He hated people who showed their weaknesses. Since I was so sensitive and so easily hurt, he had difficulty dealing with me.

With no direct parenting while away at school for such long periods, I had no emotional support. If I had ironed out my fears and concerns at home, I wouldn't have worried so much at school. I suffered through the school year and should have known better than to complain to my parents about how distressed I felt.

My parents did come back to 'Highlands' for a short time before returning for another posting in Germany. When the term finally ended, my mother told me that my father didn't have time to come and collect me, so I would have to make my own arrangements. Since I couldn't find a ride, I had no option but to hitchhike home, which Mum didn't like. The distance from Bloxham to East Meon was about a hundred miles. My mother was very nervous about what might happen to me, but I made it back safely. These days I would not attempt such a journey given the state of society and the dangers present on the roads.

I used three different rides to get home, lugging my hefty grey suitcase with me the whole way. The first ride was a rather chatty nurse on her way to work. I was surprised she stopped, but maybe she took pity on the poor schoolboy with his suitcase on the side of the road. The second was an unshaven Safeway delivery driver who was very short with me and asked me to chuck my bag in with his groceries. The last and most enjoyable companion was farmer John with his six sheep in the back going to market. Needless to say, I felt quite at home with him and learned a great deal about sheep farming.

During the summer of 1976, the weather was very hot in East Meon. Given my earlier hitchhiking discussions with farmer John, he inspired me to take a summer job on Mr. Tostivine's farm bringing in the hay and stacking the bales afterwards. Hay baling was hard work as the mechanical baler wrapped the string very tightly around each bale. Despite wearing gloves, slipping my hands underneath the string on each bale to lift them gave me painful red blisters across my palms. The work was hard, but at least I was outside.

Hiking in the surrounding countryside was my favourite pastime when I wasn't working. My mind was very troubled still, thinking about my real father, Big Dan. I had so many questions. What was he like? Did I look like him? Did he have a sense of humour? De he like the outdoors? I also had conflicting thoughts about my father: why he never talked about Big Dan. I was too scared to talk to him given how annoyed he had been with Mum.

Therefore, I used the long quiet days out in the country-side to think about my life and bond with nature instead. I gained tremendous therapy from being out there until after dark. It was my way to escape and regenerate, as nature didn't seek anything from me and was separate from the pressures of school. For a few hours each day, I was able to spend time in an oasis of pensive reflection, a place that revived my soul and took away my stresses. I explored the whole East Meon valley over the course of the summer. Most days I would start down by Ye Olde George Inn in the village, where a clear chalk stream gently trickled under an arched stone bridge. I would then walk over to All Saints Church and open the rickety antiquated wooden gate to climb the stairs up to the graveyard. The graveyard was one of those ancient places full of timeworn, moss-covered engraved headstones, tilted in all directions with illegible writing on them, some sunken into the ground.

From the west end of the graveyard, I took a path that rapidly ascended a hundred meters through a dark tunnel of emerald green trees. At the start of the climb, I always remember the imposing yew trees, classic evergreens that fre-quented churchyards and linked with immortality. In Wales, the traditional planting of yews evokes ancient Druid beliefs and customs. In England, long before the Christian era, yew trees frequented pagan temple sites, eventually adopted by the church as "a holy symbol." I would always hear Wood Pigeons cooing from these trees, the wind whistling through their wings as they flew, as if the sound of blowing on a blade of grass held between your thumbs. These huge pigeons would launch their hefty bodies into the air, often clapping their wings twice before gliding down again.

As I continued my climb, a giant beech tree struck me reaching up to the sky on my left. I counted eleven rook nests in the top. Once at the top of the path, I bore right and jumped over a stile[10] into a steeply sloped meadow. Here a beautiful song emanated on most summer days. No matter how hot it was, Skylarks sang high, unseen in the blue above. They were always singing, and I wondered how they had all that energy. I would reflect on Shelley's poem "Ode to a Skylark", in which he suggests a reason for the happiness of their song.

Shelley wrote that a Skylark was free from all that gave pain to man. It was higher up than we were, spreading joy and hope, and not affected by all that happened below. The Skylark had a means of escape from this world, and I always thought about this as I took my walks. How I wished I could be free from the pressures and emotional pains I was going through at that time. I sought solace from nature and was grateful that I could lose myself up on Park Hill. I spent days discovering, collecting, examining, and drawing the many facets of the countryside that lured me.

When I climbed further up the hill, I had great views looking over the village. I was soon higher than the steeple of the church below. Once at the very top, I could look east to the South Downs, and stretching away in the haze beyond was Butser Hill, one the highest points on the chalk ridge of the South Downs.

Another familiar bird on the hill was the Sparrow Hawk that would hover in place, and then suddenly without warning, drop to the ground to catch a mouse. I would sit on the hill for hours some days, viewing the hawks and looking over the rooftops of the village, watching early morning mist lift off the landscape, or later in the day a sunset slipping behind Drayton Pools in the distance.

On fine summer days when the air was still, I would close my eyes and listen. The sounds of the village would waft up the hill. People joking behind the old-time George Pub having a pint in the beer garden. Mrs. Coates' unrestrained raucous laughter as she joked outside the post office with a customer.

---

[10]   An arrangement of steps for people to climb over a fence.

41

The rattles and clunks of one of the farmer's tractors making its way methodically along one of the narrow village lanes. Children shouted at each other while playing on the swings in the school playground. Sometimes when it was quiet in the middle of the day, Wood Pigeons would exchange their soft coos from the beech trees. On one occasion, I heard the sheep in the meadows near the mill.

On one of my walks, I took some picture wire up Park Hill to a place called Vineyard Hole, where I set some homemade snares for rabbits. It was fun trying this out, but I was distressed and stopped when I realized what awful injuries snares caused.

On those very still, hot, hazy days, my feelings were what I called "the very life of a British summer." Wafting up that hill was the sweet smell of new hay, tossed about in the sunshine, and fresh mint from the village gardens below. It was a timeless, peaceful place to stop and ponder what I should do next in my life. What direction should I follow? Given no guidance and my lack of self-confidence, I really had no idea.

Returning to the village in the afternoon, I entered on the far side where sunken pathways riddled a valley lined with trees. Each tree had gnarled twisted roots as if giant snakes coiled around them and reminded me of the trees in the film "The Fellowship of the Ring." I also had to pass through the grey steel kissing gates, which were sometimes tricky, as this was a type of gate that allowed people to pass through, but not livestock. Every so often I flushed out Ring-Necked Pheasants that were everywhere in the countryside. They would utter a loud ke-tuk, ke-tuk, ke-tuk as they beat their wings together and launched into flight.

Later I came across the village green, where a lazy evening game of cricket would be going on, with everyone dressed in pristine whites, like a scene from classic English village life. My path then veered off through the allotment[11] gardens and

---

[11]   A plot of land rented by an individual for growing vegetables or flowers.

along the village stream, with its thatched cottages and Georgian houses. Named after the famous angler, the very popular Isaak Walton Pub appeared to my right, where I would sometimes sneak in for a "half," as they say. Aged eighteen gave me the permission to savour a pint of beer; underage only allowed me to sneak a pint of old Hooky at Bloxham. My journey finished with a short walk home to 'Highlands' along a steeply sided country lane.

At the end of the summer, I organized my notes and observations and wrote a nature trail of my personal journeys and experiences around East Meon village. I read it recently, and my words and illustrations took me back exactly to all the wonderful sensory details of that summer. It is a melancholy thought that I can never take that same walk again, because both that path and I have since changed.

6

BERLIN

The peace I had enjoyed in the landscape strength-
ened me. The harsh reality of returning to boarding
school came around once again. My father called us all
together, asked us to sit down, and told us some great news. He
had been posted to Berlin as the military chaplain to the Joint
Allied Forces. Once again, our lives would be turned upside
down, but there was a silver lining in this news for me. He
informed me there was a military high school, Windsor Boys
School in Hamm, Germany, that was worth looking at. He said
that if I was that unhappy at Bloxham, I could change schools.
It wasn't a school for officer's sons, but for other ranks, which
would suit me fine. I would rather be with regular kids than
those at Bloxham, where I was miserable. So we all moved to
Berlin, and I started my final year of high school at WBS and
took my "A-levels" (Advanced Level exams.)

At my new school I was put into Balmoral House, named after the royal residence in Scotland, and immediately met a housemaster I liked, Mr. Donavon. Academically it was similar to Bloxham, but I felt more at home socially. I learned how to play the bass guitar and joined the school rock band, which boosted my self-confidence and allowed me to feel more popular. For the first time in school I felt encouraged, and finally, I believed I could succeed at something. I wasn't among the elite public school types anymore. These were sons and daughters of the other ranks, which was a refreshing change. The faculty cared more about the students than those I had had at Bloxham. Everyone was included and treated the same way.

At the end of that first term, to travel from Windsor Boys School back to Berlin, I had to take a special military train through the Berlin corridor that traveled through East Germany and linked West Berlin with the rest of West Germany. This in itself was a huge treat, and I was excited to ride it a few times while stationed in Berlin. It was 1977 and I was nineteen years old when I first rode the "Berliner" home to West Berlin. After the Second World War, the Russians had agreed that the British should have the right to go through a corridor to access West Berlin and the military train ran from Braunschweig to Charlottenburg. The steam train left every day, except on Christmas Day, for four decades, and I still remember that journey today and the austere scenery along the way.

I would board the train in Braunschweig at 4:00 p.m. and arrive in Berlin according to the timetable at 7:45 p.m. I still have one of the British Military Train cards, handed to me when I boarded, and a copy of the rules. The train card provided information on what we would see along the way, east- or westbound.

I noticed parked in the station the two-toned painted carriages as I ambled alongside them. Above the window line was a pale cream. Below the windows, a dark green ran the length of each carriage. Exactly in the centre of the carriage printed over the dark green background were the words "Royal Corps of Transport" with the army regimental insignia above that. A Union Jack was painted near the end of the carriage where we boarded. The train had seven cars. The gigantic black beast of a steam engine with fiery red wheels was gently hissing in the station, just as they did in vintage movies.

The Royal Corp of Transport issued a train card and folder that included the rules for the journey. Because this was the time of the Cold War, we were about to cross through essentially enemy territory, so we had to be cautious. The rules disallowed cameras or binoculars during the train journey. There was no leaning out of windows either or throwing anything from the train.

There was to be no speaking with or attempting to converse with East German nationals or Soviet personnel. Upon reading this, I wondered who in their correct minds would jump off and start a conversation with a Soviet guard. Also, we had to remain seated at all stops in East Germany, but this was easier said than done for an excited nineteen-year-old. I was looking forward to seeing the Soviets and how they treated us as we passed through. Since the British Military ran the train, there was no charge for the journey, but 10 Deutsche marks were required to cover my food and drink from the dining car.

I boarded with much anticipation and found a seat in one of the compartments, adjacent to the long corridor that ran along the entire carriage. It was the kind of train compartment one saw in classic war movies such as "The Great Escape." A sliding glass door sealed passengers into a small compartment where they sat across from one another. Head cushions were thoughtfully arranged and plenty of dark wood panelling lined the carriage. I was surprised that one could actually pull the top window down slightly, but I quickly put it up again as a sticker on the window stated they were not to be opened.

Everything was rather British and understated. It was like boarding a lower-class version of the Orient Express, a train that held a lot of mystique about the journey. The military train was really a symbol of Western opulence. As well maintained and (almost) as lavish as the Orient Express, the train had no torn seats or stains on the fabric in the carriages. A clash of cultures between socialism and the decadent West! Through the window, I was about to see my first impressions of communism in the faces of the Soviet guards and in the landscape we would travel through.

All the train doors started locking with a loud clunk as armed guards boarded the train with machine guns, which was very alarming. We were ready to travel on a journey that would take about four hours to cover the distance of 145 miles from Braunschweig to Charlottenburg.

Although nominally nonstop, the Berlin-bound train stopped in Helmstedt, the last station in the West, to change engines between the West and East German Railway systems and carry out border documentation checks. I assumed this was because each side used their own engines. We continued from there using an East German engine and from then on we would be in the East corridor. It was a foggy December day, and I was looking forward to the holiday. The windows of the train were not that clean, so I had to find patches where I could rub a space with my sleeve to see out; I was lucky to be in a warm carriage insulated from the cold world outside. From my window, I saw hideous watchtowers looming out of the mist like alien creatures on legs, barbed wire hanging in tangled circles along fences, signs in German for minefields, and guard dogs patrolling fences. Scenery passed in blurs at times, as I was sure we sped up and then slowed down along the route. Outside looked like a scene from a war movie but without any action. The grey and green uniforms of the guards were dull and drab, blending in with the landscape, except for the white epaulets flashing on their shoulders and white piping on their collars. They had a distinctive green band around their caps.

There was a lengthy stop in Marienborn on the East-West German border where Soviet soldiers checked the trains and greeted Allied soldiers with salutes in a platform ceremony. British officers exchanged documents with the Russian authorities and a detailed external check was carried out, including the use of dogs by the East German border guards, ostensibly to prevent smuggling of goods or refugees.

When I saw our British officers' march past my train window looking so official and disciplined, it made me think of the security of this corridor and the protection it offered to Westerners who wanted to travel to Berlin. I asked myself what an officer's job might be like and wondered what he did every day. Maybe I should consider it. I would be more secure doing this, I thought. After all, there was no war in these times, so how dreadful could it be? I would be in charge of others and have an enjoyable lifestyle that I knew was possible from what I had experienced at home in Berlin.

From my seat on the train, I saw the British officers passing over what looked like magazines to the East German guards. It was only later when I got home and mentioned it to my father that he told me it was common for British personnel to conceal a "Penthouse" magazine with the official documents handed to the Soviets to speed up the processing. On many occasions, officers would swap cap badges and belts as well. I still have a Soviet cap with a badge and belt that my father exchanged at Checkpoint Charlie in 1977. He would travel through as the military priest to make regular visits in East Berlin, as this was part of his outreach program to help those in the East.

The train made a brief stop in Magdeburg. It all felt quite "James Bond"- like. The decrepit DDR (German Democratic Republic/Deutsche Demokratische Republik) stations still had the station signs from Hitler's time, all created in the scary gothic script. It was very much a time warp; horses and carts travelled on roads; the apartment blocks in Magdeburg looked depressing and unkempt with paint peeling off the window frames. The entire city had bland design features with no aesthetically pleasing designs, just drab, block-shaped, functional spaces. I would never want to live there and felt so sorry for those that did.

As we neared the small town of Kirchmoser, I noticed some unrecognizable dark shapes looming in the fields alongside the track. It was so foggy that I couldn't make the shapes out. Then I noticed a long barrel facing directly towards us as we rounded a bend. More barrels emerged attached to heavy armoured vehicles, dark and rusty, blocked tightly together with one after the other. It appeared to be a military tank graveyard. I asked Corporal Wilson, one of the soldiers in my compartment, and he told me we were going past a huge Soviet tank repair workshop. What followed were fields upon fields of obsolete Russian T-62 & T-64 tanks, lined up in multiple rows at least six deep. It was rather ominous and scary seeing so many military vehicles as we glided alongside the fields for what seemed like ages, rather like witnessing a silent display of force waiting to be unleashed, except these were now spent forces. Corporal Wilson told me that the repair shop was still in use but not very busy. I wondered what action these tanks had seen and how dated they were. From what I could make out, some looked very damaged, with their turrets disfigured and tracks missing on their sides. My mind wandered, and I thought of all the battles I had set up on my bedroom floor with my soldiers and tanks, and those I had burned and blown up with firecrackers when I was younger. Just imagine if I could have torched this lot and had some real fun with life-sized tanks.

Just as I was looking at the train card to see what station would be next, a waiter slid the compartment door open.

"If you would like to come through, dinner will now be served."

"Thank you," said the corporal opposite me.

This was rather civilized, as they called each carriage in turn. I fumbled in my pocket for my 10 Deutsche Mark note and had it ready. I entered the dining car and noticed how nicely it was laid out, with an aisle down the middle. There were tables either side laid out with white china and candles on white tablecloths. It was a rather cosy atmosphere with plenty of warm wood trim, curtains tied back neatly along the sides of each table.

A waiter dressed in a pristine white starched buttoned-down tunic wearing a black bow tie welcomed me; he motioned for me to sit. To this day, I still remember him as I would take that train three more times and recognize him. He was an older gentleman with slick, flicked-back grey hair. He was always very polite and treated me as if I was an adult, which was nice, and he called me "sir".

Although it was not quite to Orient Express standards, the silver service was excellent. They even had their own wine label for the dining car. Corporal Wilson noticed me and asked if I would like to sit at his table with his mates, who offered me a glass of wine, which was rather kind of them. As we rolled through East Germany, past collective farms, and Soviet army camps, the waiters served us a sumptuous meal. It all seemed so surreal though as if I were in a dining car scene in a John Le Carré novel.

We soon arrived at Brandenburg, known as the oldest shunting hump in the world. This was a huge railway yard used to separate railway cars on to one of several tracks. Plenty of antiquated carriages parked in rows covered in dirt that I suspect had never moved.

The train stopped outside Potsdam for a further detailed search by the East German border guards before they left the train. The train subsequently handed over for its arrival into West Berlin at Wannsee and termination in Charlottenburg. I saw the brightly lit Funkturm tower of Berlin in the distance, and so I knew we were finally in the city. I took this trip a few times, and every time it did not fail to disappoint. The train operated like clockwork, and the service on board was impeccable. A similar routine followed during the outward/westbound journey. Coming back from Berlin, we enjoyed an English breakfast before the train even left the station at Charlottenburg. I remember that if the menu cards were pink, they served breakfast.

My family's posting to Berlin was a fantastic time. Nobody posted to Berlin back then knew if they were safe from the Soviets. East Germany surrounded West Berlin, so everyone including us enjoyed life to the fullest in case the Russians invaded again. My mother and father attended the ballet and attended numerous fancy parties. I did the same and made regular visits to the officers' club, where we would swim, play tennis, and have a Pimms cocktail for 30 cents. We became accustomed to eating German food when out. We all particularly enjoyed currywurst (a German Bratwurst dish) on the streets, after a night on the town.

Today I realize that we lived life in a bubble, even though we didn't realize it at the time. I spent my time enjoying lounging beside the officers' club swimming pool and naturally drawn to a lifestyle that my father enjoyed. I also continued to develop my talent for drawing, as army friends paid me to create house portraits for some pocket money. It was a step up and more lucrative than the free drawings I had created for the Haileybury Ornithology Club. I mixed with all the other officers' kids and started to realize that an officer's life in the Army could be a great career for me. Could I really become an officer and marry an attractive officer's daughter? I hoped to meet the ideal girl with a ponytail.

In the summer holidays, I invited Bronny out from England. She was blonde, the daughter of an army officer, and had a sophisticated cinched ponytail, so she fit the exact mould that I was attracted to. I had seen her numerous times at the officer's club swimming pool. She moved with a shimmer; walking around the pool tossing her golden hair back, her body was as gracile as a doe. We were just friends, but I really fancied her, especially when she trained her sultry eyes my way. Invitations arrived for our first parties at friend's houses, where she crushed me going off with boys who owned motorbikes instead of staying with me.

I started to sense that bothersome stigma again of not being worthy enough to attract an officer's daughter because I was the "Preachers Kid." (They called us PKs.) The girls considered the officers' sons who owned motorbikes as more hard-core, wicked, and fiercely attractive. I still had a great time, despite failing to attract the girls I wanted to date. I enjoyed disco dancing and won a big bottle of red Valpolicella wine at the Berlin River Boat Disco dancing competition. I still have my white bell-bottom disco pants from that era.

Some people worried about PKs. Apparently, we had a reputation for rebellion, and some suggested that this was the fault of P's not minding their K's. The preacher was so busy tending to his flock that he neglected his own. On the other hand, people suggested that preachers' kids were rebellious because we lived our lives in a fishbowl. Our rebellion was the natural consequence of people having such high expectations of us, in my opinion. In my case, I had a father who never thought I would amount to anything. He told me that art and music wouldn't lead me anywhere, so he taunted me to go out and get a real job and not to waste my time painting or playing my guitar in the basement.

What I experienced in Berlin affected me greatly and fuelled my desire to join the British Army as a career. Therefore, I finished at Windsor Boys School and headed to officer training in the UK. Nevertheless, it didn't take long for me to realize the illusion I had about military life. It wasn't the high life I enjoyed living when I was mixing with officers' sons and daughters. How tough could it be after my boarding school experiences? I was about to find out.

7

THE RIFLE

After three years, my father was posted from Berlin to the Royal Military Academy (RMA) at Sandhurst in England just before I chose to enlist in officer training at age twenty. I had applied and been accepted to join Brigade Squad at the Guards Depot in Pirbright. I felt I had something to look forward to, at last, a goal to work towards, and a career with which I was familiar. How coincidental that I would end up training at the very academy my father would be serving! Maybe it would give me an opportunity to develop more of a relationship with him and make him proud. He had constantly made comments that the art and guitar music that I had so enjoyed at Hamm School would not amount to a career.

I had packed lightly for Pirbright; told to bring only toiletries, underwear for a week, and a notebook. It seemed so minimal for an eight-week course, but I knew they provided everything else. They recommended bringing nothing personal, as there would be no free time and nowhere to put it.

Brigade Squad, as it was known in those days, was a brutal training course, designed to weed out applicants who wanted to join the Brigade of Guards as an officer. It couldn't be any worse than what I had endured at boarding school, I thought, except for the physical requirements. My father shouted at me for many years before this. The course provided valuable lessons for those who completed it and assisted in their subsequent selection and further training. It was a baptism by military fire if you will, and a taste of what the ordinary recruits experienced. We experienced a shorter, more intense course. At the time, I didn't realize how tough the training course would be.

Other than moving on to officer selection, we didn't fail or pass, per se, as there was no passing out parade, promotion or other completion benefits. As candidates, we still had to pass through the Regular Commissions Board at Westbury and then complete the commissioning course at RMA Sandhurst.

I had heard that the whole purpose of Brigade Squad was to drain from us every spark of individualism, moulding us into the combined identity of a single platoon. I was about to find out what that really meant, and how they were going to destroy my personal identity. They trained us to act accordingly and conform to certain expectations. We were of no use to the regiment until we had become automatons.

I wanted to join the Welsh Guards and was the only one at the time in training for that regiment. Others were interested in the other six regiments that made up the household division. In some cases, four were trying to get into the same regiment, like the Grenadier Guards. I felt I had a better chance of entering my preferred regiment, as I had met the commanding officer Lieutenant-Colonel Lewis from the Welsh Guards, and my father knew him well. In addition, my father had served the Welsh Guards for many years as their Padré. Lieutenant-Colonel Lewis wished me the best of luck before I left.

Mum drove me to the Guards Depot at Pirbright. The imposing entrance sign was a substantial rectangular board with the Brigade of Guards insignia emblazoned on it, and it made me feel very nervous when I first saw it. I said goodbye to Mum and checked in with my paperwork at the guardhouse closest to the entrance barrier. The first requirement was enlistment in the army as a guardsman. That first day involved lots of forms, photographs, health checks, injections etc. As I checked in, I noticed Lance Ranson, another tall enlistee like I. We were all very surprised and amused that Lance, who was such a huge guy, had fainted when we had the entrance day injections. We hadn't even begun the challenges of the course yet. At the end of the day, we received a crisp plastic identity card in a see-through wallet and for once, I felt very important. We were told never to lose the card and keep it in our wallets at all times should we have to produce it. We were required to remember our new army numbers emblazoned below our names.

We also checked into our narrow wooden barrack hut. It looked like it had popped out of one of those Second World War movies. Inside, grey steel beds lined each side of a long room. On each bed were neatly folded red blankets and sheets. Everyone had a tall steel double door locker in matching grey by the side of their beds. Off to one side in the back were the toilets, this time with doors, thankfully. As we relaxed, without warning, Corporal of Horse Carter marched in. Corporal of Horse is the equivalent title of a sergeant in other regiments. Carter was from the Blues and Royals cavalry regiment and was a tall, pale-skinned, wiry guy with a high-pitched, piercing voice.

"Right, you lot, fall in by your beds," he barked.

Carter brought us to attention, introduced himself with a torrent of curse words, and made sure we knew he was thankful that he wasn't one of our mothers. He made it clear that we wouldn't get any respect from him until we proved we had earned it.

"I won't call you 'sir' until you get out of here," he shouted. "Only then will I salute you as I am required to."

I already disliked Carter since he brought our mothers into the picture, which I found unnecessary. He was a Cockney from East London and clearly liked inflicting pain on recruits and was to play a significant part in the dehumanizing process we were about to endure.

As to my fellow officer recruits, I sensed a very highbrow Etonian/Oxford presence, the aura of lords' sons and the off-spring of captains of industry. For example, there was Lord Innis-Ker, as he wanted to be referred to. Then there was Eskington Pratt-Bolton whose double-barrelled last name sounded like a mouthful of marbles. Charles Bowyer said he hailed from the Bowyer sausages family.

Then there was Surrey Swayne, who was unrelated. He didn't speak with marbles and was what I call a regular normal lad. He had come from "below stairs" as they say, which meant that he was not from an upper-class family, and he wanted to cross the divide and become an officer. This was Surrey's second attempt at the course. I liked him immediately, and he was to become a great source of advice to all of us as the course unfolded. Another person I immediately liked was Francis Hobbs, who was hoping to join the Grenadier Guards. None of us had much time to chat and get to know each other, so we all had to get on with it and muddle our way through.

The course consisted of basic recruit training, field craft battle camp, a shooting competition, adventure training, and then a final forced march before a week of preparation for the Regular Commissions Board (RCB). RCB was the Army assessment centre where officer candidates faced further but more academic challenges. One had to pass one physical team challenge, in which all six team members had to forge a stream using a huge oil barrel, a rope, and two planks. I knew that I was in great physical shape, but looking at some of the others around me, I felt some would need some help, Lord Innis-Ker in particular. Rather pale and plump, he clearly had been living the life of a lord.

The first two weeks were spent "square bashing," a term used for marching, stamping our feet, pirouetting, and twirling to the frenzied barks of Drill Sergeant Everett on the parade ground. Marching made a distinct rock-crushing sound as we crunched around all day. The sore feet from breaking in our army boots was only part of the pain we endured in those first few weeks.

Sergeant Everett was a short, stocky Welshman from the valleys, so I felt comfortable with him since "he was one of us." When formed up as a platoon, he told us that his job was to turn us from civvies into respectable, precision-focused soldiers.

"If you can't march and salute then you are of no use to any of your regiments," he shouted.

He carried a pace stick with him everywhere he went. It was a tool used to measure the stride of our marches so they conformed to a set measure on the stick. I still, to this day, remember the way he taught us how to do the about-turn, or as we called it "the Check TLV manoeuvre." When we were about to turn, we stopped first by drawing the rear foot up to the leading one. Then we pivoted around one hundred and eighty degrees, forming the letters T, L, and V as we turned with our boots. We did it so many times that it became second nature, and I will never forget it. It turned out to be my luck that I was coordinated and the tallest in the platoon, so they appointed me the right marker, the position at the front of the platoon alongside which everyone formed their ranks.

Marching wasn't easy for everybody. I recall a fellow recruit, Kelly, who was ganglier than I was and looked like he was ill. He had such a ghostly white complexion that one took an involuntary step back when he came close to you. Kelly was whiter than milk and marched like a stick insect with a hunched back. He had absolutely no coordination and was all arms and legs jumbled up. I couldn't understand why he had chosen to come on the course, as it was clear he wouldn't last long. Sadly for him, he was a target from the very first day and picked upon relentlessly. One time they pulled Kelly aside on the parade ground and made him spend the rest of the day marching past the reviewing stand practicing endless right-handed salutes. That evening we heard that he had been docked two days' pay for not swinging his arms up high enough, and for several salutes to the wrong side. I already felt sorry for him.

If a recruit did something wrong and was put on a charge, he was required to dress in full battle kit complete with his forty-pound backpack. Then he was marched double-time into Capt. Falkner's office, after which he was required to mark time in front of the Captain for a short while, and then told to halt. Capt. Falkner's words were brief, usually guilty as charged and docked pay. A recruit had limited opportunity to explain or ask questions. The ordeal ended with a double-time march out ordered by Sergeant Everett and the return to the barrack-hut.

It is fair to say at this point that none of us openly stated we felt sorry for someone. That schoolboy mentality kicked in again with minimal empathy for the weak and ordinary. Some mutterings passed between the recruits. I could already sense that the lords and fancier types were forming a clique and would become their own mini unit.

One morning we awoke at 5:00 a.m. to Carter's "soft" voice. He ordered us to be dressed in running gear in fifteen minutes. Still shivering, we hustled out for a brisk three-mile run. At one point Surrey passed the word that it wasn't usually the sand hill at this time of the morning.

"They would save that experience for later," he said.

As we rounded a corner, I saw a large sliver of yellow leading up between some pines. Clearly, this sand hill was a punishment to come, and heaven help us if they dressed us in full kit to go up it. I was in better shape than most and offered to assist various recruits across the different obstacles on the assault course. Hobbs, despite being more athletic than most, was very grateful when needing help on one occasion. We got back to the hut, huffed and puffed our way into the room. Innis-Ker was already complaining that it was unfair to be running before breakfast. We came to immediate attention as we suddenly realized Capt. Falkner was standing right there in the middle of our barrack room waving his swagger stick around. He was wearing very highly polished knee-high brown leather boots, the kind of boots you could see your face in due to the polishing. He announced that the inspection of beds and lockers would occur at 8:30 a.m. and that we had very little time to get our uniforms organized. We gathered round to view what he called the perfect locker layout. The captain then opened the grey steel doors by one of the spare beds, and there was the perfect Harrods window display of all elements of our army kit, all carefully laid out on each shelf and in perfect order! We needed to make our lockers look like this.

In the locker, shirts hung organized to the left with creases all pointing the same way. Socks were folded and carefully laid out to the right with a creased smiley face looking out at us from the shelf. Bulled (highly polished) dress shoes pointed forward, a wash kit with knife, fork, and spoon meticulously arranged, and drill jumpers lay neatly folded.

Capt. Falkner explained, "Once you are in the field for real, you must keep yourselves and your kit clean. Your men will be looking up to you and therefore you must set an example to them."

From our lockers, he then moved on to the precisely folded bedding, with blankets folded exactly to the same height, width, and depth.

"You need to use a Bedstick to prepare perfect bed blocks like this."

The captain pointed to a box at the end of the room and told everyone to get a Bedstick. Each stick was eighteen inches long and used for measuring the exact width of the blankets so they all conformed in a neat block. I still have mine today, being a unique item that allows me to tell a story. Each stick was painted in the navy and burgundy colours of the Household Division[12].

They showed us the way to fold the sheets and blankets in the approved, precise way and to prepare the bed blocks for the blankets, complete with hospital corners for the bedding.

---

[12] Seven regiments, comprising five-foot guards and two mounted cavalry.

"I want the beds so tight that I can bounce a 50 pence piece off them. Do you all understand?"

It was a lot to take in so quickly. We only had until 8:30 a.m. to prepare our own versions of this ordered system and it was already 7:30 a.m. Fortunately, we had Surrey with us, who showed us some shortcuts. He also showed us how to polish our boots and blanco (blacken) our belts and told us about 'Clear,' a banned product, which was a high gloss floor polish that would shorten the job of achieving shiny parade boots.

"Don't ever get caught using it, as it's a serious offence," Surrey said. You also had to be careful applying it as it would crack on the top coat if not applied properly.

At 8:30 a.m., everyone had created some abysmal displays of bed blocks and locker layouts. In some cases, the blankets stuck out beyond the length required by the Bedstick. Some of us were not proficient at folding, and it was truly a mess. Corporal of Horse Carter and Sergeant Everett started the inspections randomly. Bowyer was first, and immediately they flung all his bedding on the floor stating, "It looks like a homeless person had been wrapped in it."

I could already see Kelly's red lips trembling at the far end of the room as they approached his bed. They asked him what the regimental motto was for the Scots Guards, the regiment he was hoping to join, as they prodded his kit in his locker. He knew he had one boot half polished so he had turned it around so they couldn't see it. Unfortunately, they did, and Corporal of Horse Carter ordered him to clean his boots later that evening. Then they reached Gaggero's locker, who gave them a hearty Irish smile. Carter smiled back and took a closer look at something on Gaggero's shelf.

"Do you have a larder in your locker, Gaggero?"

"What do you mean sir?"

"I see a foreign edible object in your pants."

Well, the whole platoon burst out laughing at that comment. A foreign edible object?

Corporal of Horse Carter carefully withdrew the half-eaten sandwich from the pants and waved it under Gaggero's nose.

"I mean this, sonny."

"Sorry, it was left over from yesterday, and I didn't know where to put it last minute."

"Well it doesn't belong in your underwear, does it?"

"No, sir."

"Go and throw it in the bin."

I couldn't believe he got off. Then Carter and Everett turned and faced us all from the far end of the room.

"Some of you have not been called upon today. Just make sure you are ready for your time."

After they left, we all laughed with Gaggero. This first inspection passed relatively well despite what felt like a "trial by fire." While they carried out these inspections, Carter and Everett quizzed us on our knowledge of the Household Division and our regiments.

Corporal of Horse Carter asked Holland Hibbert, "What does *Honi soit qui mal y pense* mean?"

"Shame on him who thinks evil of it, sir."

Sgt. Everett asked another question, "What does *Septem juncta in uno* mean?"

"Seven regiments joined in one," shouted Surrey.

Who was the commanding officer of the regiment we hoped to join was a typical question. They berated us loudly in front of the platoon if we didn't answer these questions correctly. I escaped the first inspection with some minimal comments on poor folding. Of course, no one was perfect, except Innis Kerr. He said, "I have watched my butler do this sir, so I know the ropes."

Sergeant Everett commented scathingly that he wouldn't have a butler when he became an officer and so had better get used to doing it himself.

We didn't know what day it was most of the time, as weekends never counted for anything. We all sensed the end was not that far away but also feared we had that last major hurdle when everything would come together on the forced march at the end.

Mornings we concentrated on inside housekeeping; afternoons we saw how much our bodies could take with various forced marches around the depot in full kit. This was to prepare us for the final test at the end of the course. Physically I was holding up well, but some of the others were not. One day while we were on the assault course, Gaggero, the Irish lad, fell awkwardly and broke his leg, which was unfortunate, so he left Brigade Squad.

Kelly limped along and became even more picked upon. He would often cry towards the end of our runs because he couldn't make it, so we had to run back and drag him along. On one of our runs, he really wasn't doing well. We were about to encounter what was named the Three Sisters and the famous Sand Hill. The Sand Hill was no ordinary hill. It was a hill that would tear out our lungs and reduce our legs to jelly as one attempted to get away from the red-faced monster barking from the bottom. We knew that it was coming, but we didn't know when. We had to tackle both hills with full forty-pound packs and weapons. Kelly scraped through the Three Sisters, which were medium sized hills, but he collapsed in a tangled heap halfway up the Sand Hill. We had to unravel Kelly's legs, twirled around him like spaghetti around a spoon. Sergeant Everett told us to leave him there and shouted at him to get up and finish. Kelly said he couldn't, and so, whimpering and groaning, they stripped him of his kit. They ordered him to run up and down the Sand Hill ten times in his underwear because of his weaknesses. Kelly showed up at the hut later that evening, after taking three hours to complete the sergeant's requirements. We all knew that Kelly wouldn't last long with this kind of treatment. Some of the guys helped him undress and flung him onto his bed. I was exhausted, too, and offered to help the others on a few occasions but wasn't sure they really appreciated it.

Corporal of Horse Carter enjoyed punishing us for any minor offense we committed. His favourite punishment was ordering us to scrape the paint off the pipes below the urinals.

Carter would smile like a salamander as he ordered one of us to crawl underneath the urinals and use our toothbrush to scrub eight inches of paint off the pipe to reveal the bare copper beneath it. We subsequently discovered thinly applied paint so it came off quite easily with water. Carter was rather thick; we would finish the unpleasant job quickly and then pretend to be brushing furiously while we chatted beneath the urinals. One time someone really pissed him off so Carter meted out twelve inches of pipe for a few of us to clean. I remember him saying, "It's going to take you hours to do this, so be prepared to stay up all night." He would stomp in to check the work from time to time while we pretended that it was an awful job. After an hour, he left for the night, stating that he expected it completed by 7:00 a.m. the following morning. We scraped the required twelve inches and then turned in for the night with everyone else. The next morning we acted as if we were completely exhausted from the arduous all night punishment, and pleaded for no more.

So far, we had completed the basic recruit training and adventure field training at Brigade Squad. We still had the weapons training to finish and the final forced march at the end before the course instructors prepared us to face the Regular Commissions Board.

One night someone suddenly flipped on the lights in the barrack hut to wake us. They ordered us immediately to get outside, and once there, Capt. Falkner addressed us with a severe tone.

"Does anyone know what happened to Kelly?"

We looked at each other inquisitively. What was he talking about? Capt. Falkner stated, "Kelly's bed is empty, and there is no sign of him."

Then we saw three figures looming out of the mist on the dimly lit road. Between two soldiers, hanging off their arms, was a bedraggled Kelly. As he drew closer, we saw tears running down Kelly's ghostly white face. He made no sound; his head hung down to avoid our stares. We looked at each other but said nothing.

"What's going on, Sir?" Ranson piped up.

"During the night someone sacked him," Capt. Falkner replied.

A few of us asked what "sacked" meant. Apparently, Kelly was gagged with tape around his mouth first and then bundled into a burlap sack. It did not mean they fired him. In this undignified state, he was then dragged up the Sand Hill, and buried up to his neck in the sand and left. If it weren't for some passing soldiers who heard the moaning, he would still be up there.

Capt. Falkner interrupted our inquiring discussions by saying, "I am asking anyone who knows anything about this to step forward now. This is not the sort of conduct becoming of an officer and not acceptable at Brigade Squad."

No one flinched; there was a long pause while we scrutinized each other with suspicious faces.

"I will get to the bottom of this kerfuffle," said Capt. Falkner. "Now get some sleep. You'll need it for tomorrow's workload."

No one knew anything about the incident. We thought that maybe Corporal of Horse Carter and his buddies had sacked Kelly to teach him a lesson. I felt sorry for him, as he undoubtedly knew he set himself up for a tough course but gave it his best shot regardless. We all thought his treatment was rather unnecessary and in poor taste. Consequently the following morning Kelly left us. We found his bed and locker emptied when we returned from our usual morning run. I felt bad for Kelly, as he was a soft target for the instructors and recruits. Both could see his weaknesses early on and sought to wear him down. He really wasn't officer material, being an introvert, softly spoken and very shy. I couldn't imagine him commanding a platoon of men. He would have been better suited to a job with minimal human interaction, such as information technology.

What I detested about the Brigade Squad process was that instructors deemed it acceptable to pick on the vulnerable. I had witnessed similar behaviour too often at Haileybury, and

Bloxham. Bullying was rampant years ago and not subject to the same laws as today. Was I naive to think that the army would offer me better treatment than I had experienced at boarding school? I only viewed the outward, enjoyable facets of the military with its impressive uniforms and beautiful girls all dressed up at officer's functions.

In between random barrack room inspections, we spent the ensuing week on the firing range, getting familiar with various weapons. The largest beast was the general-purpose machine gun or GPMG. This gun featured in numerous war movies I had watched and had been in use by the military for decades. It looked very cool due to its sleek yet robust profile with splayed legs at the far end; however, it was also rather cumbersome, bulky, and heavy to carry, so we always dreaded being the one to lug the GPMG around the assault course.

The gun we had to rely upon every day was the self-loading rifle (SLR) with a 7.62mm calibre. I was very comfortable with the rifle and was a skilled shot because in my teens I had learned to shoot by practising with my air rifle at home. When I joined the Combined Cadet Force at Bloxham, I had improved my shooting skills even more. We had to know everything about the SLR, including stripping it down while blindfolded and reassembling it in the dark. We would spend hours cleaning our rifles with special rifle bore oil and rags, so much so, that if I smelt it again I would instantly remember it. Each day before we left the firing range, we stated that we had no rounds in our possession, as that constituted a court-martial offence. The SLR was quite heavy and later replaced with lighter rifles with more automatic firepower.

At last, the day came for our final battle-ready exercise. We were loaded into convoy trucks early one morning and trans-ported off to an unknown destination. At the time, none of us knew exactly where we were going. Surrey told us our chal-lenge would most likely be Salisbury Plain, a vast open terrain of undulating chalk country with hardly any trees. Salisbury Plain was roughly three hundred square miles, of which half was devoted to military training by the army. In 1943, the army evacuated a small village, Imber, located in the middle of the Plain, for military use. It had remained closed and deserted ever since, except for an annual service at the village church. About 39 square miles of the plain was closed permanently to the public due to unexploded ordinance and bombs. I hoped like everyone else that we wouldn't be training in that part.

Heavy olive-coloured canvas covered the backs of our trucks so we didn't know where we were. After a two-and-a-half hour drive, we diverted off the smooth highway and drove along a bumpy dirt road. After an abrupt stop, the instructors flung back the canvas and lowered the tail flap at the back of the truck. Ordered off, we sluggishly lumbered off with our heavy Bergen, (backpacks) each Bergen weighed before we boarded. Each of us had to carry forty pounds plus our weapons and water. We didn't know how long this exercise would last, but once again, the ever-reliable Surrey told us all about it from his past experience.

He said, "You will each be called upon to be a leader at any point during the Tab[13]. You won't know when your turn will occur, so you have to always be prepared."

Our forced march would be over four days and consist of roughly eight miles per day. The one thing they did not tell us was the lack of full meals each day, further testing our abilities under pressure. How much we could eat and how often would soon be apparent.

We would also have to negotiate fake enemy positions, enemy fire, and a river on our way. We had to march as a platoon, and everyone was responsible for each other, similar to the modern-day reality TV show, *Survivor*.

The first day or so was fine as the weather was dry and the flat terrain was easy. Our initial objective was to make our way to a rendezvous point on the map. At the end of the day, they

---

[13] A relatively fast march over distance carrying a load.

threw us a curveball and told us that we would be encountering enemy shelling at any minute. Initially, we reacted by marching faster to evade it. Then someone shouted out, "What if they are really going to shell us"?

"Don't be so stupid!" Innis-Ker yelled back.

Then like a flock of starlings wheeling in the air, everyone started to jog, some of us quicker than others did. Almost at once, we realized this was ridiculous. How stupid were we? They wouldn't actually shell us! Therefore, we slowed down. "Just cool it, boys," hollered Innis-Ker, who was always the one to try to stop any unnecessary running. The news of the shelling came as we were ready to stop for camp; we were exhausted after hauling our packs for six miles. As the shelling alarm dissipated, the instructors ordered us to march double time to cover the last two miles. A change of command took place, and Hobbs had to lead the platoon. He did a fine job despite our tiredness, keeping us motivated as we made it to camp under the cover of darkness. That night they gave us full rations but next morning only a glass of orange juice with no breakfast. Some of the guys traded some chocolate they had smuggled into their packs.

I hoped that my turn to command would be following, as I felt ready for it. But, somehow, I felt they were keeping Ranson and me, the biggest and tallest guys in the platoon, for last. Maybe they wanted to wear us down even further after we had helped others carry their loads to see what we were made of.

I remember wading through a river at one point and then emptying water from my boots, wringing my socks and walking a mile, running another mile, and then walking again. By the time we stopped, our feet were sore, blister-ridden, and verging on dry. We never knew what we had to do next as the plan was to wear us all out, and it was working. Coupled with the half rations, the daily marching, and heavy packs loads, the strain was making many of us weaker. Lack of sleep then came into play, with false ambushes occurring randomly at night. I still kept hoping I could take command soon, but they were waiting;

all this time I felt my own physical well-being eroded. I had offered to help carry the GPMG for miles as I was the tallest, and that was a mistake, as I, too, was now exhausted. Ranson had done the same, and I could see the strain written across his face. How many more days would this go on, I wondered? When I asked Surrey, he said two more days.

They reduced our ration packs. A full ration pack contained one of four tinned meal choices: chicken curry, bacon grill, rice, or soup. Then there was a biscuit pack, fruit, some chocolates, and dextrose tablets. A few dried packets of coffee or tea, and apple flakes or oatmeal block rounded out the full ration. We were limited to a half-ration pack those last two days, which consisted of the snacks but not the main meal.

For those of us who really needed food, like us tall guys, this was a major problem. What's that phrase? "An army marches on its stomach."

They gave me command of the platoon finally on the very last day, just as evening was coming. I felt relieved to know that I wouldn't have to do that much since it was a routine camp stop. Thankfully, Ranson offered to take the machine gun as I had carried it for two days in addition to my own rifle.

As we marched along towards the final camp, Surrey suddenly appeared alongside me to warn me.

"Dan," he said. "They have planned the worst part for the end. Last year they carried out an ambush with smoke, simulated grenades, and mortar fire in the village. You'll have to be on your wits and be ready."

I was tired, and it was hardly what I wanted to hear. I responded, "We haven't been trained to counter an ambush. What did the platoon do last year when they were ambushed"?

Surrey made me laugh by saying. "Remember that Monty Python movie, *The Holy Grail?* Remember the evil white rabbit?"

"Yes," I said.

"Well, they all ran away, didn't they," he joked.

"No, seriously, what did they really do?"

"The platoon leader last year careened off into an empty house and wouldn't come out or issue any orders."

"I can do better than that," I replied.

I had to have a plan so that it appeared I had command of my platoon. Everyone else had been lucky enough to take charge without any major challenges occurring. All they had to do was motivate everyone to keep marching to a particular destination.

We were about two miles from the village of Imber when the instructors ordered us to pick up the pace to rendezvous with friendly forces in the village. They expected us to follow the main road leading in. I quickly consulted the map, and since, thanks to Surrey, I knew it was a trap, I made the decision to take a less risky approach from the north, rather than use the main route. I stopped the platoon for a moment, but the instructors immediately told us to keep moving, as they didn't want me to have time to formulate a plan. They weren't aware that I already knew there was going to be an ambush. So, unfortunately, I had no choice but to circulate my plan as we marched along. My plan was that if we came under fire, we were to split into two groups and disperse onto either side of the road. We knew there was a church in the village, so I chose that as the rendezvous point. I wasn't able to tell my platoon where the church was because we couldn't stop and consult the map, which seemed ridiculous at the time. Any platoon in a real-life situation would have halted and formulated an approach plan, but not us. We would attempt to outflank the would-be attackers and make our way around to the church. Hobbs was to lead half the platoon that would split if we came under fire, and I had the rest.

Surrey got my attention again. "The ambush will consist of explosions and gunfire with no counter troops. The officers and instructors will watch where you deploy and how you command your men. Good luck." Then he fell back in line.

As we neared the village, everything was quiet. It was a cloudy night, so it was darker than usual, which was excellent, as we needed the cover. We were on the main road into the village, so I silently motioned everyone off the road and into an adjoining field. We then held close to a long, tall hedgerow that allowed us to approach the village with some cover, rather than being out on the open road. Surrey gave me a thumbs-up as we crept along the hedgerow and came to an intersection near the main road. The main road continued. A narrow lane led off it around the perimeter of the village. I knew from my earlier brief look at the map that this lane would eventually bring us to the church on the other side of the village.

As we quickly jogged one by one down the lane, suddenly all hell broke loose.

One of us snapped a trip flare that triggered an enormous burst of successive explosions. Bright white flares lit up the entire sky, and I could see flashes of gunfire coming from the windows of a vacant farmhouse on the far side of the lane. The gunfire sounded realistic, and it was rather terrifying to experience what it must feel like being in a real battle. The only difference was we didn't hear bullets drilling past our ears. Thunderous explosions ignited quite close to us, deafening our ability to communicate with each other in all the chaos. To make matters worse, a thick grey smoke immediately engulfed us before I could issue any orders. "Damn it!" I thought and screamed out for the platoon to split as agreed. My group took the nearest cover possible in a deep ditch on the side of the lane. Hobbs's half dispersed into various buildings further up the lane. There was no way of making contact with him, but at least I knew his men had followed according to our plan. I remained with Ranson and the rest of the platoon but thought to myself, *why hadn't they issued us with radios to communicate with each other?* After all, that is what would have happened in a real field situation.

We had to hunker down, reorganize, and make our way out of this. I presumed Hobbs would stay put and defend his position on the other side of the narrow lane. Ranson had the GPMG, so I quickly ordered him to set it up and cover the road ahead as the instructors were watching. I ordered my men to spread out along the ditch and be ready to oppose any incoming troops. When ambushed, we bunched up, which was not wise.

We dug in, and after what seemed like ages, there were some loud whistles, after which the gunfire and explosions stopped. The instructors appeared through the lifting smoke and came towards us to debrief us. Initially, they commended us for taking a divergent route into the village and for then splitting into two organized groups and not fanning out. In a real-life ambush, they advised that we should gauge the firepower of the enemy first before making any rash decisions. They ordered us to fall back in on the lane to march to a planned camp for the final night.

It was then that disaster befell me. Before I climbed out of the ditch, I reached for my rifle, but it wasn't beside me. I panicked and realized that in all the mêlée it might have slid further down into the ditch. It was so dark I was unable to see into the bottom. *Oh no, this is terrible!* I thought. Losing a rifle was tantamount to a court-martial offense in military law. *What am I going to, say? I have mislaid my rifle.*

"Thomas get back in line!" ordered Capt. Falkner.

"Sir, I need to locate my rifle. I know it is down in the ditch, but I can't see it. It was tucked up close to me. It had been a tight squeeze as we were all crammed in when the ambush started."

One of the sergeants had a torch, so he shone it into the ditch. To my horror, there was nothing there, simply holes in the mud from our boots digging into the bank and flat grass from where we lay. No rifle! Now I was about to be chastised in front of the whole platoon. This was the worst thing that could have happened to me at the end of the course.

My body turned to Jell-O; I was totally demoralized, my heart pounded in my chest. I was back in that freezing swimming pool again at Haileybury. Terror struck, my mind drowning, dreading the berating I would get when we returned to base.

No one said anything. Many recruits turned their faces the other way. The fancy lords chuckled to themselves behind a smirk.

Surrey came up to me and whispered, "I think one of them took it. Don't let them see you rattled, you'll be fine."

Surrey tried to boost me up, but I knew the minute the rifle was lost that my dream to join the guards was shattered. I was supposed to trust these people in a life-threatening situation, but clearly, one or two of them wanted to do me in and had another agenda.

"You realize this is a serious offense, Trooper Thomas." Capt. Falkner said firmly. "Losing your weapon whilst in the field."

Just then, Trooper Holland shouted from the other side of the lane. "I have found a rifle, Sir. It could belong to Thomas."

Indeed, it was mine, but it was in a ditch on the other side of the lane where I had not been. I protested immediately that I had not been over there, but no one listened. Capt. Falkner seemed relieved, but I still had it coming to me.

When we returned to Pirbright Barracks the following day, it was my turn to be read the riot act and marched in double time before Capt. Falkner. I asked permission to speak and told him that I had not been on the other side of the lane during the whole ambush.

"Well, how did it get there?" he remarked sternly. "You are responsible for your weapon at all times during a combat mission. You know the rules."

I knew that someone had taken it from me in all the chaos. I kicked myself for not holding onto it tightly and had to suck it up and face the consequences. It was the perfect opportunity for someone to do me in late in the course. Lucky for me what transpired was a stay of execution. I was docked a month's pay instead and so avoided the court-martial threat that could have been carried out. This incident counted as a major black mark against me, even though my performance on the course had been exemplary up to that point. I was mortified and felt I was doomed, but I finished the course with no further incidents.

When I returned home to Sandhurst, my father would not speak of the incident at all. He had evidently heard about it through the army grapevine and was disappointed, but offered no support. There was a frightening silence in the air; I hated it. I felt it was pointless to argue my case with him, so I proceeded to Westbury to take the Regular Commission Board selection course. I did well, but the die was cast.

One morning a few weeks' later, a letter arrived from RCB informing me of my non-selection. The reason given was that I needed more time to mature and be ready for the army, so they invited me back again the following year to try again. I was rejected even though I considered myself far more capable, sharper, and fitter than most of them. My reaction was "what a load of nonsense." I was pretty gutted[14]. Clearly, the establishment didn't want a mere padre's son getting in, just like poor Surrey Swayne from the other ranks, who had endured the training twice, striving to succeed and cross the line. He would have made an exemplary officer but the odds were against him. All of us had benefited from Surrey's invaluable advice at some point on the course, and many would not have got through it if it wasn't for him.

"That is it! This is the end for me!" I said to myself. "I'll have to do something else for a career."

Those who supported me tried to boost my confidence and bolster my depression. Passing Brigade Squad would have been a great opportunity to show my father that I really was officer material, but instead, I sensed that I had let him down. Again. A few weeks later, the Green Howards Regiment offered me an officer's commission, but I turned it down. It simply wasn't the Guards and the fairytale story to which I had become hopelessly attached.

I reluctantly returned to reside with my parents at five The Square, RMA Sandhurst where, ironically, all my fellow officer recruits, who had passed, were now coming to complete their training. It felt like the ultimate slap in the face.

---

[14]　To feel extremely upset or disappointed.

8

HURDLES FOR CONFIDENCE

Austin A40 Farina MK II

My confidence and self-esteem were very low. I knew I was officer material and yet had to accept what had happened at Brigade Squad, so I decided to focus on getting my driving license, since this would provide me with some freedom to explore other career options. I had been able to drive in Germany since I had taken a military driving test, but I didn't have a UK license yet.

Two years earlier, back in Berlin, my first relationship with cars had been a disaster when I purchased a Prinz NSU. It was manufactured in West Germany and had a rather boring boxy shape, or as we might say in the UK, it looked a bit "naff"[15]. From the very moment I had set eyes on it, my bad luck had begun. It was perched up on bricks, but I was convinced it was

---

[15] British slang word *meaning* uncool, tacky.

roadworthy and I could find tyres. Spare tyres and other parts were difficult to find, as I didn't know that the car had stopped production in 1962. I overlooked these glaring warning signs since the price was only 100 Deutsche Marks (about £25). Despite my poor judgement I bought it and had it transported to our driveway.

I remember being excited about my purchase at the time, but my father complained incessantly that it made our house look like a junkyard, and he was reluctant to help me find parts to fix it. Therefore, it sat there, rusting away for the entire time we lived in Berlin. Maybe this was an omen for my driving experiences to come.

Now that we lived at the RMA in Sandhurst, I took whatever transport was available. Trains and the London Underground had been fine for me, as they were much cheaper than the cost of owning a car.

My first civilian driving test took place in the spring of 1979. It was going well until I drove through a housing estate.[16] The examiner was about to test me on the three-point turn and the emergency stop. As I was driving along, I noticed in the distance what looked like a dog in the middle of the road. It wasn't a tiny dog but a massive German shepherd, who eyed me intently as I approached him. I hoped he would move as I got closer, but he decided to pause and then pull up his haunches as dogs do when they are about to do their business. "Oh no, I thought to myself. What am I going to do?" I turned and looked at John, the examiner, hoping he would say something, but he didn't. He was a rather severe-looking chap with heavy black-rimmed glasses and sat there awkwardly, like a sack of potatoes, eyeing his clipboard.

"Should I stop for the dog?" I asked.

---

[16] A group of homes built together as a single development.

John still didn't answer and raised his eyes from his clipboard and stared ahead with a straight face to see what my next manoeuvre would be.

Since the dog wasn't going to move and was taking its time, as I got closer I decided to rev the engine slightly, rather than blast my horn. It still didn't budge, so the dog forced me to stop the car and wait.

"Tut, tut, tut" said John, as he wrote something down on the test sheet attached to his clipboard.

"That wasn't a problem, was it? I mean, I couldn't run over the dog? I hope you are not taking points off for that?"

I continued with my driving test and did a great job on the rest of it. At the end, I parked in the test centre parking lot, after which John turned to me and said, "I am sorry, but you failed by two points."

"What? But I didn't make any mistakes."

"You stopped for the dog, which could have caused other cars behind you to be in an accident. You should have blasted your horn to scare the dog off the road and then kept going."

I sat there in silence as John left me in the car with my failed paperwork. *This is ridiculous*, I thought. How could a dog pooping in the street cause me to fail? Surely, this test was about controlling the car, not how to interact with animals on the road. I didn't realize until later that driving a car also meant one had to be aware of one's surroundings and be sure that one didn't inadvertently cause an accident. Later on, my friends told me that you have to stop for a dog, as one cannot simply run them over, whereas cats don't get the same privilege. Apparently, you can flatten a cat at will. I had been correct, but it was too late to do anything about it.

The second time I took my test I had to use my mother's much-loved second-hand car—a vintage 1959 Austin A40 Farina MK II, a car whose top speed was 66.7 mph. It took a sluggish twenty seconds as it dawdled its way to reach 50 mph. Instead of handle winders, one had to use finger grips to pull up or lower the windows. Mum's car had some additional issues as well; for example, it had no second gear and jumped from first to third gear. In addition, the passenger door was brittle and stiff, so one had to reach through the window to open it. The biggest concern, however, was that the car would occasionally stall for reasons we never knew. The only way it would start again was for someone to get out of the car, remove the petrol cap at the back, and then blow into the fuel tank. The car would miraculously start again. Maybe it had something to do with engine pressure, we guessed.

We placed a rubber mat beneath the foot pedals to cover a gaping hole so that an examiner wouldn't see the road as I was driving along. I just hoped that whomever he or she was would be okay with the car's deficiencies. Of course, this time, I got the crazy wild Scottish examiner, Mr. MacDonald, a man with fiery red hair, bushy sideburns and a heavy Scottish brogue that I could hardly understand, a bit like Alistair Frazier, the well-known butler from the very popular British TV series "Upstairs Downstairs." Upon seeing my car, as we strode from the testing office, Mr. MacDonald asked if it was roadworthy.

"It's like ye hae an older car, so I hope it's had its MOT (ministry of transport test)?" he asked.

"Yes, it should be fine. However, I should warn you before you get in about a few oddities. The door handle is very stiff, so you may have to bang on it first before it will turn open. If that doesn't work, simply pull down the window and grab the handle. Also, if it stalls, I will have to get out and run to the back of the car for a moment."

Mr. MacDonald said, "I see that your MOT sticker is richt thare so that is gud. Okay, let's get guing as I hae many tests today."

I neglected to tell him there was no second gear, hoping that he wouldn't have a problem with that. I started her up, and off we trundled out of the test centre. The car gave a few coughs and splutters but thankfully made it out to the main road. I then chanced it and made the sudden leap to third gear.

"What kinda gear change did ye just dae, Mr. Thomas?"

"I simply wait until she gets fast enough so I can go straight into third."

"What about second gear? I canna fail ya right noo if you are going tae skip gears like that."

I reluctantly replied, "There was one more thing I didn't tell you at the centre, and that is the car doesn't have a second gear."

"I should fail ye richt noo but since your MOT sticker is valid and the car was passed for the road I am guing to overlook the matter. Ye must get this fixed immediately, as it's dangerous and could produce bursts o`speed that canna cause an accident."

"I will, as soon as I get the money from my parents."

"Yeah," I thought to myself, "like the burst of speed going from zero to 50mph in twenty seconds was going to cause an accident."

We then started driving up the hill on the ring[17] road inside Basingstoke town centre. I knew I had to keep her going steady, as this was where she would sometimes stall. For some reason, she didn't like hills, also compounded by the shift I had to make from first to third gear. There was also nowhere to pull off, so I quietly prayed and hoped nothing would happen. Alongside the traffic lanes was a bus lane, which was an automatic fail if I drove in there. I started to hear the car choking, so I gassed her a bit more and shifted gears, just at the point when the engine was beginning to growl and being overwhelmed. We jolted back and forth half way up the hill, and the engine started to falter.

"Oh no."

"Wull ye pull off into the side street, please, before ye lose your engine, so we can park."

I panicked and missed the turn altogether as it came so quickly. I also couldn't understand what Mr. MacDonald was asking, as I was concentrating on the road, and not trying to decipher his heavy accent so I accidentally swerved into the bus lane.

---

[17]   A series of connected roads encircling a town

"Noo ye are in the bus lane an need to get out o` here richt away."

Through my rear view mirror, the humongous number 55 double-decker bus to Reading was quickly trundling up the hill behind us. "O no, this is not good!" I couldn't get any more power from the engine, and then she annoyingly stammered to a halt in the bus lane.

"Jump oot. Thar's smoke coming oot o`your bonnet[18]. Put the flashers[19] on so that the bus knows we hae an emergency."

There wasn't time for me to run around to the back and open the petrol cap, which was my first thought, to try to remedy the situation.

Since Mr. MacDonald was speaking quickly in his gritty Scottish brogue, it was hard to understand his words and this wasn't the time to ask him to speak more slowly.

"What flashers, Mr. Macdonald? This car doesn't have any!"

Now a heavy black pall of smoke was curling ominously into the air from under the bonnet. This had never happened before, so I knew it was serious.

Mr. MacDonald stood at the back of the car and waved the number 55 bus by as the angry driver sounded his horn and waved profusely while lowering his window and uttering some nasty words at us. In the meantime, I moved over to the railings in case the car exploded.

"Dae ye hae a red triangle? Ya know, an emergency road-side kit."

"No."

Mr. MacDonald joined me over on the pavement as curious bystanders came over to view the smoke billowing out from the engine.

"Do you want me to call the fire brigade?" a passerby yelled from outside a shop. That seemed like a much-needed question as the entertainment value grew for everybody.

---

18   The hood of the vehicle.
19   Hazard lights activated when a driver pushes the hazard light.

"Yes, please right away," I said.

Mr. MacDonald stated clearly for once, "This concludes your test, Sonny. I should nae have allowed the test tae start wi , wi a car like this."

I muttered back "I know the car wasn't in great shape," and then continued to watch the disaster unfold. What was I going to tell my mother, who was down at the test centre waiting for me?

A few flames started to lick out of the engine cover and spread up to the windscreen[20]. In the distance, I could hear the wail of a fire engine coming from below the town. The sound increased as the engine spun into view in the distance and raced up the hill with its lights flashing.

The car was now in flames. I remembered my jacket was still on the back seat, so too was my British School of Motoring handbook and my notes for the course. Oh well. I hadn't thought to retrieve them in all the panic.

A police car then arrived, and Mr. MacDonald immediately walked over and explained what happened to the officers.

"Stand well back from the car in case something explodes, please," shouted one of the officers.

People walking by on the pavement stopped and gawked. I hoped they didn't know it was my driving test and instead thought it was simply some unlucky car fire.

While the fire brigade doused the flames on our much-loved Austin A40, the police officers drove us back to the test centre. When we arrived, my mother was standing outside the centre looking very concerned. She said, "Gosh, what happened? You've been gone for ages and why are you in a police car?"

"Did you see the smoke coming from town down here? Well, that was our car."

"What?"

---

[20]   Windshield

"It gave up on the hill, and before I could run around to the back, we were on fire."

"Oh no! Are you okay, and where is your stuff?"

"I left it in the back of the car."

The test manager caught our attention and called us into his office. "Mr. and Mrs. Thomas, would you please come in?"

"We have not had an incident like this before, so we need you to fill out some paperwork."

Mr. MacDonald informed me that the car was not road-worthy even though it had passed its MOT.

My mother replied, "We hoped the car would be okay for the test. You see, my husband drives our main car for military purposes at the Royal Academy."

"You'll need to file an insurance claim and sign this paper-work stating that we were not liable for the fire. The Fire Chief also wants to speak to you about removing the car."

"No problem. We will do whatever you need."

"Do you need to call someone to get a ride home?"

"Yes please."

My father, for once, was not upset and thought the whole event was hilarious when he picked us up. It became a talking piece for a while with people at the Royal Military Academy.

I took a few months to recover from my Austin A40 experience and then decided to enrol in an official BSM (British School of Motoring) course. I drove around in a pint-sized, brand new Vauxhall that had a bright white illuminated BSM sign on the roof. Instead of paying a private instructor, I had Phil, the BSM instructor, who provided far more advice and knowledge to help me pass the test.

The day finally came for me to take my third practical driving test, and I hoped it would be third time lucky. Now I was driving a brand new car and the conditions couldn't have been better, with clear skies, no wind, and fewer people on the roads, as it was a weekday. Phil had taken me around the course a few times in the preceding weeks so I felt confident, as it was familiar to me. As long as no dogs came by, I would be fine.

When we arrived at the testing centre, Phil wished me good luck. This time I was pleased to see my examiner was a woman; maybe she would be somewhat easier. At least I wouldn't have to worry about trying to understand the Scottish accent or a severe-looking examiner seated beside me. Thankfully, she wasn't that attractive, so she wasn't a distraction. The driving progressed well on the first part of the course as I cruised along enjoying the fine weather and taking every turn in my stride. We were near the end of the course and I had one final roundabout to negotiate before we were back at the test centre.

There were no other cars entering the roundabout so I didn't have to wait. All I had to do was drive around making a 270-degree turn off to the left. I was feeling great about how the test had gone, confident I had passed and drove the car quickly around the roundabout.

Immediately there was a nasty scratching sound coming from the roof. To my horror, the metal tent-shaped BSM sign slid off the roof and fell onto the examiner's side of the car. The electric wire connected to it was dangling precariously across the front windscreen. The sign then scraped loudly against the passenger window like a sharp knife drawn along the surface of a rigid bottle. The examiner was irritated and had a huge look of surprise on her face.

"Wow, how did that happen?" I calmly said.

"You'd better pull off where you can, as soon as possible," she said.

"It must not have been properly secured to the roof," I remarked.

"No, the sign was fine. You simply took the roundabout too sharpish," she responded.

"I am sorry, but I know I wasn't going over the speed limit."

"That's correct. Still, we can't drive on with the sign dangling like this, so please pull over so I can fix it."

"Oh no", I thought, "Here we go again! Another incident to ruin my test!" I began to think I was jinxed. I pulled into a side road, and the examiner stepped out and slid the magnetized sign back in place. She didn't say a word to me when she got back into the car, and we returned to the test centre, where I awaited the inevitable words "failed again" for another time.

She asked me to park and turn off the engine. I then said, "You know I have had so many incidents happen like this which have caused me to fail my test. It is so unfair. On my first test, I failed for stopping for a dog, and then the second time my car burst into flames. This is yet another one, so I am sure you are going to fail me. I know I had control...."

She interrupted me and said, "You have passed."

"You are kidding!"

"No I'm not; you drove well even though the sign fell off, which I wasn't going to take points off for anyhow. You had complete control of the car and were not over the speed limit."

I felt like hugging her, but I resisted the impulse.

"Thank you so much. Wow!"

She handed me my pass paperwork, which I waved at Phil, my BSM instructor when I saw him. Hooray! My mother was overjoyed when I showed her the pass certificate as I entered the building.

Even though I was still very depressed about failing the army, I finally had my driving license, which gave me great confidence. I had turned a corner, and my future was poised to change. The license was a symbol of independent forward movement.

9

THE NOTE

ailing the Brigade Squad was ultimately a blessing in
disguise. Or to state it more perfectly, it was a shot across
my bow. I had sought what I thought was the idyllic army
career, and yet despite failing, part of me was relieved. Joining
the Welsh Guards was what I thought was expected of me. It
was the life I was accustomed to, and believed I belonged in,
even though it didn't involve my creative talents. Our army
friends convinced me this was a great career for me, but I
shouldn't have listened. Had I joined the Welsh Guards I would
have gone to the Falklands War in 1982, and who knows what
could have happened to me there? Would I really have enjoyed
a life with what others referred to as a bunch of Ruperts? A
Rupert in the British Army is a stereotypical upper class name
applied to an officer, because at one point army officers were
almost all from the upper classes.

After my army failure, the lack of a discussion with my father spoke volumes. I never bought the story that I needed more time to mature and was sure that the rifle incident had cost me my army career.

In 1979, the army posted my father from Berlin to the Royal Military Academy in Sandhurst. It couldn't have occurred at a worse time for me, as we were going to reside there as well - the very place where my fellow cadets were coming for further training. I knew this would be difficult for me to bear as it reminded me of my failure seeing them march around the academy.

Luckily for me, I had some great support and my art and music hobbies to fall back on. My most loyal fan was Sue, my girlfriend, who lived next door. She was eighteen, delectably intriguing, rather mysterious, and demure. We had an innocent first passionate love, as she was very naive. I wrote tons of soppy poems about her at that time which, looking back, I recognize was a kind of puppy love. She had wished me well when I left to take the Brigade Squad training.

I wasn't sure what to do next. I took weeks to prepare an art portfolio and applied to the prestigious Slade School of Art in London. Four weeks later, they notified me of my non-acceptance to the program, which was yet another blow. I probably shouldn't have aimed so high. Maybe I felt the pressure from school all those years before.

I was bored and played my various electric guitars in the basement of the house. My father always told me to stop, as he hated the incessant fuzzy, piercing guitar noises and my singing of songs from the band Status Quo. Being in the school rock band had brought me popularity, and I liked that, as it gave me confidence, but I doubted I could make a career of it.

I took a job on the RMA campus washing dishes at the Sergeants Mess as a way to kill time and think about what I wanted to do after. It was an awful job immersed in scald-ing hot water up to my elbows for hours on end washing an endless stream of filthy dishes. I fell into a monotonous daily rhythm of dunk, scrub, rinse, and dry. As I washed yet more dishes, out of the window I saw a platoon of growing officers marching past, all dressed in their well-pressed dark blue uniforms. I recognized two of my former fellow cadets amongst them, Lance Ranson and Robin Innis-Ker. It was simply too much for me to endure. I threw my dishwashing gloves down on the kitchen counter and strutted out, realizing I was going nowhere, while watching others progressing with their lives.

Unfortunately, things would get much worse for me.

I had confided in Sue, who had supported me up to this point, but she told me she needed a break. She was the one person I had depended upon who I assumed would always be there. As she put it, we were getting too intense and serious. She said she couldn't be there for me anymore.

My spirit was broken. Emotionally this pushed me right over the edge. What transpired afterwards was an act of despair.

One night while I was sitting in my bedroom, I looked out of my window, which faced Sue's house. I saw a young man come to her door and go inside. Five minutes later, I saw Sue give him a peck on the cheek as they left, and then she looked over to my window. I tried not to think she had done that on purpose, but it hurt all the same.

The subsequent thing I remember was lying in a pool of blood on my bedroom floor, my mother at my side calling my father to get an ambulance.

"I can't take it anymore," I cried. "I feel worthless; my life has no meaning."

"Of course it does," said my mother. "You have had some unfortunate luck. Now wrap your hand in this towel, and let's get you up off the floor and to the hospital."

"Why would Sue do this to me? Haven't I endured enough pain?"

"I know you care deeply about Sue, but you can't smother her. She needs to pursue her own life at this point, and so do you."

The glass from the windowpanes jutted out at a jarring angle from multiple points on my right hand. The pain hadn't sunk in yet, as I was dazed, disoriented, and in shock.

Each window in my bedroom had six glass panes above and six panes below. I had punched out all of the panes in the lower window. The sharp shards of glass embedded themselves in my hand as I withdrew each punch back through each pane. I wanted to erase the pain of everything I had experienced, so punching the windowpanes was my way to draw attention to myself again. Had I been at a train station, who knows what I would have done?

Today I can still see the fine white lines on my right hand where the numerous stitches received used to be. I came home from the hospital and spent weeks in my room. During that time, I could sense occasional jabs of pain in my hand, as there were tiny splinters of glass still embedded; they felt like sharp stabbing thorns. I used sterilised tweezers to remove a few visible pieces of glass and duct tape to pluck out the remaining ones as they made their way to the surface. It took weeks of constantly applying the tape before the majority of the splinters were gone.

My mother was supportive during this rough time. She said, "Life will get better. It is just unfortunate that so much has happened to you all at once, but you shouldn't have become emotionally dependent on Sue. You have to allow her some space and go out to live your own life. Maybe you can still be friends after more time has passed."

Showing emotion was something I had not dared do in school, yet I felt safe with Sue. I had opened up to her and so felt betrayed by her actions. I was devastated that she let me down at such a vulnerable time. I later heard that Sue was dating a bishop's son, so she had gone up in the world! I remember recovering from my wounds in my room, where I spent many long hours listening to music on my old record player. Gloria Gaynor's "I Will Survive" inspired me to keep going, but I wasn't sure how. I would sing along to the music, as it made me feel better for a while. I had lost all that I had been working for, so my self-confidence was at an all-time low.

Just as before, my father never spoke to me about the incident. He kept clear of both subjects, the army, and Sue, whenever we briefly spoke. He continued to complain, however, that I should go out and get a real job instead of lounging around the house "playing that infernal guitar." He also thought my art was simply a hobby and that I should pursue a real career. He never really understood my creative side, and even though his antagonism hurt me, I couldn't blame him. He wasn't wired that way.

At the end of 1979, I had summoned the courage to move on and see what the real world was like, but I didn't know how to get out of my army fishbowl. Given the stress at home and the pressure from my father, I finally decided my best choice was to leave home. There was no alternative, and debating my decision with my parents wasn't an option. There was nothing at the Military Academy for me. Why remind myself of my failings watching my friends on parade?

One morning I wrote a note on a piece of white paper and left it on my mother's bed when she was out. It read, "Gone to London to find a job, I'll be fine. Going to pursue my interests."

I never warned my parents. I packed a meager suitcase and left. I didn't know what I was going to do, let alone where I would stay, as I knew no one in London. I dressed in my polished brogues[21] and put on my best three-piece navy pinstriped city suit and set off. The station wasn't that far from the gates of the Academy so I walked there.

In my twenty-one-year-old diary entry, I wrote, "The countryside was quiet and peaceful. Butterflies and birds played in the air and all was calm. When I reached the station, it was of a stagnant nature. The churning grinding rails produced a yellow-faced monster that sniffed and jangled my nerves as

---

[21]   A style of low-heeled shoe.

it approached. It turned the air to confusion, and then doors slammed with determination. The grey sky had upset the equilibrium too since it sent a dark shadow to mask my fears. I had to board the train since it led to a new life. It pulled away taking the dreams I once had down the tracks. People at each station joined like ants in a procession, all very British and coordinated. The sweat and buildings grew, an internal cancer clogged the landscape, greenery disappeared, and concrete worlds appeared through the misty windows. Cigarette smoke hung like sheets of metal in the carriage, so I couldn't see the far end. Paper rustled on newspapers as my life thickened with dismay. We reached each station and more ghostly talkative characters joined and packed in like sardines in the early morning sun. The conductor was hard to hear on the loudspeaker as passengers dashed to board. I pushed and shoved to find a clear space but quickly realized that the fields had gone, and the grain no longer brushed against my legs. The ground was hard and unyielding. I had lost myself, and my lifestyle, and was now given over to becoming someone who wanted money, power, and success."

When I arrived in London, I waited for the Tube[22] underneath Waterloo Station. A warm rush of stale subterranean air hit me as I waited on the platform. I turned away as the dust particles tickled my face, and the noise of the train filled my ears with a hellish rattle. Had I really come to live in this place? I headed in the direction of the City on the Circle Line. At least there, dressed in my fine suit, I would fit in and find suitable employment. I got off at Chancery Lane and came up to the street level.

I bought my first *Evening Standard* near the station, and over a quick cup of tea in a local café, I immediately looked for places in the classified section. There was no looking back. I felt energized and in control of my own destiny. No one could shout

---

[22]   Otherwise known as the London Underground system.

at me anymore—my father or the military. I searched for jobs where my character and army background would, I hoped, get me in. I saw a listing for a sales job with the *Catholic Universe* newspaper, with an office that was close by, so I decided to walk. I thought my training in the Guards would be well suited to the discipline needed for a telephone salesman. I was lucky, and not only did they interview me, but they offered me the job. I wrote in my diary that day, "I think my suit and charm allowed me to rise above the other candidates," which was rather cocky, I admit. Now I had a job and remembered being over the moon.

My parents didn't know where I was going, and nor did I. All I knew was I had to get away and pursue a career to gain some confidence. I never told my father I was working for "the other side" so to speak, as he was Anglican, ordained by the Church of England, and I was working for the *Catholic Universe*. I took pride in calling funeral homes to sell coffins and called old ladies who wanted to place advertisements to let out their houses on the seashore in Blackpool. I was very elated one week being the top salesperson. Selling coffins to cathedrals was a tougher proposition, as the demand wasn't there. No one important had recently died so there would be a long wait until the required need.

I remember buying my first toasted sausage and brown sauce sandwich on the way to the office. One of my work colleagues had suggested I try one; I never looked back and bought one most days on my way to work along with a cup of tea in a Styrofoam cup. Each month the newspaper issued employees with luncheon vouchers, which we used at the local sandwich shops to save money. I am not proud to reveal that many of us also noticed how easy it was to photocopy the vouchers, so we got away with quite a bit. Working for a religious newspaper didn't deter us from committing a sin!

One busy day I was at the Rose & Crown pub for lunch near the newspaper's offices. The men on the newspaper staff would go there regularly at lunchtime to watch Clarissa, the local stripper. Out of the blue, with a pint in my hand, I felt a tap on my shoulder. It was my Uncle Toby up from Petersfield, Hants. His sudden appearance gave me a nasty shock, just as Clarissa was shocking the audience at the same time on stage.

It seems my father had become concerned where I was and what I was doing. Therefore, he sent Uncle Toby up to London to check on me. I cannot remember how my uncle found me, but he did.

I didn't know what to say to him. He quietly said, "This is an interesting divergence from working at a *Catholic newspaper*." Toby then smiled and got a pint of beer and joined me. I knew that he had been in marketing, so we chatted about his experiences and his advice about going into sales. Over a pint or two, he encouraged me to pursue a career in advertising. He suggested I try to get into one of the well-known advertising agencies and gave me a few tips. Even though he had startled me, I was excited to see him again. Before we said goodbye, I begged him not to tell my father I worked for a Catholic newspaper. I don't think he ever did tell my father the full story. I heard sometime later he had simply said I was "in newspaper sales" and doing very well.

Dad's misconception was evident a few months later when I attended a drinks party with my parents. My father introduced me to his friends as his son who worked in the tabloid newspaper business, even though I told him I was a telephone salesman. Some of the wives at the party got the impression that I was somehow responsible for the offensive nudes on "Page 3" of the maligned tabloids. I subsequently had my hands full explaining that I did not work for one of the offensive tabloids, and was certainly not involved with "Page 3." Even though I told my father what I did, he rarely really understood. I left out that I was selling for the Catholics and having lunch at the pub while watching the local stripper.

Most people who had a very strict military upbringing, after serving in the army, would have stayed close to their comfort zone when it came to getting a job. The typical jobs were as civil servants or in a security-related career. I knew I had art and music talents, so there were more opportunities out there for me. Making the jump from the military world to civilian life was quite easy. The stereotypical norms in the army held people back unfairly, like Surrey Swayne from my Brigade Squad training, who would have made a fine officer. Less class-consciousness would permit all people to achieve what they were capable of, I thought, and yet in Britain, one's class was so ingrained.

As I grew up I witnessed so much expectation of one's duty to society and family, but now I had a duty to myself to explore my creative and communications skills and break out of the mould. Given the knocks I had experienced, something inside me was driving me to find success. I knew that advertising sales was not my ideal career, but it could be a stepping-stone to the bigger and more prestigious advertising agency world that my uncle had mentioned. I did some research on the advertising industry and found out that I would need a lot more experience before any employer would consider me seriously. It didn't help that I had no degree, so I knew I would have to take night classes at some point. A tiny bit of luck was all I needed to find a company that might be willing to take me on.

10

BEDSITS

Looking back, I was lucky to find a job, but finding a place to live proved to be a challenge, as I didn't know a single person in London except those at the newspaper. As luck would have it, Sandra, one of the office secretaries, was moving out of her bedsit, so she invited me along one evening to see if I would like to take her place. It was located in Finsbury Park, which seemed miles away by the time we got there. Coming out of the Tube, I felt very self-conscious in my suit, as the neighbourhood was full of unsavoury characters. I scurried along behind her, wondering who might be following us, as some of the agitated youths at the station looked rather threatening. A bad omen of sorts had already occurred as the handle on my suitcase had broken off on the way, so I had to drag it along the pavement.

There I was, the six-foot-five-inch white guy smartly dressed in clothing that didn't belong there. Sandra took me to the house, which was at least ten minutes' walk from the station. I was able to rent her large furnished bedsit with a huge bay window looking out on the street for a meager ten pounds a week. It was a big room, wide enough to swing a cat in, with two armchairs, a single bed, desk, and wardrobe. Mrs. Trent, my landlady, explained how to insert the five pence pieces into the electric meter in my bedsit, and how to use the one-foot-square wall-mounted Belling cooking stove. In order for the water heater to work, I had to feed another meter in the hallway with 50 pence pieces. Sometimes, if I were running a bath, the hot water would give out as the bath reached half-full. In such cases, I had to traipse down the wooden stairs in my undies to feed the damn meter again. I had to feed the fridge as well with five pence coins, which was a silent death trap. This too had an indicator showing me if it was on. I would come home and find it completely defrosted with giant puddles on the carpet. Keeping a collection of 5 and 50 pence coins became a chore. I also couldn't work out how long the electricity for each appliance lasted, so I tended to over-feed the meters.

My cooking exploits would turn out to be disastrous, as the Belling stove had a mind of its own. Without any warning, it would fling open its door and eject whatever was cooking. On one occasion, a whole steaming hot roast beef rolled towards me across the carpet and stopped at my feet.

On that first day, I met the other tenants, who were an odd bunch. One was a retired RAF (Royal Air Force) officer of about seventy-two. Also in residence were a black medical doctor who smelt of curry, a pair of youthful Chinese footballers, and an alcoholic journalist living on the top floor. At least my bedsit was homey. Opposite the house was a rundown building site. It was only when I looked through the curtain that I noticed a prostitute walking slowly up the street while a car slowed down to talk to her. It seemed like a rough area and not very well lit. However, my Guards' training made me feel confident that I could deal with any intruder should I need to.

I heard Sandra saying goodbye to the landlady outside my door, and so I popped out to thank her. As she turned to close the front door behind her, she said, "Just one thing Dan. They might all seem a bit nutty here, but they are trustworthy people. They won't cause you any problems. Stay clear of the alcoholic upstairs though. Make sure you lock the bathroom door. He used to burst in on me while I was in the bath. See you at the office. Ta-ra[23]."

"Great," I thought to myself, "let's make the best of this generosity." After all, ten pounds a week was dirt-cheap. My first time in London, and here I was in a house with a load of nutters in a neighbourhood where I was likely to be mugged. The first night I sarcastically described the flat in my diary as "brilliant;" in other words "crap." A mouse had made a home inside one of my armchairs, and every time I made a move to turn the light on, it stopped scratching around inside the chair. It was as if it was intentionally doing this to annoy me. Sleeping proved problematic, as not only did my legs hang over the bed, but also a large pipe ran down from the ceiling along the entire wall closest to the headrest. Every time someone used the bathroom upstairs, I woke in the middle of the night as the pipe erupted into life, which sent my imagination into overdrive. The shared toilet was upstairs and quite a pain to have to visit at night, not to mention, I didn't want to run into a naked alcoholic or other crazy nighttime characters. I am not proud to say that I ended up peeing in my bedroom sink instead, which was not ideal! The fact that I had a sink in my bedsit made me think I was in school again, as we used to have sinks at the far end of the dormitory.

When travelling to work, it felt threatening to see all the drunks by the gates of Finsbury Park near the station. At least

---

[23]   Goodbye.

I could leave this part of London during the day and go to my job for training to answer the phones. I will seldom forget my training at the *Catholic Universe* and how they taught me to make canvas calls or "cold calling" as they called it back then. I felt as though I was finally doing something correct for someone and had even received some praise and recognition, which I hadn't ever had before. I sometimes made ninety calls a day, which was more than the average salesperson. I entered every call I made on a call sheet that I handed in at the end of the day. Work was exhausting, picking up the phone time after time, telephoning people I didn't know, but I was enjoying being successful at my job.

Some nights I dreaded coming home late, as Finsbury Park was not a safe area of town this far north on the Piccadilly line. When I emerged from the Tube, I would buy a takeout meal and an *Evening Standard*. The streets had poor lighting, so I had to be careful walking back to the house. There were always huge groups of angry-looking young men hanging out near the station. It must have been my imagination, but I swore I could hear them follow me down the road sometimes. I was sure they were going to mug me, so I often turned the corner, and sprinted for a while. I then cut through a side street to throw them off from where I lived. Each night I would run home a particular way, clutching my steaming pie and chips takeaway. One benefit: my food was still hot by the time I got home!

I sat on my bed with my black and white TV on and eagerly wolfed down my food. I must admit many nights during those times I felt lonely and lost, but I had the desire to make a career in London, simply to prove to my father that I could do it. I stuck it out in Finsbury Park until one night, unannounced, a brick came crashing through the front window of the bedsit. That was the last straw, so I decided to look for a safer place and move on.

Instead of the *Evening Standard*, I decided to look in "*The Lady*" magazine, which tended to have better places for rent. I saw an ad for a tiny room in a flat in Bayswater W2. I knew this area would be much better than Finsbury Park, and it was on the Central Line so it would be quicker for me to get to work. It was more expensive, but I felt I deserved it after Finsbury Park. I travelled to meet the woman who owned the flat, and when I approached the road, I realized that it was in an immense, well-to-do high-rise close to Hyde Park, which was a great location. So I took the elevator to the twenty-third floor and knocked on the door. A pleasant cockney-sounding lady answered, and I said I had come about the room. She introduced herself as Mrs. Butterworth and said, "It's just me and my cat, me luv. As long as you are an honest fella, which you seem to be on first impressions, there should be no problems."

Mrs. Butterworth appeared frail as she bent forward to keep her balance, resting against the door. Trying not to focus on her classic wattle neck, I noticed her crinkled-up kind smile instead. She seemed like a feisty antique of a lady, who I was sure had an interesting past.

I was very hesitant, since she was quite particular, and all I could think about was whether she was going to expect me back for dinner every night and have all sorts of curfew rules. I quickly jumped to my key question about having guests, in my mind girlfriends, to which she said, "I don't mind you having someone over but not to stay the night, and no hanky-panky, as Tommy might get upset. I am old-fashioned and don't want any shenanigans if you get my drift."

"I understand," I said.

She then talked about her beloved Tommy. "You see he's very shy and doesn't go out much, as he's not very social. I feed him well, and he scarcely complains. The one thing you must never do is leave a window open. Tommy isn't very intelligent and might fall out."

Tommy was all she had, and she would often call him while I was there talking with her. It was as if Tommy were another person to her, which was quite sweet. She even said he had a favourite toy rabbit that he carried around with him all the time, like a teddy bear. Despite my concerns about having a girlfriend over, it was a quiet place to live and very safe. It didn't have as much space to swing a cat in like Finsbury Park, but I agreed to her price and set the date when I would move in. The day came, and I managed to get my space all set up; Mrs. Butterworth was very kind to allow me to put some of my stuff in the extra closet space in her hallway.

It was the summer, and the weather was unusually hot for London, so one day Mrs. Butterworth joined her sister on an outing to the countryside. As the morning sun poured into my bedroom, I felt that opening the window would provide a welcome breeze. This worked, but I had to remember to close it, and most importantly leave my bedroom door closed, as I didn't want Tommy coming in. The afternoon passed by, and I fell asleep on the bed while reading. I suddenly awoke and forgot that I had agreed to meet Dave, a rugby friend, to go running in Hyde Park, as we were in training for the rugby season. The clock had stopped working, but I knew that if I ran fast, I could get to the meeting point on time. I quickly got dressed, pulled my bedroom door closed, and off I sped. While running along the street below, I remembered that the window was still open in my room, but I also knew I had closed my bedroom door, so things should be fine.

Dave and I had a great run; the park was lush and green, and the pathways were clear of children and prams, which I hated dodging while running. The Serpentine Lake was clear and calm, and ducks swam lazily across it. I was lucky to have this park on my doorstep and be able to run or walk there when I so pleased. The heat had been gradually building up during the day, so we stopped after three miles. I was sure it was over 90 degrees. We decided to take a detour and walk over to the Albert Hall for Dave to collect some tickets he had reserved for a concert. To rehydrate, we drank from our water bottles and rested in the shade of some trees afterwards. It felt like only an hour had passed, but when I looked at my watch, it was 6:00 p.m., so I needed to get home.

As I approached the immense block of flats, I noticed what looked like a big orange pillow lying on the grass in front. I thought to myself, *why would someone leave that there?* The maintenance crew always kept the lawn perfectly cut, and a modest fence deterred anyone from chucking rubbish over it. As I got closer, my eyes started to bulge out of my head. I started hyperventilating, my heart racing like a steam train, and I started saying in my head. "No, it can't be... surely someone else's; maybe a pair of fluffy gaudy slippers.... Not Tommy.... Oh *no*! How could this be?"

I raced around to the side of the apartment block where a gate led to the grassed-in area. I rushed over and saw to my horror that it was indeed Tommy. He had fallen twenty-three floors and lay distended on his side with a huge look of surprise on his face and his legs outstretched as if they had tried to grasp a balcony on the way down. It was pitiful, and I had no idea what to do. How could this have happened? How could he have gotten into my bedroom and fallen out of the window? I had to act quickly, as Mrs. Butterworth would soon be home. What could I do?

I did the unthinkable. I decided I would pretend that nothing was untoward. I knew it was cowardly, but there was no way I could bring myself to tell her I had inadvertently killed her cat. If I did, it would be the end, and my eviction didn't bear thinking about. I picked Tommy up; he was like a dried piece of stiff cardboard. He had fallen ages ago, and with the weather being so hot and rigor mortis doing its thing, he was flatter than the pancakes I ate for breakfast. I couldn't bend him in the middle to fit him into the bin[24] below the building, as he was so stiff. When I tried to push him down into the bin, he would simply pop up again like a puppet in a show—his face had a cheeky grin cemented on it, and it stared back at me. I was mortified and felt miserable with a great knot forming

---

[24]   A garbage holder.

in my stomach. I eventually managed to jam Tommy into the bottom of the bin. I weighted him down with two bricks and put another bag over the top of him. The binmen wouldn't be coming for two days, so I opted to put him in one of the bins used by one of Mrs. Butterworth's neighbours. I hoped Mrs. Butterworth wouldn't look in there. Tommy would simply disappear, like so many cats in the area.

I reentered the flat and walked along the hallway towards my bedroom, with the door closed. Now I was confused, so I opened my door and saw my window was still open. How could the cat have fallen out of my window with a closed bedroom door? I thought for a second that maybe I wasn't to blame and that something else had happened. Had someone broken in and killed the cat? No, that was stupid. Was it really Tommy on the lawn? Maybe I was mistaken all along, and Tommy was still in the flat, hiding, as he sometimes did, under her bed. I double-backed to the bins downstairs to check that it really was Tommy in there. When I removed the top rubbish bin, evidently, the bricks had moved, and Tommy's lifeless body immediately sprang into my face! I jumped back in shock and hit my head against the wall. I felt I deserved that for what I had done. Anyhow, I confirmed that indeed it was Tommy. A yellow label hanging off his tiny collar said "Tommy my son" in flowery homemade lettering. I returned to my room and closed my window while my mind swam with confusion.

Later I stiffened with fear as I heard jangling keys in the door. I immediately heard Mrs. Butterworth call for Tommy.

"Here, Tom Tom. Look what I bought for you when out of town today. Your favourite tuna dish!"

I kept quiet with the door closed to my room and waited for the inevitable.

After a short while, my door handle turned ever so slowly, as I pretended to be in another world. Mrs. Butterworth peeked in and asked, "Do you have Tommy in your room, as I can't find him?"

"No" I replied. "I don't allow him in here, and I always keep my door closed, as you know."

It was very painful hearing Mrs. Butterworth parading around her flat calling for Tommy. Her voice descended into one of despair as she opened and closed every door and cupboard for what seemed like hours and asking herself how Tommy could have escaped. She must have gone about the place three times at least. She then started to cry.

I half thought about doing the honest thing and confessing, but I simply couldn't bring myself to do it.

"Why would you leave me?" she cried.

It was awful listening to her, as on she wailed. I covered my ears, and then suddenly there was silence. I listened intently and didn't hear a thing. Had she killed herself or what? I was very worried and slowly opened my door, expecting to half find her lying on her kitchen floor with a knife in her.

She had left, so I took my keys and entered the hallway. Suddenly I heard a bone-chilling scream coming up the elevator shaft. I knew it was Mrs. Butterworth and quickly surmised that maybe she had found Tommy, but how? She must have gone through all the bins and he must have popped up to greet her.

I decided it was time to leave, as I didn't want to face the inevitable consequences. I made a beeline for the emergency stairs and flew out into the park. I paced around forever, pondering my fate.

When I returned later that evening, I saw the blue flickering lights of a police car. Two huge police officers confronted me when I entered the flat.

"Are you Daniel Thomas?"

"Yes."

"We have reason to believe you may have killed this lady's cat."

"Why would I have done that?"

"Did you tell Mrs. Butterworth that you never let her cat in your room?"

"Yes, that's correct. He has rarely been in my room, and if he was, I would shoo him out."

"Well sir, we found this toy rabbit under your bed. Do you recognize it?"

My face immediately dropped, and I turned bright red.

"I do; its Tommy's toy, but how come it was under my bed? And by the way, where is Mrs. Butterworth?"

"She was taken to hospital suffering from shock. She had found her cat stuffed into the bins in the basement."

He must have snuck in under my bed when I dashed to the bathroom to change for my run. When I closed the door, he sought the window as his only way out and fell to his death. I then decided to come clean and told them what had happened.

"Am I to be charged with cat slaughter?"

"No, sir. Under the law, there is no charge for accidentally killing a cat. However, I suggest you look for another place to live and decide if you want to speak with Mrs. Butterworth about what you did. She is at St. Mary's Hospital for an overnight."

Under a cloud, I left Mrs. Butterworth, and quickly found another bedsit in Shepherds Bush. Two weeks later, I rang the doorbell to Mrs. Butterworth's flat and nervously waited for her to answer. Would she even open the door for me? She opened it a crack and held it on a chain to give me a lecture on how awful I had been and how could I do such a thing. She told me never come back again.

I apologized profusely and said that I had a special gift for her. It was the least I could do, for how I had acted. She still had the door on a chain.

"Can I please show you what I have for you?" I pleaded.

She told me to get it over with and then be gone. I opened the lid to a compact cardboard box. As the flaps peeled back, a ginger face appeared over the top and meowed. At the Royal Society for the Prevention of Cruelty to Animals, I had found a ginger kitten that looked a bit like Tommy. I told her he was only six months old and had had a medical so was healthy.

She then undid the chain and opened her door to take a closer look. Her face lit up, and her icy reception melted. She remarked, "Oh the poor thing. He looks cold in that bare cardboard box. Let me go and get a blanket."

When she returned, I told her that he wouldn't make up for Tommy, but he would be a fine trainable companion.

She then blessed me with a sort of redemption.

"Maybe you are not such a bad guy after all."

I felt I had somewhat redeemed myself, and was happier walking away this time.

11

THE TERRAPINS

In the months that followed I concentrated on my job. I embraced every opportunity the newspaper threw at me. I came up with improved headings for the classified sections, such as "situations vacant" for nursing homes, and "holiday vacations to let." I even kept a copy of all the ads I sold, and I became one of the top salespeople. I got to the point where I could handle the classified advertising department all by myself. It was then that I realized that I wasn't going to go anywhere staying in classified sales, so I began to write to advertising agencies.

I also enrolled in night school to get a CAM (Communications, Advertising & Marketing) Diploma. I didn't earn a degree because I attempted to join the army. The business world would take me more seriously with this diploma. I finally got my break and joined an American advertising agency, David Williams and Ketchum (DWK) that had a great reputation. I joined as a trainee and sought to become an account executive. They liked my enthusiasm and drive. I remember my boss Les (short for Leslie) Bond, carrying his morning coffee around the office in a plastic circular cup holder with just two fingers. As a prank, the trainee account executives used to enlarge the circumference of the holder slightly and wait until it dropped on the floor.

DWK looked after me and paid for my night school courses. I worked hard creating black and white retail ads for Curry's Electrical. I was essentially the office lackey during the day, and in the evening I would take the Tube to the London School of Economics for my three-hour lecture on advertising law. After taking the long Tube journey home, I would buy fish and chips on the street before arriving at my bedsit. They were long days, but I was determined to climb the corporate ladder to success.

During my first three years in London, I lived in six different flats. I was forced to keep finding new bedsits as the leases came up. I grew tired of moving from place to place, like the life of my father in the army. The only sense of home I had known was Isyfoel our grandparent's home in North Wales. Even 'Highlands' in East Meon was now lived in by my Uncle Toby and his family.

I lived once in a luxury three-bedroom high-rise flat a rugby friend's father owned in the Barbican complex. Fortunately, the place had no pets to worry me. The flats were gorgeous and offered excellent views of the city. At one point eight of us rugby guys were living there, paying only twenty pounds each a month. Unfortunately, we had too many parties, and the neighbours wised up and reported us, so begrudgingly we had to move on.

My bedsit in Shepherds Bush was closer to DWK. I rented from a German lady, Miss Schwartz, and when I arrived to meet her, she introduced me to her two terrapins, named Boris and Becker after the hugely successful German tennis star. She warned me to be very careful when I sauntered around in the morning, as they sometimes climbed out the aquarium in the living room to wander around the apartment.

Rushing to get dressed for work one morning (and a bit hungover), I blundered through the living room towards the bathroom. As I did, I felt a crunch under my bare right foot. I didn't pay much attention to it and continued to go about my morning business. As I was about to leave half an hour later, I combed my hair in the bathroom and noticed what looked like a sandwich lying on the living room carpet. It was still early in the morning so it wasn't quite light yet. I asked myself who would leave a sandwich in the middle of the floor? I then noticed it had a pinkish colour coming out of the sides, which I presumed was the ham, until on closer inspection, I realized it was Boris. His top shell was cracked, and then I remembered the crunch earlier under my foot. Yeeks! Had I really stepped on him? I picked him up and gave him a once over. He didn't look too rough, with his shell smooshed in a few places. I did another unthinkable act with someone's pet, and placed him back in the tank, on top of a rock alongside Becker. I could have sworn I saw Becker look over at him with her mouth aghast in terrapin shock. I then left for work and hoped he would be okay. Maybe it was simply a flesh wound, as they say in the Monty Python sketch "The Black Night."

Later that day I came home to find Miss Schwartz crying and muttering something about Boris exploding in the aquarium. His shell pieces were floating on the surface.

"How could this happen?" she cried. "When I came home he was all over the tank! Terrapins don't just fall apart, do they?"

I played ignorant and asked innocently, "Do they ever shed their shells like crabs do?"

At least this time she didn't suspect me, and I wasn't asked to leave. I started to wonder if pets and I were constant poor luck. I vowed my subsequent place must not have a pet.

12

HORSES AND DATING SR'S

While I worked hard at DWK, in the evening I enjoyed socializing with friends who frequented the pubs and restaurants in South Kensington and Sloane Square. These places exposed me to a particular social group emerging in the early 1980s. They were not only from the military but wealthy people who spent weekends at their country estates.

I rubbed noses with these high-up sons and daughters of military officers. Some of these, particularly the women, were referred to as "Sloane Rangers," or SRs. Perhaps I clung to the notion of trying to find that attractive girlfriend. The exemplar female Sloane Ranger in the 1980s was Lady Diana Spencer. A member of the aristocratic Spencer family, the future Princess Diana certainly fit the stereotype of the dress and class affiliation of a Sloane Ranger.

Most Sloanes, however, were not aristocrats, but they were from the upper middle class culture and displayed a fondness for life in the countryside, particularly country sports. The women's outdoor complexions looked scrubbed and clean, as nature intended with limited makeup, fresh as the day. Viewed as narrow-minded, materialistic, and anti-intellectual, typical values of SRs were patriotism and traditionalism with confidence in themselves and their given places in the world.

The SR term eventually spread to include men as well. Male Sloanes were referred to as "Rahs" or "Hooray Henrys." One could tell a lot about a person by the way they wore their jumper. A Sloane Ranger wore his jumper around his neck and over his shoulders. A man from the London suburbs, however, might tie his around his waist, but a hardened Geordie from up north would not own a jumper, as he was a real man and hardly needed one.

I mixed with SRs at many London parties but soon became bored with their stereotypical behaviour. I also discovered that some of them didn't have much "upstairs," as one might say, which wasn't surprising given the anti-intellectual orientation of this social group. Some conversations became limited when one talked to Sloanes and centred on their love of country pursuits, in particular, horses, which were a sacred animal to them. I knew that if one of them asked me to ride a horse; I couldn't do it, let alone go near a horse without feeling nervous.

My fear of horses stemmed back to an early childhood memory when I visited Isyfoel up in North Wales. My grandparents took me over to Auntie Myre and Uncle Will's farm. Uncle Will kept horses, as his daughter Susan would often ride them at shows all over the UK.

Uncle Will would occasionally take Steve and me out to the stables to see his horses. I vaguely remembered one childhood incident when placed on a horse in the stable. The next thing I recall was lying in the straw on the stable floor, staring up at some enormous brown legs that were moving ominously around my head. I was terrified of these huge animals that one minute would be calm, chewing away peacefully, and the following minute kicking about in their stables. Even at the age of eleven, I had noticed that a horse's ears twitched before something awful happened. I didn't understand why, and was certainly no authority on interpreting horse signs at that age. However, as I was to learn later, experienced riders knew that a horse conveyed much through ear positions. When a horse's ears are forward, he is alert, paying attention and interested in what is in front of him. When his ears are pinned back close to his neck, he might be angry and about to bite or kick.

As a teenager living in Germany, I decided to take group-riding lessons at an indoor training rink. How hard could it be, as all the horses simply followed each other around the rink in a line?

I voiced my fear about riding horses to Caroline, the British instructor. She was arrestingly beautiful, tall and lithe in her fetching riding outfit, with a spiffy white polo shirt and tight, trim-fitting mustard jodhpurs tucked into her shiny black field boots. She wore a riding cap and gently tapped a slim leather-riding crop against her outer thigh as she spoke to us. I remember her silky blonde hair, tucked neatly into a bun that protruded elegantly from the back of her riding cap. By the look of it, she had a lot of hair, and no doubt it looked great once it was untethered. I had to stop imagining that so I could concentrate on the riding.

Caroline said, "Not to worry Dan, I'll give you Simon, who is our oldest and dopiest horse. He doesn't do much so you should be fine with him. He'll simply follow the others around the rink."

I wasn't ready to ride Simon, as I had no time to develop a trusting relationship with him before getting on his back. It makes sense in hindsight that this would have been what the horse would have preferred, too. We didn't know each other at all.

There was no doubt that Simon felt my fear as I approached him. I believed he heard it in my voice as I mounted him and said "Good boy Simon" and "We'll be fine, won't we?" I was a little apprehensive, tensed up, and felt my heart rate going up as well. Even though Caroline had said he was dopey, he was very bulky and could potentially act up at any moment.

Once I was on his back, his response system kicked in, so I pulled and squeezed the reins. My inclination was to grip tightly with my legs and lean forward, all conflicting and confusing cues to him, which put him on guard and made him uneasy. I was sure I transmitted my fear up and down the reins and through the saddle as well. Simon knew I was nervous from my heart rate, stiffness, voice, and other subconscious clues I sent out to him. I was trying to hide my fear from him, which made him distrust me. It didn't surprise me that he wouldn't react to my commands. I was also subconsciously trying not to embarrass myself in front of cute Caroline.

From the middle of the rink, Caroline called out, "Relax, Dan, and let your horse know you are at ease." She then addressed us all. "These horses have riders on them every day, folks. They can tell when you are nervous, so try to be laid-back."

Easier said than done, even though riding on the last horse in the group was supposedly effortless. Simon started to fall behind, so I gave him a slight kick. He broke into a slow trot, which freaked me out. Was he going to break into a canter and overrun the others?

Mercifully, he slowed down after he caught up and continued to follow the others. At least the horse hadn't thrown me. I calmly dismounted, thankful to survive the lesson. This outing didn't prepare me better for interacting with horses, and as far as I was concerned they were still unpredictable.

On another occasion, back in the UK, on a fine summer's day in East Meon, there was a village fete. My friend, Pete had two small ponies he was walking down to the village green for the children to ride. He asked if I might enjoy riding one bareback while he led it down the road. "They are short ponies and used to being ridden by the school children, so it will be easy," he said.

"Pete, there is no saddle," I said.

"You don't need one, as I am holding the reins and we'll be going slowly."

I explained my nervousness to him. "You don't know my past experiences with horses, Pete."

"There will be no issues," he repeated reassuringly.

I looked at my pony and saw his ears turned to one side. He looked relaxed, so I patted him on the side and said "Hello." He immediately was startled, so maybe I needed to make sure he was looking at me the subsequent time. I remembered Caroline in Germany had said we needed to make sure horses were looking at us before we patted them. It gave them confidence and reassured them.

Pete had two ponies to control so he had to concentrate. First, I saw those ears twitch again, which was not a welcome sign. I vaguely remembered what Caroline had told me in the rink. It was something along these lines:

"Remember, a horse is a reflection of you. Being comfortable around horses is very important. Horses are always watching and learning, so sensing you are comfortable and feeling safe sends them a positive message. If they view you as fearful, jumpy, and always pushing them, they learn you cannot be trusted, and they are not comfortable. They give back what they get."

I tried to remain very calm as I got on the grey pony's back, watching his ears at the same time. My pony's ears were facing forward and twitching minimally so I felt that was fine for the moment.

As we got to the end of the lane, which joined a busier road, I became more nervous. Then I heard a noise behind us.

Pete shouted, "Don't look back now, Dan, there is a tractor coming up the lane behind us. Just relax while I keep the ponies to one side of the lane."

I noticed my pony's ears pointed backward but not pinned all the way back, thank goodness, as that would have been an ominous sign. It looked like he was listening to the tractor behind us. I hoped he wasn't deciding to turn around and check out the sound. Then I realized he couldn't anyway as Pete had a firm hold on his reins. Pete said, "I am going to lead you both single file from the front so you'll need to take your own reins for a minute while the tractor passes us.

"Just let yours follow the brown one. I'll grab both reins back when we round the corner and the tractor has passed us."

My pony couldn't go anywhere while being confined to the side of the road, but I was concerned about what would happen when we reached the end of the lane "Pete, please grab my reins the minute the tractor passes."

"No problem. Don't worry, Dan."

Things did not go as planned. As the tractor passed, my pony became agitated and started some rapid jittery movements with its rear legs. His ears flicked back and forth, as he exhibited a heightened state of anxiety.

"Are these ponies used to vehicles, Pete?"

"Yes, they are. They are out in the village all the time."

We reached the end of the lane and then out of nowhere, my pony started to trot out from behind the lead pony. Before I knew it, we had passed Pete who looked aghast as I sailed past him.

"Grab the reins, Pete. He is moving too quickly!" I looked back and noticed that my pony's tail was jerking quickly up and down, and he seemed irritated or angry, I am not sure which. Pete yelled, "I can't run after you as I have to stay with the other one. I am sure your pony will slow down, so hang in there."

So we jogged off down the high street, that pony and I, and a lady coming out of the Spar convenience store commented how pleasant it was to see riders out in the village. I couldn't say anything cordial back and didn't want to convey how worried I was. The pony started to increase speed so I reached for the reins and yelled, "Hold up, boy!" He didn't stop. So I yelled, "Come on, boy, please stop. I am not having any fun with this now."

I had no choice! I leaned forward to grab him around his neck to try to slow him down, but this was a very bad idea. I had no control, so I felt I had to get off as soon as I could.

I ended up sliding down his left side and dragged along the gravel on the roadside. By chance, some people were coming out of the Isaac Walton Pub and saw my predicament. They immediately rushed out in front of us, grabbed the reins, and then he finally slowed down. My left knee was bleeding badly through my jeans where I had scraped it along the road. I vowed then never, ever, to get on a pony or horse again in my life.

I resigned myself to the fact that I would never make it with the horsey set. I jokingly even made fun of them and called them "Overbites," as their jaw position extended their upper lip forward of the lower jaw to easily speak that mumbly snobby Kensington accent. Everyone else I described as an "Underbite", those who extended their chins out beyond their upper lips to speak an East London accent much more easily.

I did manage two memorable dates with Sloanes. I was very lucky when I was introduced to a rakishly sleek Annabelle or "Bells" as she liked to be called. She was a brunette with piercing blue eyes and long hair held back with a navy velvet hairband. Annabelle had that typical scrubbed complexion of a Sloane with a hint of colour in the middle of her cheeks. She drove a sports car and ticked all the boxes. To my astonishment, she agreed to meet me one evening for a drink at the White Horse Pub in Fulham, known as the "Sloaney Pony." She arrived wearing tight-fitting blue jeans, Gucci loafers with chains across the tops, and a white lace-collar blouse over which she wore a green Husky.[25] Her handbag slung over her shoulder, had a Hermes scarf tied around the strap. It all combined to present the perfect military equine look that was popular at that time. As I got up to go to the bar to get us a round of drinks, I tripped over one of her legs, oddly positioned straight out in front of her. I thought it rather strange that she hadn't kept it folded under the table. As I hit it, I heard a loud "clunk" noise

---

[25]   A padded sleeveless lightweight jacket.

but thought nothing of it and continued to the bar. When I got back to where she sat, she had vanished.

Some guys on the adjacent table were laughing their heads off so I turned and asked. "Excuse me, but did you see my girlfriend leave?"

"Man you made a mess of her," one of them said.

"What's so hilarious, and what are you talking about?"

"We saw you trip over her fake leg, mate. It came right out of the socket, slid out of her jeans onto the floor."

At this point, they all burst out laughing again.

"The most hilarious thing we have seen in here for ages, mate. She picked up her leg and not to be crass, 'legged it' into the ladies room while you were still at the bar. She came out a minute later and left walking normally so she must have reconnected it."

"O, my God." I obviously had no idea what I had done. How stupid I was. I heard that clunk noise as I tripped but focused on getting our drinks, so I didn't even realize it.

"Just as well you didn't both get legless this evening mate," one of them joked.

I was getting tired of the leg jokes, so I left them and dashed outside to see if I could find her. Sadly, she had gone.

I called to apologize the following day but she wasn't home, so I left a message. I kept trying for days, but she never got back to me. In some ways, it was probably best. Had I gone to third base it might have been very awkward since in those days I was not mature enough to know how to deal with such a handicap.

My second Sloane experience was an invitation to the fancy Rose Ball at the Dorchester Hotel on Park Lane, the first debutante ball of the social season. My date, Lucinda, was the daughter of one of Britain's Olympic show jumpers and there-fore rather well known and very horsey. She was very polished, vivacious, and voguish. Her voice pitched to be heard across two windswept rugby fields. She kept her voluminous strawberry blonde hair tied in a braided ponytail gathered in the middle of the back of her head. Ponytails were quite common in the 80s, and depending on where women tied their tail, dictated whether one was sportier or had a chic personality. Lucinda had flashing eyes and skin of an inviting golden tanned colour; she was the sort of girl who would look quite at home on the bow of a Mediterranean yacht.

When I met Lucinda at a house party, she said she was into horses but also discussed her love of rugby. In those days girls liked to vet their potential partners by meeting them informally a few times before going to a formal event. Even though she exaggerated incessantly about her contacts at the Paris cooking school she had attended, I gave her a chance to see what might happen and whether I might get a snog.[26]

As we were about to enter the beautifully decorated giant reception room at the Ball, I was subjected to an embarrassing moment. The greeting staff was announcing people as they entered, and they asked Lucinda how they should address her and then turned to me. The greeters announced Lucinda as the daughter of the well-known show jumper with a prominent title but referred to me as simply Mr. Thomas. I should have made something up but didn't have the guts to do so.

My association with this social group really hit home that night. I was tired of having to be "explained," as some girls would do to those that didn't have as high a title or background as themselves. They had to justify why they were with me. I was out of my league socializing with a group that I didn't want to be part of anymore. My social life needed a serious rethink.

After mixing with SRs for a while, I never adopted their mannerisms in the way I behaved and grew tired of some of the falseness it portrayed. For example, "I rather fancy you, in fact," was the ludicrous way that a Hooray Henry would tell a girl he was passionate about her. Everything was so unemotional

---

[26] An act or spell of amorous kissing.

and full of unnecessary fluff. They were also not slow in using the vagaries of others for their own amusement and laughter.

As a priest's kid or PK, I was used to being viewed as a notch below them anyway, despite my father being an officer and holding a respectable position. I had also grown tired of socializing in the expensive areas of West London, at popular places like the White Horse Pub and the Admiral Codrington, known as "The Cod," in Chelsea where ironically I was later to meet my wife.

The antithesis of the SRs was my friend Eddy Dygoo from Africa. He was tall and thin with a cheeky smile. After meeting Eddy only once, I was surprised when he rang me and asked if I would defend him in court as a character witness. Eddie was so grateful for my help in court that he became my beck-and-call taxi driver in London. He would drive me anywhere, whenever I wanted. I hardly knew exactly what I had saved him from, but clearly, he felt indebted. He was loyal to people who helped him, even if they were not from his background. I also never asked him why he still had a 9mm bullet lodged in his shoulder after I had come to collect him one time at Charing Cross Hospital!

I found I enjoyed getting to know people like Eddy from other walks of life and subsequently realized that I was far more comfortable with them. My dream of marrying an officer's daughter with personality and a ponytail was fading, and I began to enjoy a markedly unrelated social group. I sought friends who were not impressed with daddy's position in the army, his stock portfolio, or title.

Living in London taught me a lot, whose company I enjoyed the most, and what type of career I wanted to pursue. I was feeling more positive about myself, gaining further qualifications at night school, and enjoying my job.

It seems I was finally recovering from the loss of my dreams of becoming an army officer and marrying a girl with a ponytail. At last, I began to settle into a truer path that indeed would prove to be more to my liking. At last—perhaps—I was growing up.

13

SETTLING DOWN

Eddy's Gift

Work was going well and I felt very at home in London, particularly as I was making new friends. For some years, I played rugby every weekend with the HAC (Honourable Artillery Company) Rugby Club but later moved to London Welsh in Richmond where I could learn more and improve my game. There I was selected by the lower teams but quickly worked my way up to appear regularly in the position of lock for the London Welsh Dragons. Rugby was important to me for several reasons. It provided not only a social life but also a great release from the pressures in the advertising world. After games on Saturdays, a group of us would travel up to South Kensington in central London. Two of my best friends were Dave and Pete who played as half-backs for the team and provided ample entertainment and jokes for any night on the town.

One particular evening we ventured up to town after a particularly illustrious win over London Scottish, determined to have a fun night. We ended up at the Admiral Codrington, one of my former Sloane Ranger haunts. Upon entering the pub, Dave noticed a group of good-looking blondes laughing and joking together in the corner. While we stood at the bar sipping our pints, Pete said, "They sort of look like SRs, but they're different." Just then, one of the girls howled loudly, and we caught the distinct twang of an American southern drawl. They looked like the SR equivalent, but instead of the blouses or crew sweaters of British girls, they wore Fair Isle sweaters, Lacoste polo shirts with the collars turned up, and pearls. We knew this look as American "Preppies."

Dave commented, "The one on the far left keeps turning around and looking at me. We should go over and introduce ourselves."

I said, "I agree what about you, Pete?"

"I'm game," he replied. "I bet the one who howled is from Texas. I like southern girls if that's where she's from."

I fancied my chances with the one sitting to the left of the girl who had been looking at Dave. We meandered over and asked them if they were American as we had heard an accent from the bar. They introduced themselves as Gail, Abby, Hattie, and Tricia. Gail said they were all from Bucknell University on an overseas program and were staying up the road in Egerton Gardens.

Pete asked if we could join them, and so we did. Each of us scooted in next to the pre-agreed girls we had each identified, Dave and Abby already making plenty of eye contact with a few laughs. I sat beside Tricia and gained some great first impressions.

She was attractive with porcelain skin that made her look like a British girl. In many ways, she reminded me of Princess Diana and other Sloanes I had met at that time. She seemed less flighty than the Sloanes I had been dating and came across as more outgoing and less prim than the others. Her friends sounded far more conservative and didn't appear ready for much beyond a drink. Whilst Tricia didn't quite get my British sense of humour, she tried to understand it and showed interest in the rugby, which we discussed. We boys faced a dilemma, as none of us was sure how events would progress from here. Dave and Pete seemed to be getting on well with Abby and Hattie, but I sensed the girls knew they all should stick together with Gail left out. Evidently, they hunted in packs, so trying to separate them wasn't going to be easy. That night we agreed to meet again and so bid our farewells with some lustful looks between us.

In the ensuing days, something must have happened between Pete and Hattie, because the following time we met, Pete didn't want to join us. I had a feeling he tried something on, which had not worked out. Gail didn't come along either, so it was Tricia and me, Dave and Abby and Hattie. The girls agreed to come out and watch one of our rugby matches, which was entertaining for us as they knew nothing about the game. Afterwards, they joined us in the bar for drinks and general mischievous behaviour. Tricia's and my relationship progressed quickly. I missed her tremendously when she left just before the Christmas holiday, and I longed to visit her in the US.

I felt lonely, so I threw myself into my work. London in the early 80s was becoming unsafe because of the IRA terrorist campaign. I experienced what it was like to live in constant danger. I experienced this first hand when having a drink with a friend in the Blue Posts off Piccadilly Circus. All of a sudden, the whole place shuddered as a bomb exploded up the road outside the Liberty store. It was terrifying, as in those days the IRA seldom gave much notice before a bombing strike, something they started to do much later. The worst bombing was of the Lifeguards mounted cavalry at Hyde Park Corner in July of 1982. The carnage shown in the newspaper was dreadful.

While I kept busy and avoided the bomb scares, I thought of Tricia constantly and wrote to her several times a week.

My career needed to progress, so I worked long hours until by the stroke of luck a budding recruitment manager saw my potential and put me forward for an account manager position at the London office of the well-known American advertising agency, Young & Rubicam. This was a top ten worldwide advertising agency at the time and very hard to get into. I had worked on retail accounts at David Williams and Ketchum and Y&R were looking for someone to manage their TV rental account, Radio Rentals. By this time, I had my Communications Advertising and Marketing diploma and enrolled in another night course to get the Institute of Marketing Diploma.

I was over the moon when hired to join Y&R, and at 24 years old, I was the youngest account manager they had ever employed. I had a lot to learn, but I was excited and confident. I still have my business card from those days with my name in fancy script writing.

Working on Radio Rentals wasn't easy, due to their location in Swindon outside London, and so I made regular trips to see them. Radio Rentals were also very fussy and detail oriented about their ads. We had long telephone calls about the pricing and the positioning of their products.

The Board Director who headed up our group at the agency was David Montgomery, a large, bullish man with a bald head. I will always remember his name because it reminds me that one person can sometimes be our undoing. My immediate boss, Henry, who was Account Director, was very pleased with my work, but for some reason, David rarely said much to me. I think he was jealous of something about me and always reminded me how much I had to learn and how lucky I was to be there, being so inexperienced.

Henry gave me snippets of information from time to time about how things were going. One time I had worked a crazy, long schedule as always, and on my way home, I had to deliver some ad proofs to David's house in Belgravia. These were for an important client meeting the next day. I was satisfied that

I had prepared everything ready in time and had worked hard to complete the ads.

I called at David's grand house in Eton Place to drop the proofs off, but he invited me in for a drink. After thanking me, he said those immortal words I have always hated since that day: "I have been meaning to have a chat with you."

David proceeded to tell me that he was firing me and that there wasn't a need for a six-month review, as he felt that I wasn't demonstrating the requirements they sought of me. I don't ever recall someone telling me I wasn't doing the job well. Henry had told me I was doing very well, so to hear this from someone further up the line was very upsetting, particularly as David rarely saw me work on a daily basis. Maybe he wanted someone else; I never knew. This was to be the first taste of what would happen to me later in life when someone so removed from how I worked on a daily basis would have a major say in my future. I simply hate that kind of phoniness, but unfortunately, it is often the reality in the corporate world.

At work the following day I told my buddy, Mike Coyle, in the nearest office that they had fired me. He was supportive and told me to take off to America to visit Tricia.

"Go off and explore the States, mate. Do you really want to be slugging away on the Radio Rentals account here?"

I immediately booked a flight on TWA for Newark, New Jersey. I had never been on a transatlantic flight before, so it was a thrilling experience. I remember the excitement of drinking numerous cans of Schlitz on the way over and thinking how cool it was.

I stayed at Bucknell University in Pennsylvania for a week and enjoyed the atmosphere of an American college campus. I would say, "Wow" to myself every day as I roamed around looking at all the amazing college girls. My school experiences had not included girls, and I had never seen so many attractive blossoming women in one place. I wished I could have turned the clock back and been able to study in the United States. The girls loved my accent, and I felt like a celebrity.

We visited Tricia's family in Princeton and took a day trip to New York. The scale of everything dumbfounded me. The Chrysler Building reached into the sky like a pointed, shiny glass finger. A hive of activity buzzed around me when I came up out of the subway to the street level. Everything was a blur of colour and noise but in an exhilarating way, despite the dubious street odours I couldn't identify. I toyed with the fantasy of being a big shot advertising executive here in this new, exciting world, a place where opportunities existed for entrepreneurs and maybe with less red tape than in the UK. I enjoyed my time so much that I started to wonder if this might lead somewhere; the allure of the United States was enticing.

Again, Tricia and I said goodbye, and I flew back to London. Given my shock departure from Y&R, I decided to make a career change from the high flyers in advertising and go into the "below the line" side of sales promotion. This would make me more marketable as I would know both sides of the promotion business. Advertising was all about developing a brand image, whereas sales promotion involved using more short-term tactics that appealed at store level.

I joined International Marketing and Promotions (IMP) and talked with Tricia whenever I could. It was a long distance relationship with specific phone times agreed between us. I missed America and became infatuated with her, the first girl I had met who really loved me.

Tricia had also been a huge support for me after I lost my job at Y & R. She believed in my goal of wanting to make it in the marketing world. She had a huge, welcoming family that was attractive to me, given my lack of family closeness growing up. I could picture myself in her world and that of the US, which could be a way for me to progress with my life. Like so many of my friends in the UK, I viewed America as the land of opportunity. The many American shows and films that made their way onto our lounge TVs formed our impressions. My Uncle Toby had also done business with Americans and so imparted some of that to me during our various discussions.

After she graduated, Tricia enlisted her father to help get her a job in London. His connections in insurance enabled her to get an entry-level position at Willis Faber in the City of London. She arrived in London in the fall of 1982 to join me, whereupon I took her to meet my parents.

My father was pleased, as he liked Tricia and felt that she was a calming influence on what he saw as my erratic, unreliable "behaviour." I wrote Dad's words in my journal. "She will settle you down. She is a good girl, given the girls I have seen you with. She is level-headed and a responsible girl with common sense." Having his approval influenced my decision to propose to Tricia, whereupon we agreed to wait a year to get married.

How would life go in the meantime? Would Tricia adapt to the inevitable culture shock of moving permanently to the UK? The time passed quickly, and without any worries the exciting day arrived in September of 1983 when we got married in Princeton, New Jersey.

At a family function a few days before the wedding, we were gathered opening wedding gifts in Tricia's family home, when all of a sudden Tricia's youngest sister, Kristen, came running into the lounge. She announced, "A gigantic beat-up Cadillac has just pulled up in front. The guys jumping out don't look like they belong here. You should come quickly."

We all rushed to the window. She was right. A hefty group of dishevelled men were getting out of a beat-up Pontiac. One had a Mohawk with chains dangling around his neck; others were very shady-looking and wearing various hats with intimidating tattoos adorning their arms. I noticed one looked familiar, but I needed to take a closer look.

When they arrived at the door, Tricia's father answered it. "Can I help you with something?" he asked sternly.

Suddenly from amongst the group, my old friend Eddy from London stepped forward and said, "We are here for Dan's wedding. He isn't expecting me so I hope it's okay? I brought some of my brothers with me."

I pushed my way to the front to say, "I know this guy; it's Eddy my friend from London." I exchanged a hug with him, and much to the surprise of the stunned Metzgers, opened the door wide and invited them all in.

Eddy and his brothers nervously filed past and joined us in the family room. It was extremely awkward; enormous black guys eyed up all the nicely dressed white ladies around the room. One couldn't have conjured up a motlier crew.

"Hey we have a wedding gift for you," Eddy said to break the strained silence. He placed a huge package wrapped in brown paper on the coffee table.

"We figured you'd like something classy for your new home so me and my bros got this for you on one of our runs."

Everyone glanced at each other with raised eyebrows wondering what he meant by runs!

Tricia cautiously opened the wrapping to reveal a highly polished mahogany box. She opened the lid and under some foam covering unveiled a full set of ornate silverware. We all gasped, "Wow," and I immediately said, "Eddy, this is expensive; you didn't need to buy this. It is simply great to see you. I really appreciate you coming all the way from London."

"You did a lot for me, man, so this is the least I can do for you," replied Eddy.

Tricia picked up one of the knives and quietly whispered to me without anyone noticing that they weren't our initials. We both noticed the initials "JKS" engraved on every piece. Others, too, started to realize something was amiss and then the information filtered throughout the room. Eddy was watching us and immediately broke the mounting tension by saying, "I hope you won't mind the initials. If you turn them over no one will notice."

Tricia's mother let out an audible gasp and strutted out of the room as we all gave each other questioning looks. It was definitely the most original and questionable gift we had received for our wedding. I had half the inclination to pull Eddy aside and ask him how he came by the silverware, but I didn't. Given Eddy's dodgy past, I was sure that it wasn't a legal procurement. In fact, to this day I wonder where the silverware is because I didn't see it again after that.

We held our wonderful wedding ceremony at a Princeton Episcopal church, and my father officiated. We honeymooned for a week on Sanibel Island in Florida.

Our life together continued in London, and soon after we purchased a modest one bedroom flat in West Hampstead. It was a loft conversion with great views of the city from the back window. At last, I had a permanent home that I could finally call my own, even though it was a tiny one. We both worked hard to afford our mortgage payment. At weekends we did a lot of entertaining, having numerous friends over with informal dinner parties. Our flat was a place we both enjoyed in our shared domestic life, and our friends liked visiting too. Tricia had developed friendships with other Americans where she worked, and I had my rugby friends and those from the business world. So from being unsettled and bouncing around London from bedsit to bedsit, I ended up married and a homeowner. My life was beginning to take shape.

14

THE ROYAL FLUSH

As a newly married couple, Tricia and I enjoyed living
in our new flat in West Hampstead. I felt content
with my life. My father was also about to experience
a culmination of his career with a change that would affect
him enormously. My father had served many of the regiments
of the Household Division and had been in the Royal Army
Chaplains Department for over twenty-five years. This meant
he was a senior chaplain and was therefore eligible for one of
the most sought-after clergy posts, that of Chaplain to the
Queen. He interviewed and then accepted the role in 1983,
which he was to hold until 1987.

My father invited us many times to attend services at the
Guards Chapel where he was now serving, but at that time
rubbing noses with senior military officers didn't mean that
much to me, as I had been used to that most of my life. While
I would leap at the chance today, the opportunity to sit behind
the royal family in the priest's pew didn't interest me. My

priorities were elsewhere when it came to Sundays. Often I was recovering from Saturday's rugby game for London Welsh, or I would rather lie in bed after a stressful week's work than get all dressed up for church. I had grown up with the army, and it was not what interested me anymore.

During this time, my parents had a gorgeous flat in Wellington Barracks overlooking Birdcage Walk, which is opposite Buckingham Palace. The flat was in a corner spot on the top floor of a modern sand-coloured square building with tall, slim windows. They looked like those built for archers in the towers of medieval castles. Tall black railings encompassed the building and the entire barracks, and kept the public out.

From our dining room, we had a grand view of Big Ben in the distance and the parade ground below, where the guards would assemble every day to be marched out of the gates and across to Buck House (Buckingham Palace) for changing of the guard. This meant from the flat we had a bird's eye view of the palace and the comings and goings of the royals during Dad's five-year posting at the Guards Chapel.

To visit my father at Wellington Barracks, I had to have my car registered with the guardhouse. When I arrived, they checked my ID and did a quick sweep with their bomb detection scanners before allowing me to enter. Anybody travelling with me also had to be thoroughly cleared through security.

Living next door to Buckingham Palace afforded us many glimpses of life in the rarefied air of royal living. I had the honour and privilege of meeting the royal family a few times, including the Queen, Prince Philip, Prince Charles, The Queen Mother, and the Princess of Wales and experienced what it was like to see my father serve as Chaplain to the Queen.

My father's church was the Guards Chapel set back from Birdcage Walk, a few moments stroll or march from Buckingham Palace. The Guards Chapel is not on first impression a church, as it is an enormous white rectangular building with few windows. Inside, though, the chapel is a lofty and grand space with history seeping from its walls. It boasts a striking but reserved military presence. The focal point is the stunning original apse adorned with luminous gold tesserae tiles, coloured marble, and magnificent marble mosaics that add luster to this beautiful part of the church.

All but the apse of the 1879 chapel had been demolished in June of 1944 by a direct hit from a Second World War V-1 flying bomb. The deaths of 58 civilians and 63 service members worshiping at the time shook the nation. Yet, amid the carnage and destruction, the six silver candles on the main altar had not gone out, a symbol of hope perhaps.

The V-1 was the first "cruise missile," powered by a simple jet engine and carrying a 1,870-pound warhead. Launched from northern France, a V-1 travelled at four hundred miles per hour with a range of up to 150 miles. It contained a device that counted the revolutions in a tiny propeller in its nose, and when it reached the number calculated to have brought it over its target the engine cut out and the missile fell to earth, detonating on impact. People would reportedly first hear a distant hum, growing to a louder harsh rattle, which either vanished as the 'buzz-bomb' flew on or stopped abruptly, followed a few seconds later by the roar of one ton of high explosive detonating.

The inside of the Guards Chapel is finished with white marble and is mostly lit from recessed floodlights in the roof. An impressive collection of faded battle colours dating from the 17th century hang in formal lines along the sides, many darkened, tattered and frayed with the odd bullet hole. Military memorials to each household regiment line the walls and salvaged fittings from the original bombed chapel are on display.

When Tricia and I attended Sunday services, we noticed the congregation gathered in an orderly, unfussed sort of way. They were rather formal and subdued. It was ceremonious, not a warm, fuzzy place to worship. After all, this is a military institution, so it did not have the atmosphere of a church with a regular public congregation.

At the start of the service, mellow string music set the tone, and it took me a few moments to realise this was live. The musicians played behind a screen in a gallery upstairs above the choir. A musical director led the band members all dressed in their immaculate scarlet tunics. I looked around and noticed there were brass cups on the floor and brass rings on the backs of each pew seat beside the aisle across the chapel. *What were they for?* I wondered. Maybe to hold swords for officers in dress uniform, or more likely for colours or candles.

The priest announced the Peace at the usual place in the service, but nobody moved and the service rapidly moved on. There wasn't even the briefest handshake. Though I am no fan of the comprehensive Peace that brings the service to a halt for five minutes, not having one at all seemed very stiff upper lip and stilted. Some acknowledgement and well-wishing towards other worshippers would have brought us together more.

My fondest memories of the chapel, besides seeing my father preach, were the resplendent highly pressed scarlet uniforms worn by the guards and the wonderful music from the choir and band. While we sat in our pew, my mind would wander, serenaded by the majesty and pomp of the service.

The chapel added my father's name years later to an honour roll for all the chaplains who had served there. The keeper at the church was Fred Barrett, and it was great to see him again when I visited a few years back. Fred was always a great support for my father and later would receive an MBE (Member of the British Empire) for his 24 years of service.

My father's position afforded us invitations to many royal events. In July 1984, we were excited to go with my parents to the Queen's annual Garden Party at Buckingham Palace, which was a thrilling experience.

The "invitation" was actually a command issued by the Lord Chamberlin on behalf of Her Majesty on a stiff white card. The Garden Party team worked at Buck House handwriting every "Command" in wonderful black ink. The convention is that it's a once in a lifetime "invitation." When the package arrived, it contained instructions for the day along with an admittance card, security details, car parking badge, and maps;

cameras were forbidden. We needed to bring a passport and one other form of identification. The dress code was stated as uniforms, morning dress, or lounge suits, which is what I wore. "Afternoon dress" was required for women, such as an outfit suitable for a wedding, preferably with a hat.

On the day itself, we were allowed in through the three entrances to Buckingham Palace from 3:15 p.m. (even though the invitation said 4:00 p.m.), so guests could walk through the Grand Hall of the Palace, out onto the terrace, and enjoy looking around the gardens for an hour. Tables and chairs were set up over parts of the lawn for guests to sit in. As we neared the terrace, we heard the band of the Welsh Guards playing such favourites as Beatles numbers and Lloyd Webber tunes.

Military friends told us that the Queen had personally checked everything for the party, as she was a diligent hostess! We strolled over to look inside the main marquee, where at least a hundred staff lined up along an enormous extended buffet table ready to serve cups of tea, glasses of still lemonade, and numerous strawberry tartlets, salmon sandwiches, and whisky cakes. Typically, Garden Party fare consisted of dainty crustless sandwiches, mini éclairs, thin slices of Victoria sponge cake, and tiny chocolate ganache cakes with miniature golden crowns on the top. To accompany this there was a special "Garden Party" tea—iced tea and lemonade but no alcohol. The catering staff helped serve the refreshments, but really, it was a "help yourself" buffet!

My father told me it was poor taste to take too much food, and indeed the size of the rectangular shaped plate prevented this, since our white china cups fitted into a combination[27] plate. This limited how much food I could take at one time, but I did see that some people were rather clever about stacking their plates carefully. Guests often returned for second helpings, and one ingenious gentleman, in particular, took

---

[27] A plate with separate compartments for foods.

out his napkin, wrapped an éclair in it, and then placed it in his pocket. It reminded me of the scene from the 1983 movie "Trading Places" when Dan Akroyd, dressed as Santa, stuffed a whole side of salmon inside his tunic. We quickly realized that if we preoccupied ourselves with the food, we would miss the chance to meet the royals so we made a choice.

Mum noticed that gentlemen ushers, who were members of the Royal Household, were approaching suitable guests and placing them in the spaces in the lanes where the Royal Family members were planning to walk. These guests could possibly meet the Royal Family. Mum told me that if chosen, we would have to wait in the "space" for up to an hour and forego the refreshments! Therefore, the choice was simply to meet or eat! Neither of my parents was that eager as they had met them before, so we milled about in the grand marquee picking at the sandwiches. My father kept bumping into people he knew, whereupon we exchanged pleasantries and superficial hellos before moving on.

If nature called, superior portable loos were dotted discreetly around the garden. Upon inspection, I found these well maintained and impeccably clean, compared to those at rugby matches.

The St. John Ambulance team were ready in the first aid tent, and the Queen's Bodyguard of the Yeomen of the Guard in their striking red and gold uniforms attended as well. The Yeoman marked out the routes through the crowds that the Royals would take and were always ready to guard the Queen, their traditional role if the need arose. The Garden Party ladies were on hand to help any guests who had forgotten their invitations or ID.

At 4:00 p.m. exactly, the Queen, Prince Charles, and Lady Diana Spencer stepped out onto the terrace as the band played the National Anthem. The Queen was easy to spot, as she wore a bright blue dress with matching hat. Then each Royal slowly meandered down a distinct lane of guests, zigzagging from one side of the lane to the other so that the most people possible saw them. The walk took a whole hour, due to the number of people the Royals liked to meet and speak to. My father nudged me and said, "Watch what the Queen does with her handbag." He told me there is a little-known sign that the queen sometimes gives using her handbag to tell the ushers she needs to move on. The Queen often uses her bag as a signalling device. She might switch the bag from one arm to the next, indicating she wants to talk to someone else. If she places her bag on a table, it means she wants to leave in five minutes.

A Gentleman Usher briefed any guest due to meet a Royal on etiquette in advance. Men were supposed to bow from the chin and not the waist, with their arms straight by their sides. Women had to keep their backs straight with their heads up. The curtsey involved placing the right leg forward, with the left leg back, and then a dip, without too much of a wobble. A mistake was to pull the skirt out to the side, deemed way too theatrical and rather "Hollywood." My father told me that conversations with the Queen often strayed off the rails. People who met her became so nervous that they started babbling, or became dumbstruck, in which case she filled the silence with her own conversation.

When the Royal Family reached the end of the lines, they took tea with government ministers in the Royal Tent. At 6:00 p.m., the band played the National Anthem again to signal that the party was over and the Royal Family then waved and silently ambled back to the Palace, chatting informally to a few more people on the way. The queen had probably placed her bag on a table to signal she was ready to leave.

I was shocked later when I did some research on how much is consumed at an average Garden Party: 30,000 sandwiches and scones, 27,000 cups of tea, 20,000 slices of cake and 20,000 glasses of still lemonade.

After seeing or possibly even meeting the Queen, 8,000 people travelled home very content, including ourselves. We didn't meet the Royals that day, but I did meet them on several occasions at the Guards Chapel.

Welsh Guards Remembrance Sunday.
My father with HRH Prince Charles and Lady Diana Spencer.

In addition to the normal Sunday services, my father had to organize many special royal services throughout the year such as remembrance, memorial, and weddings. Prince Charles even had a nickname for my father and jokingly referred to him as "Evil Tom." I think the evil part came from Charles seeing him as a devilish Welshman, because Charles had attended military services at many of his postings.

My father also spent a great deal of time with the late Queen Mother at functions where he officiated. My mother said the Queen Mother was so popular because she would waft around in an alcohol-induced haze. My father told the story that once, after attending a function in London, the host invited the Queen Mother to stay on for tea. The host had nervously said to the Queen Mother, "I hear you like gin, ma'am." The Queen Mother replied, "I hadn't realized that I enjoyed that reputation." In addition, she continued to say "but since I do, perhaps you could make my drink a large one."

Many stories from what I term the "royal days" make me laugh. My mother recalled a story she witnessed at Buckingham Palace, or "Buck House," so called by the military folks. My mother attended a small charity tea party hosted by Lady Diana for the Red Cross in one of the ornate drawing rooms at the palace.

My mother often attended these events, as she, as the padré's wife, was involved in many charity fundraising functions. She told me how important she felt giving her name to the guards at the side entrance to Buck House and then having her bag searched while they called her "Ma'am." She liked the youthful Scots Guardsmen calling her that. Mum loved these occasions but didn't get out as much as my father who was in the royal spotlight all the time. Thus, the tea party socials were a way for her to rub shoulders with important people. At one such event, I remember her telling me afterwards she had met Charlton Heston, whom she said was stunningly handsome.

Mum described the grand setting of the tea party. She loved the opulence and grandeur of these events in rooms that had high ceilings finished in elaborate styles, plush red carpets on the floors, and flocked wallpaper. The drawing room had the look and ambience of a period museum, a room that was stuck back in time, and probably not redecorated since Victoria's time. The gilded interior displayed ornate chairs with curly gold legs and sculpted backs. Looking down at the guests were brooding portraits of royal ancestors and a painting by Canaletto.

Things were well on their way when Mum noticed out of the corner of her eye an innocent-looking Prince William who slipped into the drawing room at the far end. William was wearing red shorts, white ankle socks, navy buckled shoes and a white top with a navy sweater. He was alone, which my mother thought rather odd, and seemed to be looking for Diana, who was in the middle of the room, socializing. The Prince, who was five at the time, stopped as he entered the room and gazed around. The light coming through the tall windows cast a bright light onto his upper body and made it seem like he was wearing radiant jewels. Those tall Buck House windows would often cast brilliant light onto the gold cornicing and splendid trim around the room, but this seemed peculiar.

Mum recalled, "It was as if the Prince was lit up like a small Christmas tree."

All heads turned to look over at him as well. After all, he was the star back in those days, and anyone welcomed the chance to see him, particularly given his surprise entrance. The glow emanating from his torso wasn't from the sunlight shining on him at all. As he walked towards Princess Diana in the middle of the room, everyone stopped talking and their mouths dropped open. Even the royal mice residing in the palace walls must have held their breath that day. All that could be heard was the clickety-clack of William's shoes on the floor and a clinking sound coming from what was hanging around his neck. Finally, Diana turned to discover her son walking to her.

Around William's neck hung several strands of pearls, some so long that they draped below his tiny red shorts. On his jumper was pinned a shiny brooch. As he walked up to Diana, the sun caught his face.

His large blue eyes looked up at her as if to say, "Just check me out."

Everyone covered their mouths so as not to laugh aloud (very unBritish) at what he was wearing, some with their hands on the sides of their faces whispering something to the person adjacent to them.

Diana couldn't help herself. She giggled and tried to defuse the awkward tension in the room. According to my mother, Diana asked William if he had been playing with some dolls jewellery in the nursery, but everyone could see quite plainly that these were no trinkets. William had obviously entered into someone's dressing room and put on all their jewels. I had to laugh as my mother described the gorgeous diamond brooch pinned to the left breast pocket of his sweater. William wore it like a toy patch, but it was, in fact, worth millions. A string of emeralds was peeking out of his tiny shorts as if he hadn't had time to sling those around his neck. Then Diana's nanny, Olga Powell, rushed into the room spluttering and apologizing as she strode over to collect William.

She said, "I am so sorry Ma'am, but he got away from me for a short while. I'll take him back with me."

Diana made very little of it except to say to the nanny that she should make sure that everything was put back where it belonged and to call one of the maids to help.

Apparently, as Ms. Powell plucked Prince William from Diana's arms, he reputedly said, "These look pretty, Mummy, as they go around in the loo."

A few guests overheard this and merely raised their eyebrows with a short chuckle. Diana said, "Oh don't be so silly. We would hardly do that, would we?"

Well, it transpired that he had! The charming little Prince had taken some irreplaceable, historically important jewels and flushed them down the royal toilets. Mum later learned this through the grapevine and had been asked to keep it quiet. In those days, many events were hushed up and didn't get out, especially if the press was not present.

To see those pearls around his neck would have been a perfect pressman's dream, but it was a private event and no media were present, thankfully. The next day my mother looked out of the flat window from Wellington Barracks and saw a line of plumbers' vehicles entering the Palace gates.

It turned out Prince William had flushed quite a few royal jewels down the system, and now the River Thames was the owner of some of that. Needless to say, it never hit the papers or the news, which was a blessing. I doubt whether Prince William would remember doing such a thing, but one never knows, and sadly my mother and Lady Diana are no longer with us.

I felt that Diana and I had some similarities. She lacked confidence, was very nervous and a sensitive type like me. She had her own struggles with bulimia, whereas I had been a hypochondriac in school but had overcome most of that by the time I left.

In 1987, I had my own personal encounter with the Princess of Wales by chance and not in church. It was on a fine hot July day when Tricia, a friend, and I attended a Guards' Polo match in Windsor Great Park. I don't recall encountering much security getting into the park except to present our car pass upon entering the grounds.

The ticket collector told us to read the warning notice on our passes, which was to cover the clubs liability.

"The holder of this pass recognises that polo is an aggressive, physical sport which, by its nature, involves a high risk of injury and damage to persons, animals, and property, not only to the persons who are engaged in playing polo but also bystanders and their personal property."

I was aware of the unpredictability of horses myself already, having had a few experiences. I just hoped that this event wouldn't add to that.

When we arrived to find our spot by the field, there was only one big building on the far side, which someone mentioned was the royal box.

We had taken a picnic with us to have on the grass beside our car at the match. The first few chukkas were fun to watch, and at halftime, the spectators were asked: "to press the divots" for five minutes. This involved going onto the field and walking around flattening the turf kicked up by the horses during the match. As I pressed my divots, I meandered to the other side of the field. I could see Princess Diana quite close, trying to stay cool on the balcony in the royal box, a stand that wasn't that huge and so the Royals were quite accessible. The royal box was a straightforward two-storey building with a sloped roof and a second-floor balcony that ran along the front. A simple white picket fence cordoned off the front with a patch of grass behind it. Diana was sitting alone, which was unusual as someone was always pestering her. She looked bored with everything that was going on and stared into space down towards the polo field full of spectators. Maybe she was thinking about James Hewitt, a man with whom she had started having an affair, or maybe she was mulling over her marriage troubles—little did anyone know that her marriage was about to collapse.

I won't forget the moment I caught Diana's eye. We exchanged a fleeting glance; I pretended to be busy pressing the tossed-up turf back into the ground while she watched me from the balcony above. When I looked up the second time, our eyes met, and she suddenly smiled at me from "over the fence." It shocked me and made my day, so much so that I still remember her smile. She gave me a warm gentle smile—as though she thought she knew me. It was a genuine smile from a friend and not a forced fake royal smile. I felt like I should wave back but didn't, as that wouldn't have been protocol.

Suddenly the whole world crowded around, breaking the connection I felt with her. Others members of the royal party returned from the halftime break and joined Diana on the balcony. I sauntered back to our side of the field, to our less privileged lives. As I did, I turned around one more time, just in case I was lucky for the third time, but I wasn't. The royal box was full again, and I could hardly see Diana in the crowd.

In the months that followed, my father provided counselling and advice to Prince Charles and Princess Diana. I could see written on his face the toll it was taking, as he and others valiantly tried to help them through their marital difficulties. He would return looking dejected and exhausted, would pour himself the first of several scotches, but he rarely said what had transpired. We knew confidentiality was an important part of his job; it was a matter of duty, and my father did his best as was expected of him. The Queen is head of the Church of England and divorce was still deeply discouraged. He felt responsible for helping them stay married, as he liked them both. Their eventual separation saddened him. It was such a shame that Diana's life ended prematurely later on.

My father enjoyed the social part of being a chaplain in the military where he hobnobbed with senior officers and enjoyed a drink or two at the many Officers' Mess functions. He was just as content to be with the other ranks as he was with the officers, and we noticed that over time he seemed to enjoy more than a few drinks. I believe the prolonged exposure to constant events, parties, and the royals fuelled his habit. He denied it, but when he retired from the military and took a post in 1988 on a small parish on the Duke of Wellington's estate outside London, I believe his drinking got worse.

He never said so, but my mother told me that my father missed the important job he had in London. Moving to a country parish was for him a major step down. Living in the countryside was a huge adjustment as he faced new civilian parishioner issues such as HIV/AIDS and domestic abuse, which he had rarely encountered in the military. My father was upset with the way that man treated his fellow man, and it came through in his sermons. He expected his parishioners to know their neighbours, help others, and stand up for what was correct. I think my father felt humanity wasn't going in the proper direction.

He also didn't like the way the Anglican Church had started to modernize, as women could then be ordained. He was also very old fashioned and thought homosexuality was a sin. I recall when he came back from the Anglican General Synod and told us how shocked he was at the number of gay clergy. He seldom discussed his specifics views about women priests, but we knew his opinion from his negative comments at home. Mum, Tricia, Steve, and I sensed he was not identifying with the changes occurring in the world around him.

15

MEETING BIG DAN'S SISTER

Aunt Heather's Embroidery

Mum was dealing with my father's drinking when she told me she was going to a funeral for Gordon, Aunt Heather's husband. My mother invited me to go along. I had no idea who Aunt Heather was. My mother told me she was Big Dan's younger sister, the only one of the Turner siblings still alive. I was pretty stunned that I was only then learning about Aunt Heather—some fifteen years after I learned about my birth father.

I felt this was someone I should have met a long time ago. I was in my mid-thirties and it seemed very odd meeting my biological family for the first time at this point in my life.

When we arrived, Heather put her arms around me and gave me a kiss as if I had known her for years. Even at her husband's funeral, she seemed a very optimistic person. I could tell she had a feisty outgoing personality with a wicked sense of humour, and I looked forward to getting to know her better. There was much apologizing between her and Mum for not staying in touch over the years.

Despite the mournful occasion, I had the opportunity to ask Heather about my birth father. Heather told me he was an upbeat man, often singing the popular tune "You Are My Sunshine" to her in their childhood. She gave me some more black and white photos of him to add to the collection I had from my mother, but unfortunately nothing else. On the walls of her house, I noticed some framed fine embroidery created and signed by Heather. Maybe that is where my creative side came from.

I was disappointed that Big Dan hadn't ever written or created anything to give me more of an insight into who he was. I knew he excelled in sports since I had his cups and a tennis racket that my mother had given me. Big Dan lived in the days before video cameras, so I couldn't get an impression of him at all, except through the black and white pictures. I left the funeral with very mixed emotions about him and the Turner family. Heather told me I should visit again and meet all my cousins, of which there were many. I couldn't believe I was discovering a completely new side of my family so late in my life.

I was a bit annoyed with Mum for not telling me all about them, but I also tried to understand how painful it was for her to go back there. I don't think she knew them that well when she met my father. After mum and Big Dan courted and married, they left England with his posting to Cyprus, so she never met the rest of the Turners back in England.

At his burial in the military cemetery on Malta, only his commanding officer and other officers who knew him well attended. It was too expensive to fly that far in those days. Mum told me it was very painful for her, so she didn't have any further contact with the family after he died and a gaping void developed.

After Gordon's funeral, Mum and I returned to Sherfield-on-Loddon and talked in the sitting room. Mum said she was sorry there weren't that many belongings left from

Big Dan. "Being in the military meant he didn't have much where he was stationed."

Later when I was upstairs getting ready for bed, my mother called me into her bedroom. "Come here a moment. I have something to show you."

When I entered her room, she asked me to come over to her wardrobe. The doors were wide open, and sitting on the top shelf I noticed the outdated battered brown leather suitcase, the one she had told me was special many years ago.

I saw some stickers on the outside and two tarnished brass locks on the front. It had reinforced corners with protective leather caps that gave it a robust look. A blue canvas strap around the middle and tightly tied with a knot told me she had wanted to keep it shut. The knot had dust on the creases, so I knew that it had remained closed for some time.

"This suitcase belonged to Big Dan," Mum said. "I never told you that did I"?

"Wasn't this the suitcase that was in the back shed in East Meon years ago?" I asked.

"Yes, that's correct. The reason I asked you to bring it inside that day was this suitcase is very special to me."

She explained that after Big Dan's death the military sent all his personal possessions back to her in Wales from the hospital in Malta. "All the lovely memories I had from my brief time with him I sealed in this suitcase. I vowed never to open it again as it would cause me too much pain."

I said, "It must have been difficult for you, and I can't imagine what that must have felt like. You were married only about three months, right?"

"Yes, and there was no warning about his illness. It came on very quickly. I didn't even make it out from Wales to see him before he died, so he died alone in that military hospital."

I noticed tears in her eyes. "You are all that I have left of Big Dan."

I gave her a gentle hug.

"Someday in the future, this suitcase will be yours but only after I am gone. I hope you understand that."

Back in my bedroom, I thought about our discussion. When posted to Germany and beyond she had moved that suitcase all over the place. All the time it remained locked and unopened since 1958. I wondered if she had talked about it with my father, in which case he must have just left it alone. Had he been the one to put it back in the outside shed in East Meon, or had she? I had so many unanswered questions about that suitcase. What was in it? Did it hold any surprises about my birth father? I felt I couldn't ask my mother anything more at that time. It would simply have to wait until another day.

Little did I know it, but I too was about to consider using my own suitcases soon after that day.

16

EMIGRATION AND NEW YORK PRESSURE

The "Blanche Currie" Cufflink Box

M y life was moving in the perfect direction in 1992, as I was doing well in the promotion marketing business, rising from an account manager to become a director at Clark, Bubear, Hill (CBH) a well-known promotional marketing company in London that I had now worked at for five years. Tricia and I were also enjoying our two children; Amanda was four and Robert was two. We had moved from our first tiny flat in West Hampstead to a tiny row house in Wimbledon. Since we both worked, we discussed hiring a nanny and were lucky to find Madge, whom the kids adored. Even with two kids, we still entertained our friends whenever we could and hosted many dinner parties on the weekends. I tried to find time to play rugby, but life became so busy, and other commitments often got in the way.

My daily drive to work in central London was about ten miles. Despite my continued progress at CBH, I was concerned about what to do next in my career. Our cramped house forced us to think about moving, and I couldn't go any further in my company. CBH told me after five years that I would never make partner as the owners would not make room. All they could do was give me a few pay rises here and there, but it wouldn't mean that much professional progression, as I wanted more for my family and me. I had also finally completed my BA in business studies, after eleven years at night school since 1981 to get various industry qualifications.

I now had two degrees and a diploma in advertising and marketing and was even, finally, somewhat proficient in math, having scored highly in the statistics part of my business degree. My school math teachers, Mr. Backhouse from Haileybury and Mr. Fiori from Bloxham would have been gobsmacked[28] as we say in the UK. My mind turned to the US; after all, that was the "Holy Grail" for promotion companies and marketing. Now that I had a degree, being hired was easier in the US, since most people at my level had one. In the back of my mind, I considered that the US might be a place where I could start my own company. My in-laws in the US were supportive of our coming to America, so I began writing to companies in New York City to see if they had any openings.

I knew I would kick myself in the future if I had never tried to make it in the US. I was at an age where my skills would be useful in advertising, so the timing seemed appropriate. Tricia's parents were prepared to sponsor me in my entry to the work-force and had agreed to vouch for me as an asset to the US.

My emigration to the US was a whirlwind. Comart, one of the leading promotional marketing agencies in the US, quickly offered me a job. I had been fortunate since Comart had a London-based affiliate, Kingsland, Lloyd, Peterson, and one of its partners had interviewed me first. They sent a favourable report to their New York office recommending me.

---

[28]   Utterly astonished; astounded.

It was all such a rush, as Comart gave me six weeks before I started my job in New York. We, therefore, had to sell our house quickly and arrange to move all our belongings overseas. We sold many of our unwanted belongings at a car boot[29] sale; the rest we had no choice but to put into storage, especially the electrical goods which would be of no use in the US. Looking back, I wish we hadn't sold our house, as we didn't get a great price for it. Years later, friends of ours who lived not far from us told us that houses like ours had tripled in value over the years.

Before we all departed, on the final weekend I visited my parents for the last time. Mum gave me a special gift, a white porcelain cufflink box. On the front was the image of one of the great cutter sailing ships that used to cross the Atlantic Ocean regularly. She explained that the ship was the Blanche Currie and had transported slate from the quarries in North Wales to America. On return to Porthmadog, she brought back giant stone boulders as ship's ballast. This was the closest major port to Borth-y-Gest where I had lived as a child. Receiving this gift felt so very poignant, given that I was about to travel to America. It was a reminder that I, too, would be taking possessions to America as well as bringing items back when I returned to visit later.

It was particularly difficult saying goodbye to Mum. I worried about her health, as she had picked up a kidney infection while on a trip abroad. I had concerns about leaving her with my father, who wasn't much help since he continued to drink heavily. I was torn between feeling guilty for not caring for my parents and the desire to make a new life in America. To secure my family's future, however, I had to look forward and do what would be best for them.

Tricia, Amanda, Robert, and I left on Virgin Atlantic Airlines on August 2, 1993. I still have the plane ticket from that day. It was a life changing decision, but I didn't sense I was

---

[29] The selling of items from a car's boot.

leaving Britain forever, even though I knew I was embarking on a momentous move. After all, airfares were quite cheap, and I could fly back when I liked.

At first, we stayed with my in-laws in Princeton, who were a great support until we found our own place. My father-in-law provided helpful advice as I transitioned into the American way of working. He stated that workers got up early here, and everyone was used to the commuting schedule. It all seemed so intense to me. He turned the shower on at 5:00 a.m., and daily proclaimed as he came down the stairs, "Another day of opportunity lies ahead." He was gone before me in the mornings.

I commuted every day from Princeton Junction into New York on the 6:15 a.m. train, often not getting home until 9:00 p.m. at night. It was a tough adjustment, as I had previously driven my comfortable company car into London to a private garage.

Settling in the New York tri-state area and commuting to New York City in the summer of 1993 was quite an eye-opener. My initial impressions were overwhelming. Everything happened so fast, and the pace of life picked up enormously compared to London. Life seemed hectic in the US—or was it just where I was living? Everyone rushed about their day and crammed as much in as they could. I didn't hear people complaining as I rode the train, except when there was a train delay. I remembered how busy New York had been when I visited previously on summer vacations. The city was vibrant, pulsing with purpose, and had its own particular smells, such as the honking smell of summer garbage lying in black bags and baking in the hot sun on the sidewalk. The unmistakable whiffs of sweat and urine in Penn Station mixed with fast food was quite a combination to decipher. Enticing cooking scents wafted from broiled hotdogs on the Sabrett food carts, and hard-to-classify odours blasted out of subway grates and building vents on waves of hot air. The air was heavy and stuffy, especially in the bowels of Penn Station when I came off the commuter train. It was that same smell of musty, heated, stale dust I remembered when I left home in 1979 for London and entered the underground system in Waterloo station.

I was now in the Big Apple and working for one of the leading promotional marketing agencies in the US. What's more, I was working on their most important account, Philip Morris. Working on the Marlboro cigarette business would give me great experience and make me more marketable going forward in the US. A tobacco account was not my ideal choice, as smoking was not something I supported or liked. My parents were both smokers and Steve and I had endured their smoking for many years as children.

I was ready for my first day at work and arrived at Comart to find there was a welcome sign on my desk with my name on it, with the US and UK flags illustrated side by side. It was a touching gesture that made me feel welcomed and at home right away.

My boss was a tall, attractive woman by the name of Lori Brandon. I remember she owned a luxurious full-length fur coat, wore a massive diamond ring on her left hand, and was very organized and put-together. My secretary, Brittany, was a nineteen-year-old from Staten Island. It was Brittany's first job, and she was proud of her typing skills and her ability to quickly change the golf ball letter device on the IBM typewriter.

On my first day, I made an innocent mistake that paved the way for a series of misunderstandings as I merged my language and cultural background with that of the US. I asked my secretary if I could borrow a rubber[30], something we were used to doing in the UK. I didn't know that a rubber in the US means something else. How could one word mean something completely opposed in two countries that spoke the same language? Brittany immediately turned red in the face and dashed down the hall to Lori's office to complain. Lori couldn't conceal her smile as she tactfully told me that rubbers in America were

---

[30] Eraser.

condoms. Afterwards, I apologized to Brittany, who thankfully was understanding of the mistake.

It was just as well I didn't smoke so I never asked for a fag[31], which would have got me into even more trouble. A fag in the US refers to a gay person, but a fag in the UK is slang for a cigarette. It was also what students were called when acting as personal servants to the most senior boys or prefects[32] at Bloxham.

To meet with our client, Philip Morris, Lori and I would take a luxury Lincoln Town Car from midtown over to Park Avenue. I would sink back into the luxurious deep leather seats, and the stress of my day would immediately subside for a brief moment on that journey. I thought, *Why couldn't we merely take a leisurely tour of the city instead of going to a stressful meeting at Philip Morris?*

Lori was scarcely one to take the subway if she could avoid it. I remember many times carrying her bags (like a fag) and trying to be the perfect English gentlemen. At my first client meeting, Lori introduced me to a room of fifteen executives sitting around an endless conference table on the 28th floor. Given my accent, they kept asking me to speak, which was very off-putting, but I had to appear unruffled, as I was their new management supervisor. I didn't want to put a foot wrong, so I worked the extra hours and did what was required and some. I had to think through and prepare for every important meeting ahead of time, with Lori being very demanding and a perfectionist. The pressure on me was enormous.

It didn't help that trains were often late at Penn Station, and delays often occurred when the weather was lousy, so I would get home some evenings well after 9:00 p.m. Fortunately, Comart was only a ten-minute walk from the station, which was a blessing at the end of the day. The only thing I enjoyed

---

31   Personal servants to the most senior boys.
32   Assistants in the smooth running of the school with the student body.

about the commute was my reading time on the inbound train. I worked out exactly where to stand so the train doors opened in front of me, and then dashed on to find a window seat. Coming home my strategy was to wait for the platform announcement in the corridor underneath the main concourse. I knew what platforms the Princeton Junction train departed from, so I was always ready to make a dash for it when they announced the train. Once I had my outbound seat, I was often asleep before the train emerged from the tunnel.

I learned the ropes day in, day out, by listening to Lori and absorbing as much as I could about how high profile business worked in New York City. Two account supervisors assisted me in managing my other accounts, which were Reckitt & Colman, Banana Boat Sunscreen, and Scott Paper.

During this very busy time, Tricia and I purchased a house not that far from her parents, and our third child Charlotte was born in 1994. Now we had our hands full. My job was crucial since my wife was not working. There was no time for me, which concerned me, as all I did was work and had no time to unwind on the weekends. When I discussed my frustrations with my father-in-law, he simply said that this is what everyone does when they commute. After all, that is exactly what he had done for twenty-plus years. I had to become used to my stressful existence, leaving the house at 5:45 a.m. every day and many nights not getting back until after 9:00 p.m.

Back at Philip Morris, something colossal was brewing, which would eclipse both The Marlboro Adventure Team and Country Store promotions. The managers of the Event Marketing Group were the main engine drivers of any Marlboro promotion campaign and coordinated all the work with the field and sales teams, so were critical to the success of any promotions. They held meetings in a smoke-filled room where they coughed and wheezed as they told us that Leo Burnett, their advertising agency, had come up with an incredible, groundbreaking "Huge Idea", which would garner huge support for the brand. The challenge, though, was how to make this event come alive.

It was 1995, and Philip Morris invited Comart to pitch for a huge promotion named, "Project Thunder." There was intense secrecy at that time surrounding this project, and it sure was fun to work on it because of that. Would we be the agency to win this business and therefore become the most recognized promotional agency in America?

Along with Lori, I was responsible for briefing several creative teams at our agency. Afterwards, my account team and I had to coordinate everything for the presentation to Philip Morris, including preparing the proposed timeline and budget.

The "Huge Idea" centred on building a special smokers' train for regular customers that would run through "Marlboro Country." Exactly what termed "Marlboro Country" was difficult to agree upon as they discussed various routes in meeting rooms filled with heavy cigarette smoke. We even had to work out the best route for the train and negotiate with railcar manufacturers. Many routes were very controversial, such as laying track in the Grand Canyon, but eventually, they decided to run the train from Billings, Montana, to Denver, Colorado, which epitomized the ideals of "Marlboro Country."

They sought our ideas for the creative rendering of the train, the sales brochures, the salesforce incentives, and the themes for each carriage of the train. We proposed a sky-viewing observation car, with a retractable roof where smokers could sit in recliners and puff away while they viewed the night sky above. We also proposed a dance car that had specially reinforced glass on all sides and an observation car that allowed maximum viewing of the countryside. This train would spearhead the promotional effort from which many other events would spin off.

For the presentation, we drew up what we termed "marker concept boards" in those days. One board had the visuals for all the kick-off incentives and prizes, and the creative department came up with the idea of creating a round case that replicated an authentic train wheel. Inside was a special railroad jacket similar to the previous Country Store denim jackets. We also proposed making replica railroad spikes like those actually used on the tracks and using them as awards. Instead of being made of steel, the spikes would be made of a lighter material, then coloured gold or silver and engraved.

The plan to run the train through Marlboro Country and even along the bottom of the Grand Canyon was controversial and ambitious. If anyone could pull it off, Marlboro could, but we at the agency felt environmental issues and logistics could present problems. After all, the Grand Canyon is a sacred place, and there was no way Philip Morris would get permission to lay a track down there, but we continued with our ideas regardless.

Unfortunately, Comart didn't win the promotion, and we hardly heard anything more about it. It never left the station, so to speak. We heard it had run into some major legal or logistical problems, not to mention issues with the cost of the project.

Comart wasn't doing as well as I believed. We had been losing existing business, including parts of American Express, Ciba Geigy, and Scott Paper, and then Reckitt & Colman started to pull back as well. We were also top heavy, with senior management drawing huge salaries. The combination of these factors indicated to me that the writing was on the wall, and significant changes were about to occur.

There were rumours of a company purchase and possibly layoffs. Working on the most profitable business, Philip Morris might save me. I had been in the US only nine months, so it was a harrowing time. I needed the stability of a reliable job and my family feeling more settled.

What transpired was an odd situation. Victor and Robyn Imbimbo, a sister and brother team, owned Hadley, a promotional marketing agency that purchased Comart. They laid off most top management at Comart, including Lori. I was the only management supervisor retained because of my knowledge and contacts at Phillip Morris.

Hadley moved us downtown to Houston Street. My commute became unbearable since it involved taking three trains into the city and then walking fifteen minutes to the office. The new working hours and the pressure to succeed with less staff only added to my misery.

I felt torn between the expectations and duties in the US and the need to be back home caring for my parents. I felt maxed out; work was stressful and uncertain and on top of this I spent my weekends ferrying the kids to sports activities and social events. There was no time to relax. I really wanted time with the family at home instead of always being scheduled; even church became a weekly drudge.

To provide myself with a break I decided to join Princeton Rugby Club to get back into rugby and take my mind off work on the weekends. I had played at quite a high level for London Welsh back in the UK and it would be a great outlet for me, give me some exercise, and a chance to make some new male friends after living and working with women all the time. I played a few games, but then Tricia became concerned that if I was injured, it would affect the family and we would have no income, so I felt pressured into giving it up which was a shame.

Fulfilling my need for rejuvenation wasn't possible, and this put a strain on my relationship with Tricia. I was living a very prescribed lifestyle and Dan was not part of it.

I stayed at Hadley for six months and then decided to move to a marketing agency near home, Quincy, Lipsky, and Mitchell (QLM) in Princeton. I would have no more commuting and instead could take a short drive to work.

QLM appointed me to work on the Heinz business. I learned only on my first day that the Heinz account had not come on board. Instead, they appointed me to work on new business because of my Philip Morris connections, so this kept my job safe for a while. After a few months, QLM, like many established large agencies, started to experience a downturn in business.

Large agencies at that time were all overstaffed and resting on their laurels as fresher, aggressive creative marketing agencies emerged. These upstart agencies charged less and didn't have such a massive overhead. I started to think about starting my own agency. QLM paid scant attention to the smaller accounts I serviced, and wouldn't miss them if they came with me when I left.

17

THE PADRÉ'S DOG

Our family June 1997
Left to right, Steve, Mum, Me, Dad, Matthew

I t was around that time that the news from my parents back home was not great. My mother's kidney infection had got worse and now she had partial loss of one kidney, so she had started dialysis. I was annoyed at the National Health Service (NHS) because no one had diagnosed the problem earlier. My mother told me that my father wasn't much help as he was drinking more than ever, and was being verbally abusive towards her on occasion. Mum said he wasn't physically abusive but his words were just as harmful. In the spring of 1997, I spoke with Mum at length and could tell from her voice that she wasn't doing well. It reminded me of my younger days when she would hold back her emotions when we left Germany to go back to school in England, and now I could sense that hesitation in her voice again. I always felt Mum wanted to be more emotional about farewells, but instead, she maintained her decorum and kept her feelings hidden. She wouldn't tell me she wanted me home and put that pressure on me, but I knew she did.

She made light of the subject by telling me a funny yet sad story about Percy, a delightful old man from the village who looked after mum's garden during the week and always brought her a plant from his own garden. He was also an avid train spotter and loved to spend time at Basingstoke station watching and recording what trains he saw. Mum recalled how one day Percy sat beside my father on a bench on the station platform. As the 1:15 pm train to London came in, my father turned to Percy and asked whether he had recorded it. Percy sat looking straight ahead and didn't answer him because he was dead. I didn't know what to say so I asked her what my father did when he realized Percy was dead. She wasn't sure if he dashed and got help or carried him to his car and took him to the nearest funeral home. All I could think of was my father giving Percy a fireman's lift and carrying him through the station like a hysterical Monty Python sketch with everyone wondering what was going on. The story provided some light relief to end our call.

Tricia and I spoke about my taking a trip back to England on my own.

I was excited and relieved to go back home in June of 1997 as it was a break from my usual routine, however, I prepared myself emotionally for what I might face. For a change, it was the perfect English summer with temperatures in the mid 70's with warm sunshine, the garden at the rectory was in full bloom and I could see mum had spent time arranging her much-loved geraniums on the back porch. One day we had a family picnic and took some photos in the back garden. Someone found a weird longhaired blonde wig from somewhere in the house and we all laughed at who looked the silliest wearing it. Grannie was with us and my brother Steve with his stepchildren, Cassie and Tom.

In every one of those family pictures, Dad had a glass of scotch. If he wasn't holding it, I could see it below the bench on the ground. It is a painful reminder of just how accustomed we were to seeing him always with a drink in his hand. It had been a steady downward spiral with Dad's drinking, but thankfully he wasn't physically abusive to Mum.

Mum was battling her kidney failure on top of my father's alcoholism, which must have been very stressful for her, but she was a fighter and was determined to live as best as she could given the circumstances.

I explained to Mum what I was experiencing back in the US and the concerns about the way my family life was going.

I felt stifled and not able to be myself I told her. "I can't do things that allow me to regenerate and there's this constant pressure to work hard with not much rest."

It hadn't helped that Tricia's father was a workaholic, as I saw it, and that, in turn, affected me.

"When I do have time off on the weekends, all I do is run the kids to numerous sports activities. There's also scarcely any time to do activities as a family as it's all about fitting in with everyone else."

Mum said, "I have told you before, stand up for yourself; I am sure Tricia will listen."

Standing up for myself had been a recurring theme in my life but I had been brought up not to question authority so I wasn't used to it. "That's easier said than done," I said. "Tricia is very stubborn and gets her way on most decisions. She doesn't want to deny the kids involvement with all the activities that their friends do. My point is we need to spend more time as a family and I need time for myself as well."

Our conversation ended with no new suggestions from Mum. She simply finished by saying, "It's tough living with your Dad as well, he is stubborn, and won't listen to me about his drinking. As you well know, he always disappears into his study where he remains in his own world, watching "Match of the Day," his favorite football program."

One Sunday morning Dad wasn't up as usual for the Sunday services he conducted. My youngest brother Matthew woke him and found him in an awful state. His small bedroom sink was full of blood. We phoned for an ambulance to transport him to Basingstoke Hospital. I was due to fly back in three days so I knew his being very poorly created enormous worry and stress for us all. Over the following two days he was stabilized and the day before I flew back, Mum saw him, taking some fresh clothes and smoked salmon as a treat, which they enjoyed together, just like some special memories from their past.

I was leaving Matthew, my half-grown brother by twelve years, as the caregiver with a lot on his shoulders. Both Steve and I realized that he was now grown up and not a kid anymore, very different from the many years we viewed him as an annoying pest. In fact, we used to be very cruel to him, and on one occasion, shot at him with our air rifles when he was up a tree after dousing him with water from the garden hose. Now he was a mature growing man, very analytical and studious, often off researching and writing, but now his focus had to be on Dad.

When my turn came to visit Dad in the hospital, I knew this could be the last time I would see him alive. He didn't want to get better or seek help, which was a shame as we had all been trying for years to assist him. Dad had never acknowledged he had a drinking problem. We had given up trying to encourage him to see a way back.

I visited him first thing in the morning on the day I was due to fly back to the US. Given my experiences with hospitals for my teeth and adenoids, I wasn't looking forward to it as I always found hospitals to be environments that were impersonal, cold and full of despair. I had had my fair share of lousy hospital experiences myself.

I entered the building and saw that nowhere was the chronic underfunding of the hospital system under the NHS more evident than in the hallways. They were, for the most part, crammed with patients on trolleys, some tended by stressed out relatives and some lying alone. Each patient was lying on his or her back, strapped in, eyes staring up towards the naked fluorescent tubes above that flickered as if they were on their last legs. Insipid ghastly green walls had been deeply gouged by metal framed trollies as well as by bored children who had rubbed their hands on the corners. Cheap prints hung on the walls, framed in plastic, depicting some waterfall scene or mountain landscape, as if the images would take one away from the experience one was having. The confined spaces magnified the groans and wails, but nothing came of this vocalized misery since the nurses had seen it all before and were immune, hardened by repeat exposure and overwork.

I made it up to Dad's ward, which he shared with five other patients. He looked so frail and weak, compared to the shouting monster I had endured as a child. The alcohol had ravaged his body to such an extent that his skin was a pale yellow from liver disease and his face sunken and sad. As I approached his bed, Dad was reading the Daily Telegraph newspaper, wearing his usual wonky black glasses that had a piece of Sellotape[33] holding them together at the nose bridge. He was now a shadow of his former scary self. He had become weak and quiet in nature, not as fearsome as I remembered him in my childhood. I couldn't help but marvel at the power of alcohol to do so much to someone.

I believe Dad's habit stemmed initially from the great social life whilst in Berlin, attending regular parties, and being the centre of attention in his role as the priest to the joint forces. He then continued to be in the spotlight at the Guards Chapel where his status was even more elevated with exposure to the royal family. So many people depended on him and had high

---

[33]   Scotch Tape.

expectations that I think he managed the day-to-day pressure to perform successfully with alcohol as a crutch.

He never admitted he was an alcoholic, and he never told us why he drank so much. As I sat with Dad in his hospital room, we chatted about life in general in an unemotional way.

He said, "Your mother brought me some smoked salmon yesterday, which was a pleasant surprise. Are you looking forward to seeing the children when you get back?"

"Yes. This has been a fun visit, with all those photos in the back garden and that crazy wig." I couldn't help thinking to myself that the wig was a fun way to mask the real problems that were going on at the time. At least it had provided some amusement on the day. I tried to make light of his condition and skirted the subject of his health.

I said, "I am sure that Matthew will bring Mum down quite a bit to visit you."

He then asked if I was going to be busy when I got back.

I replied," I have quite a bit of new business and my company is doing well." It would have been an opportunity for him to say how well he thought I was doing, but that never came up. Over the years, he had softened his approach to me, as he realized that I had made a success of my life.

The nurse then came by and checked his chart and examined him, and for some reason I started to reminisce. I remembered the heavy smell of nicotine that always hung in the air in the living room as Dad used to smoke with us in the same room. Unexpectedly, I started to experience a series of forgotten memories about him and remembered some of the fun times. He did have a wicked sense of humour, but we rarely saw it until we were more grown up. One crazy thing he did was in 1988 after we three boys watched the grand slam rugby match on TV between Wales and France. It was near the end of the game and Wales were about to win, when suddenly Wales let France through to score and France won 10-9. Dad was so furious he quickly disappeared from the lounge. The following thing I recall was hearing the chainsaw motor in the back garden. To take out his frustrations he was sawing down our gorgeous apple tree, so we had to rush out and stop him before he took all the trees down in our garden.

I recalled a memory, which placed Dad in the heart of Welshness, Bethesda, where he was born. After Taid died, Steve, Matthew and I joined Dad for a drink at the local pub. Dad was dressed in his full-length sheepskin coat and wore a country flat cap so looked like a local farmer. Before walking in, Dad warned us to be quiet and not to say a thing in English until he said so. I soon realized why, as we entered a smoke-filled saloon full of working-class Welshmen chatting. Everyone immediately stopped talking and stared at us inquisitively while we made our way to the bar. Whereupon Dad ordered our drinks in Welsh after recognizing an old school pal serving behind the bar. The bartender was a strange character as he translated the price of our drinks into pre-decimal prices and asked Dad for 30 old pence. Apparently, he always did this with customers even though they paid the correct price for the drinks. A minute after Dad spoke in Welsh, everyone continued talking again as we were accepted.

On another occasion, Dads tooth fell out of his mouth in church while he was preaching in the pulpit. He continued to preach while he ducked below the pulpit to find it and then reappeared with a broad smile on his face like a scene from a Monty Python clip. Dad used to refer to some of his parishioners as three-wheelers, those that came to church only three times, after they were born when in a pram, when they got married in a limousine, and when they died in a hearse.

I remembered Dad's voice most though, for he ruled us with it when we were small. He wasn't a large Welshman but, boy, did he have a loud voice when he got angry; his raised voice was enough to send tremors through us. It reminded me of being in school again when the masters used to shout at us. Dad was also very stubborn and had to do things his way. He would even smoke when we took our own kids to visit him, assuring us that no harm would occur. These days we all know the dangers of second-hand smoke. On one occasion, when he and my mother were babysitting our children, Dad couldn't get my son Robert to sleep. Therefore, unbeknownst to my mother, he went into the kitchen and put some of his scotch into Robert's milk bottle. When we got back from our night out, Robert was lying on his back with his mouth open, flat out cold on my mother's lap. Luckily my mother told us about that one, so it didn't happen again. My mother rarely got her way as Dad dictated all the decisions.

The nurse suddenly interrupted my reminiscing and day-dreaming for she had finished checking on Dad and asked, "Would you like a cup of tea, sir"?

"Yes, that would be very welcome. Sorry, I was in another world, thank you."

I always find it amusing that in the UK a cup of tea pro-vides the perfect social filler for many occasions. Often these are awkward or uncomfortable when the cup of tea comes in very handy.

I considered talking about our relationship. I wanted to say I hoped he thought I had turned out the way he wanted. I wanted to give him a hug and show more emotion, but our long-standing passive relationship suppressed me. I wanted to break tradition and say more, but I feared any discomfort. Eventually my dilly-dallying became awkward, and it was time for me to leave, so we bid each other a rather strange farewell.

Dad just wished me well—as if I would be back tomorrow—and asked me to give his love to the children. As I reached the door to leave the ward, I turned around and could see he was already looking down to read his Daily Telegraph again. It was business as usual. His eyes hadn't followed me leaving and it appeared he had simply moved on. I lingered a moment at the glass door looking back into the ward, hardly for a moment, hoping he might look up and over my way, maybe a last smil-ing glance from a father to his son, which would have been at least something memorable to take with me as a comforting memory of him.

I was in a daze; the smells and sounds of the hospital wafted around me as I strode out. Doors whirled open, trollies rolled on squeaky-clean floors, disinfectant was as thick in the air as it was on the tiles, but I hardly noticed it.

When I left Dad, it was as if I moved to my rightful place in the periphery of his life. He was able to separate himself that quickly from what was a defining moment in our lives. Had he held his emotions in check? Or as I mostly suspected, was this the way he was wired? I couldn't answer that question, but I thought about it for a long time as I travelled home to the rectory. I had seldom seen Dad really show much emotion during his life unless he was cross with us boys, which was often. Even when his parents died, he rarely showed any break in composure to us. He would retreat to his study to contemplate and think, for he didn't give much away, always controlled and rather stoic. Although he was Welsh, he was also very British! Stiff upper lip! A total opposite to me who wore my heart on my sleeve.

Two months later, on August 28, I was standing in our kitchen in America when a phone call came from England. The ring was shrill and quick, piercing my memory now as only those calls do. I had a hunch when I saw mum's number what it meant, so hesitantly I picked up the receiver and my mother calmly told me that Dad had passed away.

Dad was a pillar of strength to all those he helped over the years, and yet, he had become so physically weak himself. He seemed to have been wrestling with his own demons as he declined in health. Diana too had her own struggles with bulimia and self-confidence. To the outside world many of us appear strong and in control, not showing the slightest sign of stress, and yet our inner selves may be in turmoil. This happens to those who seem to have it all, like Diana, and my father who rose from life in a small Welsh village to be the Queen's Chaplain.

I shed my own quiet tears and flew back to England to be with my mother. One of us, I forget who had to go to the hospital to collect Dad's personal effects, which were in a standard blue hospital bag. Apart from his watch and some other miscellaneous items, he had eleven pounds in his trouser pockets. Matthew suggested we use it to buy fish and chips from the Trawler Man takeaway in Chineham. It was a place we used to go to, and we pictured Dad standing there while we decided what to order and heard his typical words, "Get on with it boy." We all thought that Dad would have approved of that. My brothers and I stuck around for a few days to help Mum with legal matters and funeral arrangements.

Dad had a simple service and at his request was buried with a smooth slab of inscribed Welsh slate under an enormous cedar tree in the churchyard on the Duke of Wellington's property. He had the perfect view looking over a quiet private trout stream below, and his dear friends from the village were all near him, including Percy who had died next to him at the train station. In Dad's memory, Mum paid for the installation of a new water spigot at Sherfield-on-Loddon Church, which helped the gardener water the flowers in the graveyard.

Whilst we all loved Dad in our own way, we all had a sense of relief in his passing. My mother could finally have a life of her own and could do what she wanted now, even though she was very sick herself. The burden of caring for him had been very stressful for her, and for Matthew, who was at home a lot of that time. Caring for Dad hadn't seemed to affect Matthew yet, but I was sure he would realize later on just what a toll it had taken.

Dad never talked to me about not being my birth father, not once in all those years. We never discussed it, and it might have made for a better understanding between us had he done so back in 1975 in Grannie's flat. I don't think he knew much about my real father, so maybe it was awkward for him.

I felt down, but also slightly renewed and invigorated for some reason. Maybe I was relieved that I no longer had to report in on how well I was doing as I had done since I was a boy.

It was an amazing coincidence that Dad died two days before Princess Diana on Aug 28th in 1997. He had tried so hard to help her during his time at the Guards Chapel. I was dead asleep when early in the morning on the 30th I heard a voice suddenly calling me, as I lay in bed upstairs. It was my mother saying "Diana is dead, come down immediately." I honestly thought she had lost it with everything going on, so I joined her downstairs. I will always remember the awful news that morning and where I was, the immense shock for the nation, the silence, and sobbing that permeated a world at half-mast. After sitting together watching the news, Mum said, "Well, she didn't want to be down here with this lot, so your father has welcomed her up there with him."

It was wonderful to witness how the British public changed its behaviour when Diana died. The entire nation decided that the dated notions of reserve, decorum, and restraint be abandoned in favour of emotional release on a grand scale. The outpouring occurred everywhere with a huge sea of flowers laid outside Kensington Palace. Like Diana, I am a very emotional person and I identified with her struggles. She made it acceptable to have feelings and still be a royal. In effect, she gave the country permission to mourn and weep in public and I believe she did an enormous favour for the British people by helping them to remember they had feelings and could express them.

We, three boys, helped Mum plan Dad's memorial service. We had no idea how popular Dad was until we held his memorial service in the local church at Sherfield-on-Loddon. We knew he was as comfortable with the other ranks as he was with lords, ladies, and officers so we expected a cross-section of people.

Many important, high-ranking officers came from the armed services, and even some lords and ladies. The church was full, and the Queen's lady-in-waiting had to sit on a deck chair outside the church amongst the graves. Dad would have liked that since it was rather comical to have senior dignitaries sitting outside.

My mother was very touched that enlisted men wrote down their army numbers in the condolences book. Huge numbers of guests came and wrote down their special memories of him. Sadly, the lords and ladies did not do so, nor did they leave a note in the condolences book. A mere representative (not the Duke of Wellington himself, for whom my father had served) attended the service as a matter of duty. There was no doubt that Dad's ministry had touched many people, as his values had in some indirect way, become their values. That is the blessing of a life well lived for it is present even when the person is not.

We, the family, sat in the front pews and anxiously awaited the padré's sermon. A much-loved Anglican Irish priest, Roy McAllen, gave this. We had known Roy and his wife for many years and he couldn't have been a better choice for this job. As everyone knows, an Irishman can sometimes tell the best jokes, and certainly, a priest can add his own spin. Roy was a great Irish priest with a wicked sense of humour. I was in a daze until I heard Father McAllen ask what happened to the padré's dog, which quickly brought me to my senses. The air filled with anticipation as a packed church listened in silence.

Before I recount this, however, it is necessary to understand the role that dogs played in our family. One dog, in particular, was to have a leading role.

Growing up we always had dogs in the house. It was commonplace for a padré or chaplain in the army to have a dog, a sort of sidekick to take around on pastoral visits, and part of his charm and mystique. Officers had them too, but they were often small, purebred dogs like Scottish terriers named after some battle or past military general. Officers wouldn't dare have mutts as we had. We had various mutts over the years because my Dad thought they had more character. One we named Tessa, and there was a massive Black Labrador, Gordon, who used to sit on my father's lap as he drove the car around the Irish countryside.

Dad also liked Jack Russell terriers, as we would encounter them at the farms we visited in North Wales, where the dogs kept the mice and pests at bay around the house. Jack Russells were also great guard dogs, to the point they became annoying, barking at every sound outside they heard. At one point Dad had a Jack Russell named Sharne or Sian in Welsh. Sian is the English equivalent of Jane.

My mother had a dopey sheepdog, Emily, which responded to no commands and was as thick as two short planks. Emily was the sort of dog that looked impressive on the outside but there was "no one home." In fact, she spent most of her time lying sprawled out across the living room carpet in front of the fire. It was as if she were a true lady from a former life, except we kept tripping over her. Emily was simply an attractive accessory and more of a show dog.

Like my parents, the dogs' behaviours were poles apart. If an intruder were to break in, Emily would sidle up to them and lick their hand, whereas Sharne would go nuts and chew their legs off. This crazy coexistence continued for some time as the dogs lived in the roles my parents cast out for them. Emily stayed inside, whereas Sharne roughed it outside with the other village dogs. Whenever I visited my mother, I would always hear her telling Dad to get his filthy dog away from her perfectly groomed Emily. I was relieved when a change finally took place and Mum grew tired of Emily's indifference towards her and her dopey lethargic behaviour. She had become far too high maintenance and so Mum found a new home for her in one of the country houses where she would be more suited.

Emily's departure made way for my parents to find and agree upon a new dog that truly was a Heinz 57. Tobes, as we called him, was a mix of heaven knows what. I can't remember where they got him. He was a sort of dark Collie with a face that literally had a human expression that he would cock to one side when one spoke to him. Whatever mix he was, it seemed he had inherited the combined personality and intelligence of multiple breeds. Not much to look at, he was a straggly mess of long grey hair with an inquisitive face. He smelled like that "dog smell" people talk about. When my father temporarily lived in Balham, South London, before they had the apartment opposite the palace, every day Dad took Tobes with him in the staff car to Wellington Barracks. One time Tobes disappeared up in London and Dad came home to tell us all the dreadful news. That night as we all sat around unhappy and forlorn in the living room, we suddenly heard a dog barking at the front door. Sure enough, it was Tobes. He must have memorized the entire route the car had taken each day and made his way the nine miles from central London to the flat in Balham. His poor paws were sore and bleeding from the journey he had made across the concrete jungle, dodging all the traffic. His sandpaper skin wore away so much that Mum had to wrap his paws in bandages for him to heal. It was an amazing feat and a prelude to what was about to happen later on.

He was clearly quite a clever dog, very determined and mischievous. He would cock his head to one side with amusement some days if one said "Good Boy," to show you he understood you. If he knew he had been naughty, he lowered his body with his head drooped, before being spoken to, and darted over to his basket like a scolded child.

Tobes had plenty of curiosity, which would sometimes unfortunately get him in trouble. Every night when Dad needed a cigarette, he would take Tobes out for a walk around the barracks. Since Tobes had a greyish black coat he could easily slip away unnoticed in the dark. His only giveaway was if one shone a torch his way, he would look back with an impish grin. Dad said Tobes disappeared one night on one of his many barrack walks, and was sadly never seen again.

"Does anyone know what happened to the padré's dog?" we heard Father McAllen say at the memorial service.

"Tobes"

After a prolonged and hushed silence, he then proceeded to tell the story to the packed church. I nudged my brothers who in turn nudged Mum on the end of the pew. We all looked at each other in silence with questioning faces as if to say, "Where did this come from?" None of us had the faintest idea that he would be bringing this up. We shrugged our shoulders in disbelief. As the story unfolded, it resulted in a number of laughs and a few raised eyebrows from the royal household guests, who did not approve.

It transpired that Tobes had been getting loose quite frequently on his barrack walks. Dad had often left the flat after a few drinks and so wasn't always that coherent or aware of his surroundings. Sometimes I was sure he didn't know whether Tobes had come back with him or not. After all, my mother would sometimes hear the dog barking at the flat door later on.

Many times the guards on duty at the main gate called the church office the next morning and said that Tobes was with them. They stated that he often looked completely exhausted from whatever nighttime escapades had occurred.

Father McAllen then said that the guards noticed that Tobes had managed to wiggle his way through the heavy black iron railings that surrounded the high-security Wellington barracks. Tobes made his way over the busy road between the two complexes and in doing so crossed Birdcage Walk, which was a very busy thoroughfare. He then made his way into the private quarters behind the palace where the Queen's Corgis lived. A great gushing gasp came from the audience as they heard this. I turned around in the pew at this point to see how people were reacting to the story. A few of the ladies had their hands up to their mouths in disbelief. Some of the other ranks were smiling but one of the high-ranking palace security officers was not. His face was stone cold and very pale; he seemed agitated and muttered some obscenities under his breath to an officer beside him.

Roy McAllen with his very strong Irish accent leant the story even more hilarity by then adding, "Well, I'll be damned; some news was leaked later that a rather strange litter of corgis had been born in the royal household. Maybe it was a new breed of imposters," he declared as some stuffy generals coughed in disapproval.

"Was there to be some unroyal blood in the family? Heaven forbid."

Needless to say, Father McAllen told the riveted audience and a few embarrassed royal guests that Tobes had mysteriously disappeared around that time. Dad scarcely mentioned much about it to us boys except to say he had got loose and maybe killed by a passing taxi on Birdcage Walk. After all, Tobes had a dark coat and wasn't easy to spot. Dad, too, never knew what had transpired.

Roy then suggested that maybe the Queen had requested that Tobes be taken to a place outside London, and was done away with. As the phrase goes "Every dog has his day," and Tobes had thought that slimming down to get through both sets of high-security railings and then negotiating a busy road was worth it. He is still AWOL but at last, we knew in front of a packed memorial service what had happened.

After the service, I approached Father McAllen and asked him about the story. He simply said that the other ranks at the Sergeant's Mess knew about the incident at the time, but no one had the heart to tell my father what had happened. They knew Dad cared very much about Tobes and they didn't want to speculate about what could have happened to him. In many ways, it was easier to say he died in the busy traffic on Birdcage Walk.

They didn't find his body. To this day, I prefer not to think of Tobes hit by a taxi rather that he is up there in Corgi heaven, finally living a dog's life with the royal Corgis. He made it to the top of the dog world from being a lowly mutt. He crossed the class divide and sowed his oats in the ultimate doggy way. I can see still the impish grin he occasionally showed us when we called him a good boy or when he was skulking off having misbehaved. It is no wonder the guards at the main gate loved him so much and took an exhausted dog back to my father in the mornings.

Dad would have loved the story told by Father McAllen. How Dad would have chuckled had he seen the reactions on the generals' faces. Tobes and Dad were the ultimate underdogs.

18

OUT OF THE ASHES

The Chameleon Logo

I had mixed feelings leaving my family behind in the UK because I wasn't sure of many things back in the US. My work was not stable at QLM and I had major concerns about my family life. I quietly considered a dramatic change in my working life, that of starting my own business. My work at QLM had all been new business-focused, and the agency was suffering more account losses when I returned. I felt I had nothing to lose and wanted to act before they fired me.

Within weeks, I made the decision to start my own promotional business out of our house, essentially working from our bedroom where we had a computer desk set up in the corner by the bathroom. It was a scary financial move as I had a wife and three children to support with bills to pay, but I felt the time was ideal to give a start-up company a go.

I looked after a few meager accounts that were not loyal to QLM, so those came with me, and I formed an agency,

Chameleon Marketing Inc, whose positioning statement was "being adaptable and flexible to market changes." I asked one of my art directors to design a funky logo using a chameleon, and so out of the ashes from Dad's death came a new beginning.

Gail Johnson, the brand manager on the Marlboro account, gave me a lucrative research project, which started me on my way and provided three months of income. The rest was up to me. There were challenges in working at home: I would be on a conference call while Tricia was close running the shower, or the kids would wander into the bedroom when I was on a client call. The months passed by, I managed to get projects here and there, and clients who stuck with me gave me repeated work. Tricia was hugely supportive of my endeavours and did her best to keep the children occupied while I worked upstairs.

Come the New Year I had built up enough money to afford to rent a tiny one-room suite in an office block in Princeton, near my old job at QLM. Immediately I felt enthused and legitimate, finally, with my business name prominently displayed in the entrance lobby. Clients could now come to me, although that wasn't that common, and suppliers and designers could come for meetings at my office. Perhaps the most important benefit was my ability to concentrate with no kids running around and the domestic life several miles away. It inspired me to work on building the business and developing relationships with those I depended on, like my designers and printers.

As I threw myself into my new venture, a rift grew gradually at home with Tricia, for a number of reasons. The need to keep a careful watch on our money created stress between us, as we had opposing views about saving money, and where and when to spend it. My income came from projects and was not consistent because I had no retained clients, so it was a constant worry about what money was coming in. We lived hand-to-mouth and watched every penny.

Another rift between us was how our children spent their time and what we did as a family. They were signed up for too many activities—in my opinion— that kept my weekends too busy driving them back and forth to ballet, soccer, baseball, basketball, or the numerous birthday parties held at the sports complexes or Chuck E Cheese. This meant very few times together as a family. I wanted our children to experience some hobbies I liked to do such as going outside to fish, walk, and camp, but they conformed in another direction.

It didn't help that the expected norms were to follow everyone else. God forbid we didn't toe the line and do what all the other families did on the weekends. Conforming to what everyone else did, grated on me badly as it reminded me of all the expectations placed on me as a child. When I expressed my opinions to Tricia, I didn't get any understanding. She was becoming rigid and inflexible about the schedule, and it concerned me. She pointed out that this was what the kids wanted, and it gave them exposure to all kinds of diverse activities as she had had as a child. The pattern was established, and I did not argue.

In addition, I felt exhausted as I had no time for me and felt I was simply a money-earning machine that kept the house going. The real Dan was not in his marriage anymore, and I wondered where that fun college girl had gone that I had met back in London. How we had changed over the years and how our new lives together in America had brought new pressures on the marriage.

Our family didn't need to be living this way, but we headed down a path I didn't like, and I felt helpless to change it.

I did, however, enjoy the connections we had with St. David's Episcopal Church. I related to the families who attended the church because the dads shared a commute like me and faced similar pressures, so we had something in common. Tricia and the kids had friends there, many of whom attended the same school. I enjoyed one particular social activity called Seekers, where we would meet at different people's houses in the evening to share a potluck dinner and discussion. It was an opportunity for me to develop some friendships with guys, something I desperately needed with all the stress of running a business. I looked forward to the monthly gatherings, having a few beers and the enjoyment this provided. One person I met at Seekers was Debbie Hennel, who offered me great support when my father died. At these casual gatherings, I noticed she drank beer and had studied in Germany. She had even been in Berlin at the same time as I. I looked forward to seeing her in church every week.

The Seekers events were not enough, though, to counter the stresses that occurred during the rest of my week: the pressure to bring in business, find reliable designers to create brochures, and printers to finish the work. I was the chief cook and bottle washer and looking back I should pat myself on the back for what was to become fourteen years of successfully running a marketing communications agency.

The stress between Tricia and me was temporarily relieved when Mum and Matthew paid us a visit in 1998. I was over the moon that, despite Mum's poor health, she decided to make the trip over. It was very brave of her to administer the bags and catheter required for her dialysis. But she was determined to visit her son in America and live as normal a life as possible. Looking back, I seldom really considered what she had to go through on a daily basis.

I have some very fond memories of her visit, especially her grand entrance to the US. As I greeted her in the arrivals hall, she remarked that they were lucky getting through customs. Matthew was in a bit of a state, as he said Mum had brought something over that was totally forbidden and outrageous. Mum said, "I hope it's still ok to eat." It transpired that Mum had smuggled a whole leg of frozen Welsh lamb in her suitcase. Tricia and I howled with laughter when Matthew carried it into the kitchen and placed it proudly on the kitchen counter. Typical of my mother, she was always willing to take a risk to do something wonderful for us.

A few days later, we took a trip to New York to visit some of the popular sites. Our boat trip to Ellis Island and the Statue of Liberty holds a particular memory. After we had toured both places, there was an opportunity to have a photo taken as a souvenir, transposed onto the face of Lady Liberty. It was so very kitschy, but Mum insisted on having the photo. I came across it one day when going through some photographs, and it made me laugh, just like the photo of Mum using an American high-powered leaf blower in our backyard. She was always willing to have fun and do something a bit ridiculous and had such a zest for life, which was why her kidney infection was so unfortunate.

Their visit was over in a blink, but it did give me a much-needed boost to keep going and for the moment made me forget the issues between Tricia and me.

That year, Chumbawamba's song "Tub Thumping" came out. The lyrics summed up my feelings, and I used to recite the words in my head often.

He sings the songs that remind him of the good times
He sings the songs that remind him of the best times
(Oh Danny Boy, Danny Boy, Danny Boy)

I get knocked down, but I get up again
you are never gonna keep me down

While these lyrics echoed in my head that year another song buzzed around our house from a new artist by the name of Britney Spears. My elder daughter Amanda, of course, was a fan. One day she came home from school to tell us that her friends' parents were taking their children to see her in concert. Her tour "Baby One More Time," was performing at the former E Centre in Camden, New Jersey.

Of course, I felt the pressure like so many other times to organize a family trip to see Britney in concert. One evening I broke the news to Amanda that I had tickets, and everyone was excited.

When we arrived at the arena there were many young families there, with a ton of excited teenagers. After the opening act, the organisers announced Britney was running late. When Britney did eventually come on stage an hour later, the crowd weren't quite as excited as before. I think the parents had had enough by this time, as it was nearly 10:00 pm.

The massive light show and pyrotechnics were impressive, but when she started to sing, it didn't sound okay. I could tell she was lip-synching part of her concert, and other parents began to notice as well. All said and done, it was a lousy performance. We got out of there at around midnight and I was glad, as it had been a very long draining evening.

We made our way like everyone else to the parking lot, relieved to get back in the car. After sitting on the grass for five hours, we were overjoyed to get back into the comfortable seats of my brand new silver BMW 328, one of the perks I had allowed myself. Instead of following the rest of the traffic leaving the parking lot, I decided that it might be quicker to cut through a neighbourhood that brought us back over to Route 95 more quickly. We were so tired that we welcomed any shortcut at that time of night.

When I turned right out of the parking lot I proceeded down the road and made a left into a poorly lit area that looked shady. Tricia said that she hoped we would get out of the area soon as it didn't look safe at all. She reminded me of how dangerous Camden was by quoting the murder rates. Then I started to notice groups of young black men standing on the corners as we made our way through the back streets. Some of them even came close to my car and pointed at it. A spotless shiny new silver Beamer coming into their neighbourhood must have looked enticing. Just then I felt a sudden jolt from the passenger side of the car and noticed the car was listing downward somewhat. Oh no, I thought, I hope that is not a flat.

"Don't look out," I remember saying to Tricia.

She noticed people now pointing to the car. It felt like a flat, as I could sense the rim resting on the road so I must have been driving on it. We had to get out of there quickly. I reached a traffic light and tapped the steering wheel quickly hoping for the light to change, the car surrounded with scary-looking people. One came up to the windscreen and said,

"We can fix your car, Mister, for you and your lovely Missus. Simply pull around the corner."

Tricia told me not to lower the window and keep driving as quickly as I could even with the loud scraping. Drawing attention to ourselves with the noise was not going to help us. I began to notice a few sparks coming off the road and heard one black man say, "Wow, he's got a cute white lady in there."

I tried not to look scared and forced myself to appear in control for the kids' sake. I told them to close their eyes and try to sleep but Amanda sensed danger and suddenly asked if we were going to die. Tricia told her to sit back in her seat and stay away from the window. I assured Amanda that we would be fine, and no doubt a gas station or 7-Eleven would appear soon. Well, it didn't, and we got lost. We found ourselves driving into an enormous deserted parking lot with few lights. Now we were out in the open and there was quite a crowd building around our car so we all became very scared. People banged on the windows, and the kids started to cry.

Tricia cursed me out for choosing to take another route instead of going the way everyone else left. "How was I to know we would get a flat tire"? I yelled back. I really didn't need that at that time, and it was typical of so many other flare-ups we had. I was tired of the blame for things that went wrong, and this incident seemed to compound everything that was not okay between us.

All of a sudden, a huge black SUV pulled up directly behind us. Out stepped an enormous black man, just like Mr. T from "The A-Team", with a Mohawk and black beard. I thought, "This is it. He's the gang leader and he's now going to shoot us all."

He said something, and people immediately moved back. Who was this guy? Then he strode over to us. I was expecting the worst. He tapped gently on my driver window and asked,

"Need some help? You are in the wrong part of town, Mister. You don't want to be around here."

It was not what I expected to hear; even so, I didn't roll the window down to talk to him.

"I can help you change your flat." He said as he pulled his coat open to reveal a large gold cross swinging from his neck. Above that, I noticed a white clerical collar.

"I am a priest and was out making my rounds when I noticed your car over here. Just step out. I really am here to help you." I couldn't believe it and honestly felt like an angel came to save us that night.

Everyone around our car had backed off by this time and was heading back to wherever they had come from. After our rescuer and I had changed the tyre, he said, "You don't know where you are, do you? I'll get you back to Route 95. Simply follow me."

I did just that, and to this day will rarely forget that kind priest who showed up by chance. I never asked him for his name. It really was a miracle that we made it out of there without any harm.

Just as the music from Britney Spears was fading from my head, something was fading in my heart. I couldn't go on living like this with Tricia and didn't like the disharmony and arguing that was present between us many days.

The worst disagreements had to do with how we brought up our children. I was a taxi driver on the weekends for the kids' numerous activities, so we scarcely had time to chill as a family. It was an accepted norm of life in West Windsor Plainsboro, New Jersey that parents drove their kids around to different activities on the weekends, which I hated.

How we used our money also became a big problem. Tricia had a big family and consequently, gifts for others required a constant allocation of our money. It was something she insisted upon and over a year ate up a lot of disposable income. In fact, we used to rely on the tax return to cover our debts, which made me uncomfortable.

Tricia and I could not agree on how to work through the issues so we agreed to go into counselling. After seeing three separate counsellors we couldn't work out our problems but I felt they heard my concerns. One counsellor suggested we have some date nights as a possible way to bring back a connection between us. I felt she was less vulnerable because she was obsessed with controlling the way our children lived their lives. I tried to understand her point of view but I couldn't. Maybe it had something to do with the cultural divide. The children's activities were more important than me. Even though I still cared for Tricia, it was hard to like someone when they were so controlling.

I reached a point where I was acting out of character. I began to work longer hours at the business and hung out in the bars in Princeton and wouldn't come home until later in the evenings. I was lost and really not sure what to do, but I did know that my marriage was on the rocks.

On one occasion I was having a drink at Mediterra, a popular bar in the centre of Princeton, when I glanced to my left and recognized someone from my past. At first, I couldn't place him, but his face was familiar. I glanced back again and recognized a friend from my Berlin days back in 1978. It was Mike Allison, whose father had also been an officer back in Berlin. Mike had been one of those guys who rode motorcycles and had always garnered the better-looking girls, which I had aspired to. Now he was in Princeton dressed in a smart suit. We immediately hit it off and reminisced about Berlin and about owning our own businesses. In the ensuing months, I would hang out with Mike in the bar and then go from place to place having a great time. Mike was married but he, too, was having marital issues so we were a great support to each other.

Tricia and I proceeded with the divorce paperwork, and I moved out of our family home in Christmas of 2000 and rented a modest apartment not that far away. I saw my children during the week and every other weekend and remained as involved as I could in their daily lives.

At least my business was doing well, so I was able to provide for them all financially in the years that followed and pay for college. In fact, my company became very successful, especially after I broke into the pharmaceutical market. Writers and designers who had worked with major companies like Novartis and Pfizer joined me under the umbrella of Chameleon Marketing. I felt a great sense of achievement in how Chameleon had progressed, something that would hardly have been possible in the UK.

19

DEBBIE

The Note for the Plane

Feeling rather aimless and lost, I continued to hang out in my free time in the bars in Princeton. I felt torn about the decision I had made to end my marriage and couldn't see a way forward except to keep my business going to look after the family. I had few friends other than Mike Allison whom I met regularly at Mediterra. Well, there was one friend I ultimately would trust most of all, Debbie Hennel from St. David's.

I had always noticed Debbie in church as she had an alluring incandescence about her that had nothing to do with her blonde hair. She was not mainstream, rather bohemian in the way she dressed, chic, fun and approachable. Debbie even spoke German, the language of my youth. I found her friendship and advice invaluable. I felt I could tell her everything that was going on and she wouldn't judge me but offer sensible, common sense suggestions.

Sadly, when her husband's job required a move, Debbie and her family left the area and the church, so our lives became separated. On Mother's Day, I attended the service at St. David's with my family, and had a surprise encounter. As I walked up the aisle to take communion, I reached the last row and a hand reached out and grabbed mine. It was Debbie. I hadn't even noticed her sitting at the front of the church as I was in such a fog. It was such a wonderful surprise, and today I still think of that comforting warm hand from a dear friend reaching out to me. We reconnected that moment.

Some months later, I was in Bernardsville, where Debbie lived. I called and asked her to meet me at the Stone Tavern. We hadn't seen each other in a while, so we had lots to catch up on. She was very concerned when I told her I was spending my time in bars and dating all manner of crazy women. She told me I needed space to think through in which direction I headed and to concentrate on my children instead of drowning myself in alcohol. Luckily for me, Debbie was ultimately the only one who gave me encouragement, made me see some sense, and saved me from doing more harm to myself.

What I didn't know was she too was having issues with her husband. Over the ensuing months, we helped each other see the reasons for our marriage problems and discussed ways we could improve our lives and move on. Debbie also knew Tricia from St David's, and she could add a women's perspective on what Tricia might be thinking.

We were friends for many months before we realized it was more than a friendship. Our relationship blossomed. We gradually learned over time to trust each other and became very close. We both healed, blessed with the understanding of someone who heard and saw our pain. We listened, supported each other, and took a risk to be very open with one another, so a solid foundation for our love developed.

Apart from being a beautiful natural blonde, the one thing that set Debbie apart from many women was her sensuality. This became apparent in the choice of fabrics she chose in her clothes, which she used to devastating effect on me. I recall many memorable outfits that I enjoyed seeing her in, and which added to the deep connection we were developing. Two items of clothing in particular stand out, a straight fuzzy grey wool skirt, and a green silk blouse.

She even looked stunning in a cheap ten-dollar dress I had bought in a New York Flea Market. It was very figure hugging and sexy so we nicknamed it the snake dress. One day she showed up at my house wearing it as a surprise, with her hair fluffed up. That was quite an evening.

Debbie and I had shared interests in loving the outdoors and creative interests like art and music. She understood my creative side and encouraged me to get back to the art that I had so loved in my youth. I had not painted for years, and I started to do that again with Debbie's encouragement. She helped me to see who I really was and encouraged me in all my endeavours. It didn't hurt that we both loved Germany as well.

I noticed Debbie's generosity, often writing me wonderful handwritten letters and creating custom cards. In one of her many sweet handwritten notes, she described digging me out of a hole and having to peel away the petals on a flower very gently so that I would open up to her. One time she used Valentine's Conversation Hearts to spell a loving message to me. She also did many sweet things for other people.

We learned that we were born within three weeks of each other in the same year. Our mothers also had names that shortened to "Nan". Hers was Nancy and Mum was Rhiannon. We coincidentally had girls with the same name; each having a Charlotte, and Debbie had an adopted child, Katya, from Russia.

Debbie didn't judge me, and we both accepted each other for who we were. She didn't laugh at me either like my father had, as we are both very sensitive individuals that don't like being out of kilter like most Librans.

In September of 2001, I travelled to the UK to celebrate my mother's 70th birthday with the family. Debbie was excited for me, as the trip was a chance for me to bond with my family instead of being preoccupied with my divorce issues in the US. On the day of my departure, Debbie showed up at the airport to see me off. She wore a beautiful denim skort with a colourful red and blue blouse, practically the colours of the Union Jack. She handed me a note with strict instructions not to open it until the plane was at thirty thousand feet or I had my first drink. It was one of the nicest and most memorable notes I had ever read. She stated that it was the opportunity for a new beginning, how she was pleased that I was much happier with my life and that it was time for a celebration. Inside the card was a piece of rustic linen tied with a ribbon that contained a beautifully pressed thistle and a handwritten message. Debbie knew that I would get the "Braveheart" thistle reference. The thistle was a Celtic symbol for the moments we loved together, something free that was growing in a meadow. In her note, Debbie asked that I bring her something back that didn't cost money like a shell or stone or seeds from a meadow.

This was the first of many notes that I would read at thirty thousand feet over the coming years. On another occasion, she included a sticky-note pad to flip through, with everyday gifts written on each sheet. The words on the front of the pad said, "The best things in life are free (or almost.)"

I came back from that family trip sensing a monumental change had occurred inside me. I decided to concentrate on my business—not hang out in the bars—and get my mental state focused so I could take care of my children and enjoy my time with Debbie. We grew even more together towards the Christmas holiday and took a Christmas picnic with us to Island Beach State Park. It was the first of many Christmas picnics we shared over the years.

I believe my love for her began on the beach, a place we both love. It was there that we wrote our words of pain on sea-shells, tossed them into the ocean, watched the heat lightning from a lifeguard chair, or took lingering walks searching for sand dollars. The water reminds me of our connection to each other. The constancy of the waves is like breathing together. One time she gave me a beautiful memory from one of our beach trips, a tiny box containing all the unique shells she had found while we were there.

In February 2002, I took Debbie with me to England where I introduced her to my brothers and we stayed in a wonderful bed and breakfast in Wales called Glangrwney Court. When we returned we saw each other on weekends as we both had very separate lives in distinct locations and were not involved with each other's children, which we kept separate from our relationship. Debbie supported my concerns about my children's welfare and my need to do the appropriate things for them.

We took a few camping trips, which made me realize that here was a woman who actually enjoyed being outside. I hardly thought I would find someone who shared the same interests as I. I had wasted so much of my life looking for the perfect Sloane with blonde hair and a ponytail. Debbie made me laugh when she said: "All you have needed was a Girl Scout who is not opposed to sleeping outside, isn't afraid to get dirty, and can light a fire with one match."

Debbie, wonderfully spontaneous, would shock me by turning up at my house wearing an alluring outfit or kidnap me halfway through a day trip to take me to a wonderful bed and breakfast at the end of the day. We always call each other at the end of the day no matter where we are in the world. We would be content together in a cardboard box as long as we are together.

We began to take weekend escapes to the beach at Ocean Grove and to one of our favourite birding places, Brigantine National Wildlife Refuge. We would stop and get McDonald's breakfast to go and head to Brig where we would spend hours driving the loop and then have a picnic lunch. Sometimes we would stop and have a wonderful meal at the Oyster Creek Inn at Leeds Point nearby before heading home. It was special trips like these that brought us closer together and allowed us time to get to know each other.

Over time Debbie persuaded me to stop beating myself up about my marriage and pointed out that the reasons for its failure were not all on me. She provided much needed emotional stability and trust at a critical time, and I think I did the same for her. She ultimately divorced as well so we were able to help each other through the process. In fact, both our marriage difficulties and who we were, mirrored each other.

One day Debbie said something very profound, "We can still be fine parents for our children even though we are no longer married. We have to strive to do what's best for them and help them through this."

I was very fortunate that Debbie came along, as heaven knows where I would be today if it weren't for her guidance, support, and love. I referred to her then as my angel, and I still do.

20

MUM

Tryfan Mountain

In 2003, I turned my attention back to home in the UK and wished that an angel would help my mother. I had flown over to the UK six times in the course of nine months, to see Mum, who was not at all well and wasn't improving. Her dialysis was protracted and difficult, she was prone to constant infections through the catheter that took fluids into her body. The dialysis put a strain on other organs, especially her heart. When I flew over in August for my brother Matthew's wedding, events took a turn for the worst. Mum made it through the wedding but collapsed afterward, so I had to rush her directly to St Mary's Hospital in Portsmouth from Hyssington in Shropshire, a distance of two hundred miles. It transpired she had another infection in the catheter that provided the fluids to her body.

Debbie came over for the last part of my stay and provided much-needed support at a difficult time. We took a short trip to North Wales, partly to fulfil my childhood dream to finally hike up Tryfan, that indomitable, scary block of grey that had always beckoned me from the car window when I was a child. I invited Debbie to climb it with me, as she was the one person special enough to me who would take it on.

I had an outdated guidebook that provided a number of routes up the mountain so I chose the Heather Ridge which was rated a slight challenge but not difficult. It turned out to be a tough hike due to the rocky terrain, but at least we didn't need ropes. From our high vantage point, it was amazing to hear the trickle of a stream running down in the valley and the bleating of sheep hundreds of feet below us. We came across the prehistoric-looking mountain goats with scary faces that lived high up on the mountain. We hadn't passed a soul on our ascent, but we found a ton of people when we reached the summit. It was then that I realized that we had taken one of the longest routes up the mountain and not the easier one from the parking lot on the other side. We sat for an extended time watching the clouds roll over the top of Glyder Fach. I never did jump from the two rocks named "Adam" and "Eve", as it was too scary.

Ascending Tryfan was a defining moment for me. I had wanted to climb it since I was a boy. Now that I was finally on the top, it was primeval as if all my ancestors were up there with me. The last time I had climbed, was up the hill behind East Meon. I was a confused teenager back then and the hill was my place to escape. I was now on top of a mountain I loved, confident and happy with my life. What a difference each climb had meant. Debbie has scarcely failed to remind me, that she did that for me. After an enjoyable break from all the stress with Mum, Debbie and I returned to the US. Within a month or two, Mum's health rebounded, so I travelled back to see her and enjoyed a week of reminiscing and discussing fun times.

A month later while out fishing I received a call—not unexpected, of course—on my cell phone from Steve in Wales.

"You better get on a plane. Things are not okay with Mum."

I rang Virgin Atlantic as there was no time to lose, and pleaded a family emergency case to secure a last minute seat. I was lucky and got an upgrade as well, which helped my anxiety level. That night I flew out from Philadelphia to Heathrow. Steve hadn't told me how ill she was, so I was desperate to speak with him the minute we landed to find out more.

I called his cell phone from the baggage hall.

"Is she all right?" I asked.

Steve replied, "You are breaking up. I'll tell you when you are through."

I knew Steve was dodging the question by the tone of his voice. My heart jumped; she had died, but I didn't want to accept it until I reached Steve. I blamed myself for not flying over sooner so I had missed her and she had probably passed while I was in mid-flight over the Atlantic. I rushed through the last double doors into the arrivals hall and the look on Steve's face said it all.

I was right.

Steve's was a look I will always remember, somewhat not wanting to look me in the eye and staring blankly across the room.

"Sorry mate," he said. "She passed this morning at five thirty. You wouldn't have made it anyway had you got an earlier flight."

I was numb. We didn't speak much as we walked to the car park.

"They have left Mum in the ward for you to see her one last time."

So we travelled in silence to the hospital with hardly a word said. The only comfort for me was, at last, she was with Big Dan, so they could continue their close and joyous relationship. I thought of the people who told me why people choose to die in the early morning as if they wished to depart before facing the burden of another day.

We arrived at the rather grim square-shaped hospital, and let the front desk know who we were. I will hardly forget the look on the nurse's face who showed me into Mum's ward. Her name was Tina, she had a kind, caring manner of genuine concern. She said she would make us a cup of tea when we were ready, that instant soother of sorrows and strife.

Mum didn't have a room to herself. Unfortunately, this was the general healthcare system and not a private hospital, as many prefer these days. It was the old-fashioned NHS (National Health Service), so she was in a room with three other patients. The nurses had pulled a green floor-length curtain around Mum's bed for privacy. The other patients in her ward were solemn and remained quiet out of consideration, one quietly reading and the other solving a puzzle. It appeared they all knew the family would be coming to pay their last respects. I recall it was bizarre having an audience of strangers in the same room as I was spending a last poignant moment with my mother. I gulped when I slowly pulled the curtain back and entered her bed space. Mum looked peaceful and simply asleep like I had seen her many times. I was suddenly trembling but had to control my emotions as I couldn't speak or utter a sound with all those other people in the same room. There was only a thin piece of fabric separating us, and I wished I had her all to myself. So instead, I fought to hold every tear back, every word I wanted to say to her inside me, as best I could and said a quiet prayer for her to myself. Seeing my Mum in that final place with a curtain pulled around her bed was one of the most emotionally challenging moments I have ever had. I told her that she could now be at one, joined with Big Dan and that the pain of all the dialysis that she had so bravely fought was over.

As I gazed upon Mum's face, memories of her came into my mind. I smelt my favourite meal of chicken à la king she used to prepare on the last night of the holidays before we journeyed back to school. I saw the delight and concentration on her face as she sat in the Berlin Opera House intently watching her beloved opera "Tosca". I watched her struggle to manage her own dialysis. I remember the night she told me she was afraid to die and was determined to live longer, despite her condition. These moments and more came to me and reminded me that they would always be with me to ease my pain going forward. As I left the ward, I summoned the best British decorum I could and walked out to the hallway, passing the other patients on my way, who gave me resigned sorrowful glances without saying a word.

It was only later when I reached the crisp outside air in the parking lot that I finally cracked and was overwhelmed with emotion. I could have filled that parking lot with tears, but the rest of the family was arriving, so I held them back for the moment. It was hard for me, as I felt I had let her down by not being with her in time. Steve reminded me again that she had died in her sleep at 5:30 a.m. and there was nothing I could have done to get there sooner.

Exhausted, weary, and shell-shocked, we arrived home to Mum's house back in Sherfield-on-Loddon that evening. When Steve retired to his room I sat alone in her lounge with tears running down my cheeks. All her pretty antiques filled the room, photos of us all together. It was hard, very hard. The next morning there was a lot to organize to keep our minds busy and we hardly knew where to begin. My youngest brother, Matthew, was still on his honeymoon trip in South America, so we had to reach him as well. He cut his trip short and flew in two days later.

21

THE SUITCASE

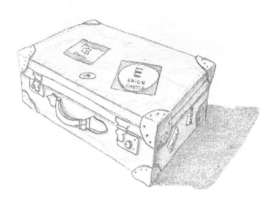

During the days that followed, I knew there was one item I was taking back with me to the US. In Mum's bedroom, I located that vintage brown leather suitcase from the top shelf of her wardrobe. Sealed in it were special memories between two people caught in time. Steve and Matthew knew about it and understood my need to take it back with me. Other family items we agreed to share out and those discussed and agreed upon over a period of time.

My mother had never been able to open that suitcase; now it was finally mine to open in my own time. She had last shown it to me after Aunt Heather's husband's funeral back in 1992. On many occasions since that date, I had casually noticed it and always wondered what it contained. I surmised that it was too painful for my mother to look at anything from that time with my father, the husband she loved, who died after only three months of marriage.

A week later, I lugged the suitcase back to the US and boy, did it weigh a ton. At the luggage check-in counter, the airline staff gave me some odd looks when I lifted the antique suitcase onto the weigh scale. I just commented that it was a family heirloom.

Looking back, I imagined that I was Newt Scamander from the movie "Fantastic Beasts" having his suitcase inspected at the airport, after all, Mum's suitcase was just like the one from the movie. It weighed so much I was sure it contained many items and concerned about someone searching it and the contents pilfered by a baggage handler. Since I didn't know its contents, I wouldn't have known otherwise. Luckily, it made it through fine and I placed it out of the way under my bed for a week until my life calmed down, and I was ready to confront whatever was in there. I could have opened it earlier with my brothers but felt I needed to do it on my own. Then when I returned I felt like I needed Debbie with me as I was going to be rather emotional. Unfortunately, she wasn't available immediately due to our family schedules.

As the week progressed the suitcase started to bother me; it seemed as if it was calling me. My mind began to play tricks on me. Was Big Dan calling me and begging me to release him from it? I had dreams about what it might contain and knew that I had to face the moment and open it soon.

Debbie said, "It probably contains some neat belongings from your mother and Big Dan, so you should open it soon. If you can wait, I would love to be with you."

"Of course I want you to be present when I open it. Having a second pair of eyes will be helpful as I am likely to be rather emotional when I do this. In fact, you know, I am afraid of what's in there."

One night I awoke at 3:00 a.m. by the phone ringing. It was pitch black outside and before I heard it, I had been engrossed in a deep dream about my mother. When I heard the ringtone, my first thoughts wondered if Debbie had a problem, or perhaps one of my kids needed me urgently. After all, who would call me in the middle of the night? So it must be an emergency.

Then a strange sensation came over me. It was so ominous so I was scared to answer. When I did, there was silence on the other end. Not a sound, no voice, not even a hang up. It was truly eerie and it freaked me out. I couldn't get over the feeling that my mother had just contacted me, but even if it were somehow true, why would she do that? Maybe it was her message that it was okay to open the suitcase or maybe she was simply getting in touch. Whatever the answer, I felt so lost without her, like a ship with a broken rudder drifting around in the night, looking for its harbour.

I chose to open the suitcase later in the week. The evening arrived and Debbie and I placed the suitcase between us on the floor. For so many years this was the moment I had waited for and now it would reveal its contents to me. It was a time capsule from 1957 and I was about to have a conversation with that time in history.

I joked with Debbie that it might contain a massive sum of cash. I had never closely examined all the stickers and labels on the outside so that's what I did first.

The stickers were multi-coloured. One read "Syracusia, Hotel Des Etrangers," which was a 5-star hotel in Sicily, across the sea from Malta. Another sticker from the "Roma Continentale" was a 5-star hotel in Rome. I had no idea who had travelled to either place, but I hoped my mother and Big Dan had done so together and enjoyed themselves. There was also a sticker that said "Union Castle Cabin," which I later found out was a prominent passenger shipping line around Europe at the time of my mother and father's marriage. I presumed that my mother had taken that ship over to Cyprus since my father would have travelled separately with the military. Also, there was a Pickford's[34] sticker that meant luggage going somewhere

---

[34]   One of the UK's oldest functioning moving companies.

with eight items listed in the lot. Presumably, these were my mother's suitcases going to Cyprus.

We were about to unpack history one item at a time. There would probably be memories of where my parents had been, and all they had done together.

The blue strap was still wrapped firmly around the middle of the case with a knot at the front. I once again looked at the heavy reinforced corners and tarnished water-stained locks. The case had withstood many batterings but was in exceptional condition given its age.

I remembered the precious belongings my mother had given me here and there along the way, Big Dan's wooden Slazenger tennis racket, and his sports trophies. They were like breadcrumbs leading me up to this day. Photos always showed him chipper and joking, just as Aunt Heather had once said, he always sang that song "You Are My Sunshine." For such a supposedly outgoing and upbeat man it was a shame he died alone in a military hospital in a foreign land.

Up until this time, I had allowed others to paint a picture of who Big Dan was. Now he was calling me to open the suitcase and inviting me to discover more about him. It was a surreal experience.

I slowly undid the blue strap and then realized that the locks to the case simply flipped up when I moved their latches, so it was unlocked after all this time. I gently levered it open and was surprised to see it wasn't full, so the weight must have all been in the suitcase material itself. An odorous musty smell immediately wafted out like the damp smell of a basement, yet it was perfectly dry inside.

Maybe it was a suitcase full of her pain. Sitting on the very top, I was surprised to see the note I had left my mother in 1979 when I ran off to London. When she put my note inside, it must have been the last time she had opened the case and made me wonder why she had decided to save my note. Maybe she was afraid that I, too, was going to leave her life as well.

Then I lifted out Big Dan's preserved military identity. A clear bag neatly stored Royal Signals Regimental military insignia, taken from all his uniforms. There were buttons, cap badges, epaulettes, and the coloured medal bars from his uniform, even a set of three miniature military medals worn on his mess uniform.

Next, I found his clear-faced watch with a white canvas strap and a silver mechanical pencil.

Then I lifted out a formal looking square white box. I opened the lid and saw that tissue paper surrounded a light-weight item inside. As I lifted it out Debbie said, "I think it's your mother's wedding veil. Look at the delicate lace pattern on it and the fine miniature pearls and beads adorning the headpiece." The veil was simple but classy, just what Mum would have liked. I felt so sorry when I gently lifted it out and had to swallow hard to keep myself together.

My mother had put everything possible from that time into the suitcase, no matter how minor. There was correspondence from every person at the wedding and a detailed list of every wedding gift that they had received. A compact red book contained a detailed list of who had sent a gift, who had sent a card to the hospital, and to whom Mum had written to afterwards. While it was great to have this treasure trove of memorabilia from my parents' brief relationship, it was also heart rendering to see how Mum had painstakingly put every trace of my father and their relationship in this suitcase. It was as if nothing should be left out, lest she come across it accidentally another day to remind her of that time. She wanted it sealed and put away. There were telegrams, wedding thank you notes and letters from her mother from Spain. Beneath the white box containing the veil was a gorgeous white linen tablecloth embroidered with delicate silver wedding bells on the corners, obviously from their wedding. Wedding invitations that spelt out their names in silver script also lay close by.

I then opened a small plain cardboard box and saw for the first time a colour photo of my parents together. My father had his arms around my mother in a casual pose and they looked blissful together in the sun. There were more 35 mm slides and photos contained in some leather-bound albums that gave me even more clues and insights into my father. Through his smiles in the photos, I could hear his laughter and see his happiness. There was even one photo where his tongue stuck out as he concentrated, so I knew where I had got that habit. There were cheeky looks between my mother and father in the wedding photos. The way they held each other told me a great deal about how connected they were.

The most poignant find, however, was yet to come. Wrapped tightly in an elastic band was a pile of letters and telegrams. Debbie and I read each one intently, piece by piece, and then we came across intimate handwritten letters that my parents had written to each other hours before their wedding. My mother wrote in her letter, "Only a few hours, and we shall be together for always. Oh! Darling I'm longing to be your wife." In a way, I felt I was violating something very personal.

They were short messages of love and hope for a new life together. Their choice of words was very formal compared to today's way of speaking, and so carefully considered and delicately put. I wasn't part of this experience. Only their voices spoke to me from the grave like I had never heard before. If they could have talked, they would have had a lot to say.

Amongst some other papers, I found a page cut out from a magazine, which showed a person in his bathtub. My mother's handwriting on the page stated said that it was DOT (Daniel Oswald Turner) enjoying his bath, something I guessed he enjoyed. When I flipped the page over I was amused to see an advertisement for an out of style dining suite, then a price list for swimsuits from the Riviera Swimwear company from 1956. Presumably Mum had looked into buying one while out in sunny Cyprus.

Having Debbie present as a second pair of eyes really helped me make sense of stuff. She loved genealogy and history, so she worked out the chronology of events, and looked closely at the dates. There was even a brochure in the suitcase from the Ledra Hotel, where my parents had honeymooned in Cyprus. I also found a rent receipt for the apartment they occupied for a month while my mother was over there. A detailed, hand-drawn floor plan of the apartment illustrated where everything was located.

Debbie and I then noticed a plane ticket dated February 25th, 1958 from London to Malta. My father died on February 23rd so Mum had not made it over to see him in time. In one letter a close friend stated that at least she had been able to fly over and see him at peace before he was buried in the military cemetery on Malta. The letters Mum kept after Big Dan's death show plenty of correspondence with his military commanders but no correspondence with the Turner family, which I found rather odd. I can only assume that Mum wasn't that connected to my father's family.

Debbie was not as emotionally involved as I was, so she caught things I missed. She saw the dates and noticed when events happened, and then asked me questions to fill in the gaps.

After opening and going through the suitcase I felt a great weight lifted off my shoulders as heavy as the case itself. I remarked to Debbie that there wasn't any future in there, nor, sadly, did my parents have any time to formulate any dreams, but I took some comfort in knowing that at least my mother was now finally with Big Dan.

I still wear my father's wedding ring on my right hand. My mother had given it to me in 1992. Engraved on the inside is "forever" and the date 16 Nov 1957, which was their wedding day. It was ironic that my mother died on November 15th, a day before the anniversary and the start of their short-lived marriage.

I placed each item back in the suitcase and sat still for a while to take it all in. I had learned how connected they were, yet I had not gained much additional insight into Big Dan other than viewing his smiles and gestures in the photos and reading the love letters between my mother and father. If anything, the contents of the suitcase raised more questions for me. His passport stated he was born in India, but what was the family history there? I had heard my grandfather was head of police in India, but not much more than that.

I jotted those questions down for another day and remembered there were several other items I had asked my brothers for before I left England. One of those items was Mum's sewing box. It was a reminder for me of how thorough she was in that department, as she was always sewing some clothes for us boys. The box contained nametags she had sewn into my clothing for boarding school, elastic for trousers, and spare zippers. Anything that someone you loved has used is comforting and a memorable item to keep. I still have my mother's garden clippers, her sewing box, tools from my father, and a letter opener from my grandmother.

What I didn't know was that buried in a plastic bag in that sewing box was Mum's white silk nightgown. When I pulled it out, I noticed there was a slight tear in the fabric and evidently she had wanted to repair it. Also when I opened the bag the scent of my mother immediately drifted out and enveloped me. That was the scent I would smell when I bent down to kiss her goodnight. It was as if she was exactly there with me, and I had no idea that something as simple as that could make a person come across as real again. I felt heartbroken and missed her terribly, so I quickly tucked the nightgown back away in the sewing box, as it was too much to take.

Some months later I unpacked some cushions from my mother's sitting room that I had shipped to the US. The cushions smelt of her house in Sherfield. It was a scent that put me precisely back to that place and time. It amazes me how scent can immediately conjure up a mental image of a memory of a place.

There would be many occasions when an event or place reminded me of my mother. Some would occur when I least expected them.

22

BACK TO MY BRUSHES AND
LEARNING TO FLOURISH

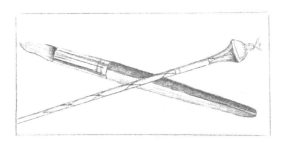

T he pressure to bring in income from my business loomed
every day. So I looked for ways to relieve the stress.
        Like other working parents, raising a family kept me
very busy, but I could have used a personal break like painting as
I used to do it in my youth. Coincidentally a few signs occurred,
that I believed were from my mother and grandmother, that
inspired me to begin painting again.

When we cleaned out Mum's house after her passing, I came
across a surprise beneath the main staircase. As my brothers
and I were going through the stored boxes, we discovered some
watercolour art supplies. I remember being very choked up about
it, as Mum never told me she dabbled in painting. One time
Mum had said she was interested in taking a watercolour class
but I wasn't sure if she did. A mini box contained her supplies,
a white mixing plate, some sea sponges and two red Winsor
& Newton paintbrushes. The two brushes now form part of
my brush collection and I look at them occasionally and even
use them to finish details in a painting to remind me of the
constant encouragement she gave me for my art over the years.

Another item came into my hands not long after, which also encouraged me to paint again. After my grandmother's death at age 100, we cleaned out her writing desk, where she used to sit to write her letters. I came across a round magnifying glass with a black handle that she used every day to examine words or phrases she couldn't read. One time I remember her saying that it was useful to look at the details in photos and I thought it was the perfect tool to examine the minutiae for my paintings, so I use it in my art studio alongside the two red brushes from my mother. These tactile objects I keep close to me as Mum and Grannie are still here with me, encouraging me to paint through the items they left behind.

I began to take an in-depth interest in watercolour, so I purchased various books online and watched a number of YouTube videos to teach myself more about the medium. Debbie suggested bringing my paints to Ocean Grove for one of our holidays; I created a quick watercolour of the pier as we sat on the beach. I didn't like my first attempt; the seagulls were out of proportion, and some of the people were not realistic enough, but Debbie wouldn't give it up, and so it still hangs in our home today as a reminder of my first plein air painting.

Perhaps the most poignant message for me to pursue painting occurred at an assisted living home where I was showing some of my UK paintings. A reception enabled me to meet the residents. It was a well-attended event and wonderful to get positive feedback on my work.

At one point I looked up from talking with a guest and glanced across the room to the entranceway that led out to the hallway. I saw an aged woman turn around for a split second and face me with a broad smile. She had the same hairstyle and her face resembled my mother's. My heart skipped a beat. I couldn't move. Did I just see my mother? She was the splitting image of Mum as she walked out into the hallway. I tried to assume it must have been some resident who coincidentally looked exactly like Mum, but how could she be so similar?

It shook me so much that I immediately strode over to the entrance and took a lingering look down the hall. The lady (Mum) had vanished. This was especially puzzling because there were no doors along the hall or an exit at the end. A chill passed through me as I gazed down that corridor. Had I dreamt the whole thing up or maybe wanted it to be my mother because I was thinking about her?

I don't think so.

To this day, I believe it was no trick or dream and that my mother had appeared to me briefly that evening to support me. Some might think I'm crazy, but I do believe family or friends who have gone before us sometimes find ways to let us know they are still here.

Painting became more enjoyable, which was at odds with how I pursued it in my youth. Back at school, it had allowed me to lose myself in another world, and temporarily blot out some of the unpleasant experiences I had encountered.

The business climate for Chameleon Marketing grew tougher. The news reported declining house prices and mortgage defaults climbing. My clients cut back on the number of marketing agencies they used, so I couldn't get as much work. I, therefore, had to find other ways to make money, and art was something I knew I could do. Even though I still had a lot to learn and selling paintings would not bring in the same income as a salary, it would prove to be a much-welcomed boost to my earnings. I subsequently signed up for numerous art shows and attended many local fairs.

I entered the prestigious annual art show at St. John on the Mountain Church in Bernardsville. I chose to enter the non-juried part of the show in which one could have up to six matted art pieces for sale in one's portfolio. I chose some of my Bernardsville watercolour scenes.

At the last minute, I showed Debbie a painting I had done back in 1978 when I was twenty while living at the Royal Military Academy Sandhurst.

The old cricket pavilion 1978

I created the painting of the traditional cricket pavilion during a rough time for me when I came back from failing Brigade Squad. The scene depicted a classical wooden cricket pavilion of a typical build, hidden away on the Sandhurst campus. This was a place that no one outside the British military world would know of, let alone anyone from the US. I spent time improving and fixing the painting, as my skills back in 1978 were not as refined as they had now become.

Debbie said, "Why not put it in the portfolio? You never know, someone might like it."

I thought it was a ludicrous idea at the time, but wouldn't you know it, that watercolour was the first piece of art I ever sold. Who in the US would buy a painting of a cricket pavilion of all places, and one that no one knew about? I imagined that the buyer must have recognized it immediately, must have been British Military, or there was the odd chance that they simply thought it was a great painting. It was a good omen for the start of my art career. My father had always told me to stop messing around with art, go out, and get a real career. If only he could have seen how I had progressed.

Sandhurst had been a rough time for me. The selling of the cricket pavilion painting led to another encounter with the military. Only this time the experience worked out well and led to what was in effect leading a platoon down Fifth Avenue in New York.

Debbie plays the bagpipes, and in 2004 she joined The Guard Pipes and Drums from Basking Ridge, New Jersey. I had attended one of their annual fundraising events and was impressed with their military uniforms. The band founders heard from Debbie that I had been in the Welsh Guards, so they asked me if I would consider training as a Drum Major to lead the band. Could I really consider joining what was akin to being in the army again? Even though I knew it wasn't the real thing, we still had uniforms, parades and marching just like I was accustomed to.

It involved special Drum Major training before I could command the band on the street. It also required learning the tunes and knowing exactly when to give the signal with the mace to cut off the music. The Drum Major role also required knowing how to tie uniform plaids, the heavy piece of fabric worn over the shoulder. I successfully completed my Drum Major training, and the band welcomed me in 2005. At first, I was nervous, as I had to get used to seeing the Pipe Major give me a sign to cut the music off. I learned how to read the street, so I knew when to stop the band and when to mark time.

Eventually, my role became second nature and I enjoyed flourishing with the mace at the front of the band. It is ironic that thirty-one years later here I was, leading what amounted to my own troop, and I was the star of the show, just like I had been right marker in the Welsh Guards.

My favourite event leading the band up 5th Avenue
in New York on St. Patrick's Day

The New York City St Patrick's Day parade was a memorable experience. Marching in the first division, we assembled on 47th Street, along with members of the New York City Fire Department and a large high school marching band. Members of our band kept us informed via their iPhones on how the parade was proceeding. Huge roars of applause echoed in the distance as performers made their way onto 5th Avenue. The air resonated with bagpipe tunes. We were sheltered in the relative quiet of 47th Street, the only sounds coming from the occasional band practicing or calls from the fire department to line up. Performers formed a snaking line to use a row of Porta-Potties at the entrance to the street. Due to the length of the parade, no one wanted to stop. Roughly assembled in the bustling street we awaited the order to move up. Every so often, I looked down the street and eyed a vast array of flags waiting to make the turn. At that point, I knew we would be off.

I had no idea what to expect. I had seen the parade on TV many times and every time noticed Fifth Avenue packed with viewers. Our time came; Jim, our Pipe Major, formed us into the line of March. We proceeded with a street beat (just the

206

drums) up the narrow street, the drumbeat echoing off the tall buildings on each side. I couldn't wait to be in the warm sun of 5th Avenue. As we drew closer, a wall of cheers hit us—a combination of clapping, yelling and screaming with the backdrop of New York sirens. The cold shiver from the shadows on 47th Street dissipated as we neared the sunlight. The multi colored flags waved ahead of us, catching the afternoon light as the high school marching band made its turn onto Fifth Avenue.

We were next. A lump formed in my throat. Now I was really in the spotlight. I worried whether the band would hear my commands above the noise. Time sped up, and before I knew it several New York City policeman beckoned us forward. Jim immediately called the street beat as we left the sheltered protection of 47th Street. All at once, a vast space opened up and the overwhelming view of Fifth Avenue appeared before me. Never had I seen this major Manhattan thoroughfare empty of cars, taxis, buses, bikes, and pedestrians. I felt tiny on such an amazing stage; a wide tarmac runway flanked by New York's finest buildings beckoned to me. I gazed down at the distinct green line painted down the center. The sunshine bathed the spires of St Patrick's Cathedral as if the heavens too had blessed this day.

"Gosh, I am standing in the middle of Fifth Avenue," I said to myself.

My stomach rumbled like a plane about to take off, but it was Jim's voice barreling at me from the front row. "Dan, 'The Irish Set.'"

I yelled the command, "By the right quick march." As we stepped off, the noise was deafening, and the crowds cheered and hollered from both sides of the street. A sea of green bodies packed in at least fifteen deep, bespeckled in leprechaun hats, shamrocks and green T-shirts, everyone holding up iPhones to record us marching. Heavy steel barricades kept spectators confined to the sidewalks, unlike other parades we had attended.

I was on autopilot, trying to block out the distracting photographers that came close to my face. We marched for what seemed like ages in a blur of sound and movement. I saluted the reviewing stand and probably the TV cameras as well. The crowds diminished slightly as we reached Central Park, where a strange peace overcame me. I marched in a more relaxed state as the cadence of the drumbeat took us to the end, spent and exhausted. What a showpiece and what an incredible day.

23

CHINCOTEAGUE

Watercolor of Main Street

As a break from work and the busy marching season with the band, Debbie and I took a trip to Chincoteague Island on the Eastern Shore of Virginia. The name "*Chincoteague*" is reputedly an Indian *name* meaning "beautiful land across the water". The island is approximately 7.5 miles long by 1.5 miles wide, and roughly six feet above sea level at the highest point. It covers 37 square miles of which only 10 square miles are dry.

This unpretentious, quaint seaside town reminds people of days gone by with plenty of Americana architecture, such as the Roxy movie theatre built in 1945 and the Watson House. This is not a beach town one typically finds along the East Coast. There isn't a vast selection of restaurants, boutiques, spas and high-rise hotels. In fact, the rule for new builds on the island is 36 feet high, which makes for a more pleasant skyline than many beach towns on the East Coast. The beach has no real estate development at all. There isn't even a boardwalk filled with tacky souvenir shops and arcades. There are only three traffic lights on the island and the speed limit is 25 mph. The Chincoteague Ponies are the major tourist attraction.

Given our shared interest in birds, and enjoyment of fun escapes, we decided to try camping as we had taken some previous fun trips with our gear in New Jersey. We slept in our tent for the first two nights despite the wind and rain and then treated ourselves to a comfortable bed at Miss Molly's Inn Bed & Breakfast, where we met the owners, Lin and Sam Mazza. Both would play a supporting role in our lives in the years that followed.

We fell in love with Chincoteague as it offered so much that we enjoyed. There were more bird species on the wildlife refuge than I had seen anywhere else. In one day we chalked up many new species particularly the variety of ducks that congregated on the ponds. Even though it was the end of March, and still cold and windy, we took trips out to the beach where we strolled along the expansive sand that stretched for miles. It reminded me of the runners sprinting along the flat sand in the movie "Chariots of Fire."

Many who come here fall in love with the diversity, the extremes of the marsh landscape, and the sense of peace and tranquility, in effect nature on a grand wide-screen TV. The outdoor enthusiasts may walk, kayak, fish or hunt at specific times of the year. It also provides beauty for artists and photographers to capture. The commanding views around the island offered me inspiration to pursue my art with so many scenes I could paint.

The island is an enchanting place, in some areas beautifully wrapped up in clapboard and watermen's cottages, with great conch shells arranged in rows in gardens and along walls. It makes one think of nautical telescopes, hidden treasure, hibiscus and random footpaths that lead to secret romantic places.

The eclectic stores in town were full of homemade crafts and decoys. People had great creativity to create such amazing decoy carvings.

We thought our kids would like it so we planned a summer trip with them. We rented a townhouse looking out towards the lighthouse on the east side of the island. We played board games at night, visited the Fireman's Carnival, caught crabs, played mini golf and rented bikes to tour the refuge.

We rented canoes one morning and paddled over to the other side to Assateague Island where we were able to view the ponies from offshore. The experience spurred me to create a watercolour of the view from our townhouse.

I brought my paints, and one evening I held an art lesson on the back porch for all our children to create a painting of the Assateague Lighthouse. The view was idyllic with the marsh extending all the way out with crisscross channels leading out into the bay. As twilight came, the Clapper Rails began calling from the marsh and made their frantic scurrying appearances along its fringes. The lighthouse light came on and provided its familiar beacon of safety, emitting a regular arching beam over the marshland. As we fell asleep, its sweeping motion scanned our bedroom wall in a comforting fashion.

After a wonderful break, we reluctantly returned to our busy lives in New Jersey.

24

THE FRYING PAN

I began to think about my legacy and what I would leave my kids after my day. I also realized that living in the US was permanent and so I had better think about my longer-term status. My thoughts turned to applying for citizenship so that I could have the rights of an American. I wasn't that familiar with voting, but I did want to have the protection citizenship offered should my career change, and to protect my estate. I obtained the paperwork and started the process, which I knew would take some time. Throughout the yearlong citizenship process, I felt lonely, despite knowing it was an immense honour. My kids didn't know I was applying for citizenship but I told Debbie, the only one I told. I didn't want to make a fuss.

In 2008, I became a US citizen after living in the country for sixteen years. On the day itself, I focused on how everyone else was feeling at the ceremony instead of myself. I wrote in my diary that day that I felt "wowed but alone." I found it to be a very moving experience to watch permanent residents from thirty-six contrasting countries sworn in as new citizens. Some experienced the moment more dramatically than others did, for example, there was an Indian woman who fell crying beneath the US flag.

For me, the most poignant citizenship story was the young man with the compact brown leather box. For most of the day, he had sat and waited in the rows of seats, clutching the unique box on his lap, staring down at the floor, and seeming in his own world. One by one, we interviewed for the last formalities, and then the officials addressed us as a group. I was in a daze by this point and kept staring at the ancient box on his lap. My mind wandered back to Haileybury School because the man's box reminded me of my dated tuck box filled with the possessions that had been dear to me and that I had protected all the time while I was in school. But I had to admit that his was much older and better made with ornate leather trim. Here was a man cradling his as if it contained his last possessions. I was curious as to why he clutched it so intently and thought to myself, "Why bring a box here when everyone else had folders with their papers?"

It was only later when I overheard a woman ask him about it, that he revealed his story. She said, "Excuse me, sir, but I am curious as to why you have an antique leather box on your lap? You have held it close to you all day. Does it contain something very important?"

He replied, "It's a family tradition that started with my great-grandfather Stasevich back in Russia. When his daughter emigrated to the US, he gave this box to her. It contained all the family documents and she carried it when she came through Ellis Island before passing it onto me. We have never had any bad luck in getting approvals provided we had this box with us and later on it will be passed to family, still in Russia, and whoever needs it after me."

"Wow that's a cool story," the woman said. "Thank you for sharing that with me."

"You're welcome. It's a special day for me. I have been waiting for twelve years to become a US citizen."

I thought to myself how boxes have so many roles in our lives. For me, a box meant security in school with my tuck box. Then there was the suitcase, which held my unknown history about my birth father. For this man, a box was the means to carry himself on to the subsequent chapter in his life in the US.

After becoming an American citizen more changes took place in my life. My new chapters may not have been as dramatic as for this man, but nonetheless, they affected me greatly.

That year the financial markets crashed in the US. The 2008 financial crisis hit most people hard, but especially those who were close to retirement and therefore lost a lot of their savings. For me, it signalled a change in the business environment. My company Chameleon Marketing began to falter for the first time in eleven years. The major pharmaceutical companies started to cut back on the number of agencies they were using and the smaller ones, like mine, were the first to go. I had enjoyed a great ride for eleven years but knew the writing was on the wall.

The money I generated from running my own business helped me educate my children, and I had fortunately set enough aside for a rainy day. Despite my persistent efforts, it was getting harder to bring in new clients. I was also tired of working as a moneymaking machine and fed up with the way some people treated me, particularly the younger generation in their twenties who became frustrating to work with, as they thought they knew everything, but didn't.

Clients knew small companies were desperate for business and so capitalized on that by working us even harder for our money. It was time to think of turning to something new. Fortunately for me, I had the time to transition from running my company into a new job.

I had thought for some time about teaching. I felt I would make a fine teacher, and certainly a more encouraging teacher than those who had taught me. I could put my business and worldly knowledge to better use, and encourage students to start a business and see a future in an increasingly competitive world.

I quickly found out that not many people from the business world moved into teaching later in life. After all, why go into something with more stress and less pay? Nevertheless, I signed up for a teacher certification course, which would take me a year to complete. Fortunately, I managed to keep my business going while studying, so I had some income and savings to fall back on. I was also lucky that the state of New Jersey had newly mandated that all high schools have Financial Literacy as a required course. My timing was therefore ideal, as schools looked for teachers with financial experience at a time when most teaching jobs were hard to find.

Debbie was already a German teacher at one of the top high schools in New Jersey, so she put a good word in for me with the principal, who telephoned me for an interview. We hit it off right away, as he liked my worldly experience and my business background, so he hired me to teach financial literacy.

Before the start of my first school year in 2010, Debbie and I took a trip back to the UK and Berlin, which we had promised ourselves years before. We shared a Berlin connection because she was studying abroad in the late 70s when I was living there. We joked that our paths could have crossed years before.

We started our holiday in England, and in order to see the most friends in one place, we asked my friend Sally Tindall if we could hold a gathering at her house in Twickenham. It was the perfect way for me to see many of my cherished friends I hadn't seen in ages. Debbie baked two cakes for the occasion, one with fruit on the icing depicting the colours of the Union Jack and the second cake had icing showing the American flag.

This unique gathering became a cherished memory for many reasons. Firstly, the people who came were from a cross-section of my life. Some came from quite a distance, such as Catherine

Davern, a marketing colleague from Eastbourne, and Mike Reed, another work colleague, and his wife Penny; Mike had been a great support in the business world. I was thrilled to see Gerry and Anita Robinson, neighbours of mine when I lived in Wimbledon. My fishing buddy Mark was there and Andrew one of my rugby pals. I got to see friends who were around at pivotal times in my life such as Francis Hobbs from Brigade Squad and Paul Bridgland from my Berlin days. There was also another new cousin from the Turner family, Rosemarie Lacey whom I had never met.

Francis Hobbs told me something I didn't know about my past, a fact that I had long suspected but hardly wanted to acknowledge. He casually told me more about the night I lost my rifle. He said that he had heard later on there had been a plot just before the final exercise on Salisbury Plain to hide my rifle for a short while. He didn't know whose idea it was, but he was sure it was true, and it confirmed what I had thought all along.

I can see in hindsight how that event had set my life on a new course and I was fortunate that events turned out better for me. Francis had gone on to win the Sword of Honour at Sandhurst and climbed right up the ladder to become *Aide-de-Camp (ADC)* to the British Stadt Commandant in Berlin. Francis remarked that he was pleased that I had moved on and clearly made a great success of my life. Of course, had I become an officer, I would never have expanded my horizons in the way life had unfolded for me. Francis also told me something rather amusing, a Facebook page created by fans of that famous Sand Hill, soldiers that used to run up and down it in full kit. Why would anyone still like to remember that? I learned the army closed Brigade Squad in the 1990's, which didn't surprise me due to the way they ran it.

Debbie remarked that every one of my friends at the party was distinct, yet they all mixed surprisingly well. I had friends from a wide cross-section of backgrounds and places, which was typical for me, as I rarely stuck with one kind of person, after moving on from socializing with Sloanes. I valued people from all walks of life. How enjoyable it was for me that day to see so many of them talking together. They all meant a great deal to me in their unique ways. It was somewhat overwhelming and I wished I had had more time to talk in depth with them all. Saying goodbye wasn't easy, as I had no idea when, or if, I would ever see them again. So many of them had made the effort to come and see me that day so my gratitude was immense. Debbie said afterwards that it showed that I had some wonderful friends who cared deeply about me, and that meant a lot.

After our wonderful stay in London and visiting family in Wales, Debbie and I took a couple of days to revisit Berlin. It was amazing to stand beneath the Brandenburg Gate at two in the morning on the night we arrived and to see places that had been walled off with barbed wire during the Cold War. The street vendors were there as usual, and it was fun to sit on a comfy sofa outside a bar drinking a large Schultheiss beer and eating a currywurst simply like I remembered from the 1970s. It transported me back to my teenage years again.

After our wonderful trip, I started my teaching job.

My pay was great for a teacher, but boy, was I about to work hard. I was about to jump right out of the harsh business fire into the equally challenging teaching frying pan. There were excellent perks at this job for they allowed us a greater degree of personal freedom than in most districts. For example, one could leave the school grounds to get a coffee or food during your lunch or planning period. There was an element of trust, but with the "No Child Left Behind" accounting standards, everything we did came under intense scrutiny, including our lesson plans, parent communications, and goals.

The school expected a great deal out of us, and we were under pressure from parents most of the time as well. The students were largely white, from affluent, educated families, and some were very privileged. God forbid they didn't get an 'A' which was pressure put on them by their families.

My supervisor was Steve Maher and despite his serious nature, I liked him initially, as he seemed supportive and liked my real-world experience. He was rather intense though and seemed way too connected to his love of technology.

I was one of the few new teachers who brought in some creative flair from the outside world, which I found the students enjoyed. Since there was no textbook for my course, I had the freedom to source and develop my own content. This allowed me to show videos and introduce real-world projects to the classroom.

I organized an entrepreneurial project whereby the students could form businesses in the school and provide services to students and teachers. This went very well. Some served coffee to teachers and others sold baked goods and other food items in the commons area where people gathered and socialized. It gave the students a taste of the real world and how the market dictated how to price their products.

I also organized an interesting field trip to visit a local green geothermal business.

I started a new school club that became an instant hit, The Executive Society, which focused on proper etiquette and learning how to act appropriately in different business and social situations. For example, we talked about how to dress for an interview, etiquette at the prom, and formal dining out etiquette. In the club's first year, we had over 30 members with students appointed as officers. We also took a field trip to Giants Stadium to discuss etiquette on the sports field.

One semester the principal asked me to teach a course for which I wasn't certified. It involved a steep learning curve to master three multimedia software programs over the summer break and be ready to teach Photoshop/ Dreamweaver and Flash in the fall. I had no choice but to do it, as the administration called the shots.

The introduction of the new multimedia course progressed well. I used my marketing contacts and invited one of my former Chameleon creative directors to come in to grade the students' final projects. The students had to come up with a name for a marketing company and then design a new product using all the software applications I had taught them. In spite of feeling like I was simply one step ahead of the kids on the software, I was very pleased with the results I achieved with the new course.

The first two years had passed quickly, probably because I was so busy and threw everything into my new career, building my rapport with students, as well as a reputation for creativity in the school. Students looked forward to taking my courses, so I expected tenure after my third year.

Then Mr. Maher told me he wanted to make some changes to what I was teaching. Given his intense interest in digital literacy, which covered all kinds of software apps, he wanted me to teach "his" preferred curriculum to my students. The school wasn't willing to pay me to write the curriculum, so I was therefore reluctant to do it. My colleague in the department supported me and said I shouldn't write and develop a course without compensation.

Early in the second semester of my third year, Mr. Maher told me that he had heard about a student who was unhappy with something I had said in class. The student had taken his complaint to his student assistance counsellor. This was news to me, since no one had come to see me about the problem, as I would have been more than willing to talk to the upset student and allay any concerns over something I had,perhaps mistakenly, said.

The student was a troubled individual who had just come back to the school after a stay in a psychiatric hospital. It was difficult for students to relate to him as he openly dressed as a woman, often in a skirt, and wore makeup and lipstick in class. I took great care to make sure he was comfortable in my class. For some unknown reason he singled me out for his insecurities in school and I became the one who supposedly made him feel embarrassed. He fabricated a series of lies to the faculty and his counsellor about words I had supposedly said.

I had genuinely tried to help him, but who would believe me? This put me in a very tough spot and led to several meetings with the school union rep who was determined to help me defend my job. There was no proof of anything I had said, so time passed and I hoped that the matter had been resolved. Then unexpectedly the principal summoned me to meet with Mr. Maher. They simply told me they were not renewing my contract. Apparently, I was "not a good fit."

Just like Sandhurst as I had to look out through those windows of the Sergeant's mess and watch my fellow officers doing their training, now I had to face another four months teaching at Chatham knowing I wouldn't be coming back in the fall. Both were painful experiences and both were cases where one individual changed the course of my life.

The principal of the high school had scarcely seen me teach; he had rarely stepped into my classroom during the three years I was there. His decision made, and I never really knew the real reason. "Not a good fit" was all I knew.

The principal subsequently handed me a piece of paper stating that I could ask for a meeting with the board to know the reason for my non- renewal. My NJEA (New Jersey Education Association) union rep strongly recommended I take this meeting, given the bogus reason they had come up with, and there would be union representation to defend me at that board meeting. Ominously, my rep stated that a board had very rarely gone back on a superintendent's decision in all the years he had known, so my chances were slim. He felt I had a strong case, however, given my great record during the two-and-half years there.

The media became involved, as they sensed injustice due the students talking, and came to the board meeting as well. Prior to the meeting, the local paper published an article supporting me. At the meeting I found it very difficult to hear Mr. Maher lie to the board, stating that my teaching wasn't acceptable, especially as it simply wasn't true, but to whom would they listen? To say they forewarned me was a complete untruth. I presented every stellar observation I had, but the board members had no time to read them. Numerous students and parents spoke on my behalf, many of them very upset with the decision.

My students told me later that the troubled student had boasted on Facebook about getting me fired, but the school was more concerned that they might have a suicidal student case, rather than defend a well-liked teacher.

It was as shattering a blow as the rifle had been in the Guards because in both cases the systems in place pitted more than just people against me. The army had its court martial laws, and school systems had to defend vulnerable students. In running my own company, however, I had controlled my own system, so I was grateful for that at least, and for the money I made over the years.

In my last months, I dreaded going back to school. One day as I laid in bed longer than usual, I had an itch on my right hand so turned over to scratch it, when I noticed for the first time in ages the fine white scars from punching my windows out back in 1979. How coincidental that I should see those again, so I promised myself that this recent incident wouldn't make me feel hopeless again.

I turned to face the bedroom window and noticed that the red cardinal sun catcher I had purchased for Debbie was glowing in the bright morning sun, casting a red shadow on the far bedroom wall. It was a sign of hope that there would be light at the end of this tunnel. The light that day shone even more brightly for me when I entered the school. The emotional moment of the sun catching the ornament prompted me to write a poem.

"The Light Catcher of Hope" March 9th, 2013

As I lay restless, churning in my bed,
playing over and over recent events in my head.
I turned to face a light that brightened my bedroom wall,

for there, brightly cast was a brilliant red cardinal.
A red buoy to return from my ocean of doom.
A marker that offered me guidance.
A sun that warmed my weary heart.
The cardinal faded and disappeared as the sun rose
nevertheless, I knew he was still there.
Hanging still, a sunlit cardinal that gave me a sign.

Given all the stress of those weeks, Debbie suggested we take a weekend break to get away. It was a trip that would change our lives forever.

25
LUCK & RISK

The Delaware Memorial Bridge

I was in need of a lucky path after the stress of Chatham, so Debbie and I set off on spring break to Chincoteague Island. Debbie set the odometer on her car to zero to record the mileage down to the island. On our earlier visits to Chincoteague, we had enjoyed its tranquillity and a slower pace so much that we thought about living there. It offered everything we enjoyed doing, the outdoors, birding, and the perfect place to pursue my art.

Taking a particular path has provided a way forward for many people. Some examples are true, and others pure fantasy such as the Wizard of Oz with its yellow brick road. The Bible tells us about the parting of the Red Sea. Frederick Forsythe wrote the book, 'The Shepherd' about a fighter pilot finding his way home after a raid in the fog. Perhaps the New Jersey Turnpike was leading us to the next chapter in our lives.

We made a gentle wide turn to drive off the mainland onto the four-and-a-half mile causeway to the island. We became excited as the scenery opened up before us. The causeway is nearly at sea level so it felt like we were driving on top of the water, which was on both sides of the car. We were so close to nature that we could practically touch it. We felt its calming effect, allowing our shoulders to sink and relax. Giant clumps of Loblolly Pines stood out on the horizon and from their dark green canopies, a blackness descended into the woods below. All around was a beautiful vast, wide-open vista, with an endless sky set above the marsh, a view with no reprieve, iPad flat and unadorned. The only way to navigate here by boat was through a complex system of channels that twisted, grooved, and furrowed their way through the marsh. The grand setting enveloped us, cleared our minds, and took away the stresses from the mainland, leading us to a quieter place, which I certainly needed after my teaching experience in New Jersey.

Debbie turned to me on the causeway and said, "Guess what the mileage is on the odometer"?

"I have no idea, maybe 250 or thereabouts."

"It's 222, my Dad's lucky number. Maybe it's a sign from him that I am meant to be here." She continued, "I have experienced many times when 222 occurred and I thought it was a message from him."

The snapshot of the 222 on the odometer that day

We arrived on Chincoteague and settled again into Miss Molly's Inn Bed & Breakfast. The following day we took a quick walk around town and popped into Sundial Books, which is a popular place to meet people. Jon and Jane always provide a warm welcome, and the charm of the place becomes immediately apparent. Islanders describe their store as the soul of the downtown area and a bit like an intriguing rabbit warren as the ground floor leads one through to back rooms piled high with books, and then upstairs to explore any genre further, where one can lose oneself happily in comfortable nooks and crannies for hours.

If one scans literature over the years, it is interesting to learn that the popularity of books written about islands far outweighs their share of the earth's surface area. Islands can conceal deep mysteries and are the settings for many adventure stories, so they conjure up a romance all to themselves.

We had been looking online at Chincoteague real estate for years and in an attempt to divert attention from the ugly situation in Chatham, Debbie suggested that we go out with a realtor, something we had hesitated to do on past visits. Lin and Sam at Miss Molly's recommended Tom Cardaci at Dockside Properties. Tom is a jovial gentleman and knows the realty business inside out. It was a whim and we did not expect to find anything desirable but figured it would give us an idea of what our Jersey house money could get us on Chincoteague. Tom was very helpful and introduced the types of properties on the island and their locations.

Initially, Tom showed us a cheap fixer-upper house up the north end of the island, which was dark, dreary and damp with diminutive rooms. It was quite depressing and didn't bode well for the day. The subsequent home was at 3594 South Main Street and when we turned the corner, we saw it was a real gem. From the moment we drove into the driveway, we were attracted to the house's historic character and charm. Tom explained that the owner, Loraine, had kept the house in excellent condition and had installed many upgrades. Despite the heavy wallpapering, dark Victorian furniture, drapes everywhere, smaller rooms and closets, we loved the original features and atmosphere of the house. The clear wide-angle view of the marsh and bay in the front was spectacular. Loraine owned the waterfront lot across the street and was willing to sell it, but we didn't have the money to buy that as well.

We fell in love with it from the first moment we saw it. When we entered we overlooked the wallpaper in every room, and the dated, but immaculate, kitchen and baths. It ticked all of our boxes and we quickly imagined where our furniture fitted, the best spots for our garden plants, and where Debbie's piano would fit. We were so excited that we needed to bring ourselves back to earth and think seriously about how we could buy it. The hardest part was both of us still had houses to sell and neither of us had jobs on the Eastern Shore. It would be a huge gamble to say the least, but we were confident we could make a go of it.

Tom Cardaci introduced us to one of his realtors, Lynne Ballerini who he thought would be perfect to help us, as Lynne was from "De Bronx." She had come to Chincoteague in 1995, fell in love with the place, and moved down two weeks later. We immediately loved her fresh "tell-you-how-it-was" approach to life. "You's will love it here," she told us at our first meeting. We discovered that Lynne isn't always on island time, meaning she isn't laid back and slower about the way she does things. She has an acute sense of business and is one of the more astute realtors on the island.

The house was built during Queen Victoria's reign from (1837 to 1901) and lived in by William C. Bunting, Sr. and Hattie Mumford Bunting, and was referred to as a traditional *Victorian* home. In 1889 the first child was born in the house. It had endured many awful storms since it was built in 1889, so we knew it was solid; nonetheless, we did have some trepidation about moving into a place close to the water. It had only four owners in its 127-year history, mostly involving the Bunting family, which we would learn more about.

Our House

We needed a second opinion so we asked our friends Lin and Sam from Miss Molly's to come and see the place. Their response was "You'd be stupid NOT to buy this place." In one of Lynne Ballerini's emails she wrote, "CI is waiting for you's" and boy, was she right.

We met the owner of the house during the summer of 2013. Loraine behaved in an unfriendly manner the first time we met her. She answered the door and seemed unwilling to let us in to view the property. After a discussion with Lynne, she gave us permission to look around.

To make a long story short, with the help of some creative financing and some further awkward moments with the seller, we decided to purchase the house in October 2013, six months after we first looked at it. Who would have thought we'd make such a quick and important life-changing decision at that time? It would require a complete uprooting of both our homes and our lives in New Jersey and the start of a new life in the south. We were optimistic early on. I knew that Business/Financial Literacy was required in Virginia schools, but Debbie would be giving up teaching German. We agreed that we would put my house on the market, while we would both keep working. I would continue substitute teaching in New Jersey until I found a job in one of the local Virginia schools and could move down. We visited our new house on weekends/breaks and started to get rooms ready before we moved our furniture.

Unfortunately, I had to reduce the price of my house in New Jersey to sell it. Lynne Ballerini was encouraging. She wrote, "I know it stinks to reduce but the island breeze is calling you's. You's two discuss and let me know your thoughts." She followed that by writing, "I know a coupla artists but you's my fav! I miss you's guys."

When we closed on the purchase of our new home, we learned more about the quirky nature of the seller. Loraine had given us a number of headaches during our contract negotiations. She had behaved in an unfriendly manner the first time we had met her and seemed to have a dual personality, so we never knew which Loraine we would meet. While walking through the house with our realtor for the last time, Loraine told us it was haunted and we should not sleep in the front bedroom. She explained she had never slept there because of Hattie, the first owner of the property. Rather, Loraine had placed a rocking chair in the bedroom by the window and told us, "That is where Hattie Bunting used to sit."

Loraine told us "Hattie was waiting for her husband to come home", as he'd run off with one of their servants. She continued by telling us that she could have sworn that the lid on her trunk opened as it was lifted into her truck that day and that Hattie's spirit had climbed into it. I looked at her son who was helping her move on that day and he just shook his head as if to say, "don't believe a word of it." This confirmed our suspicions that she really was quite odd, and was OCD about everything.

A stunning shock was yet to come, however. After we had wandered through our house and signed the paperwork, Loraine sprang a rather nasty surprise on us and informed us she had decided after all to build on the property directly across the street from us, thereby obscuring much of our beautiful view.

She also showed us the plans for her new house while we stared at each other with our mouths open.

The architectural plans for her house didn't appear to be that large or imposing, and with the required setbacks we hoped we would see either side and hopefully under as well. We were naturally stunned and upset that she revealed her decision on the day of our closing, but also determined that it wouldn't ruin our new life on the island.

Even though Lorraine is quirky and OCD, she had written a short history of the house, which she gave to us at closing. We celebrated our purchase with Lynne Ballerini and a glass of champagne. Debbie got out her pipes and played a few tunes on the front porch, much to the bemusement of those driving by. After a few photos on the porch, we retired to Miss Molly's Inn to drink a toast with Lin and Sam.

We came down for our first winter to be acquainted with the ambience of the house and to do some initial decorating before we moved in. If Debbie and I could redecorate as much as possible before we moved our belongings down from New Jersey, so much the better. We enjoyed stripping the wallpaper and painting each room at a time. Cold high winds flew in unobstructed off the bay, due to the vast open space in front of us. We also experienced our first significant winter storm, which reminded us of the awful wind that we had endured during Hurricane Sandy in 2012 back in New Jersey.

High tides and a full moon made an island storm worse, as the water in the bay came over the shoreline to flood areas without bulkheads. The cold high winds drove relentlessly into the tops of our front windows and came in through the corners, despite the tight-fitting, double glazed insulation. We tuned into the wind on the island, more so than in our former lives on the mainland, as the changes in the wind speed made us listen to its timing and its relative strength. During that first storm, the house exhibited a form of yielding to the wind, nearly bending to its power in the time fashioned way it was used to. Since its construction in 1889, the house had experienced many weather events, including a few hurricanes.

We were confident we could address the draft issues and make it a warm house to live in. The living room was repainted, and we started decorating the family room.

For a vintage house, the floorboards hardly made a sound, unlike the windows that creaked during the storm. When the heating system kicked on, however, the huge York heat pumps drove so much air through the vents that the house sounded like a 747 on takeoff. The new washing machine we inherited sounded like a jet plane passing overhead when it cycled down. It was a monstrous size with all kinds of fancy buttons, some of which I hoped might cook a roast dinner while clothes were washed.

In certain places around our house, my 6′ 5″ height bumped into the low ceiling lights so I had to watch my head. The kitchen cabinets were poorly organized and there was a nasty cold draft behind the cutlery drawer, which we had to investigate. We suspected this was due to no insulation in the walls behind the cabinets where a chimney had once been. Also, it wasn't easy living without a dishwasher, which we planned to install.

During our stay, we met Anne, our neighbour. Anne Davis was the granddaughter of Hattie and William Bunting and the only living Bunting descendant that we knew of. According to Anne, her grandfather was quite a character, a very honest man and wonderful at business, but he liked women and his bottle. "He had girlfriends on the side", Anne told us. When her mother was only two years old he left home and as Anne put it "went with a lady named Ms. Mary who used to sew for my grandmother."

In Anne's words, found on the Chincoteague Library oral history archives, she stated, "Ms. Mary lived down the street here and so at night when it would get dark in the winter rather quickly, my grandmother would tell my grandfather, will you walk Ms. Mary home, it's too dark for her to be out.

Well, he kind of liked Ms. Mary and so one time he simply didn't come back."

Anne continued to say, "My grandmother was therefore left alone down the marsh here."

Now we knew the context for the story Loraine told that Hattie used to sit in a rocking chair in the window upstairs, waiting for her husband to come home. Despite Loraine's warnings, we have not yet experienced any strange noises or encounters in the house. Maybe Hattie likes us better than she likes Loraine.

We made a few trips down with various items and on one occasion we nervously towed my new sailboat and placed it in the backyard.

We began to understand more about our island home. A dichotomy that existed on the island, whereby the northern part of the island had some very expensive homes, and not six miles away, in places like Inlet View, the south had some homes that were not in such great condition. There are those, however, that love Inlet View and cherish it as their piece of heaven with few rules. Everyone had their opinion of what they preferred. In fact, there were numerous run down trailers on various parts of the island.

As we were now residents, we found out we could get a two-dollar discount to see the movies. This was a welcome surprise given the cost of movies these days. When I signed up for my library card, I received a simple flyer with the library hours. On the top of the flyer was written, "Toes in Sand, Nose in Book, Life is Sweet." It kind of summed up the place. When I begrudgingly visited the dentist, a sign at the main desk said, "You are on island time now."

Over a year we condensed our two four bedroom houses in New Jersey into one, along with all our kids' stuff. Over time we had to reduce everything we had collected over the years.

Right away, we learned that by putting screens in every window, the house breathed wonderfully and we avoided much use of the air conditioning system. Our house is a typical

Eastern Shore design with tall sides and windows on all sides that invite a cross breeze. Ventilation flows through every room, even the attic.

Rising early is the way to live as the seagulls woke us anyhow, and the construction of Loraine's new house opposite started promptly each morning at 6:30 a.m. There was also the natural music of the island as each day we experienced distinctive smells and sounds such as the omnipresent duck noises, Willets settling on the clam beds out front with their distinctive calls, and the salty sulphurous marsh smell in the air as it wafted over onto the front porch.

When we purchased the house we enquired as to whether I could run a business from it and found out the house is located in a mixed-use area, so I was able to get a license. Part of that license also required that we had space for parking four cars. I dug out an immense area and then ordered three hundred cubic feet of crushed shells, which I spread to fill the space. The shells smelt awful as many still had marine life living in them but people told us the smell would die down after a few months once the hot sun and repeated crushing by our cars had worked its magic. The great thing about running my business out of the house was the opportunity to see what sales generated from our location. Depending on our success, we could decide later if it warranted building a dedicated business space in the back of our property.

So here we were, together, beginning a new chapter in each of our lives, living on an island five miles off the mainland, about to find out what it meant to be islanders and not tourists anymore. We had summoned the courage to make this dramatic move but now Debbie and I had to embrace it and live it. What was it going to be like running a business and mixing with the community? What would this culture be like? Who were the main characters on the island? What happened when the tourists left in the fall?

26

A NEW CULTURE

Chincoteague Waterfront Watercolor

In doing research for the title of my book, I asked local Teaguers the origin of the words "Come'ere," which was what the locals called visitors.

A *Teaguer* specifically refers to a person born and raised on *Chincoteague* Island. Many couldn't state a definitive way to spell it. What I gleaned was its verbal use to distinguish themselves from the visiting tourists. Many Teaguers agreed they used it in the early days, not in a pleasant way, as there was quite a bit of resentment towards the incoming visitors. When speaking with Teaguers Judy and Terry Howard, Terry said that if he were to write it down in a letter, he would put a dash between the two words, and use quotation marks around it. Judy, on the other hand, stated that since Teaguers talk so quickly, she would write it as one word like I have.

Rarely written down there were no precedents for the phrase. I checked with the island bookstore, Sundial Books where we scanned various Chincoteague publications to check if it occurred in print. Over time more "Come'ere's" have been moving to the island and have added to the arts and cultural aspects of the island, whilst still respecting the culture of the Teaguers themselves.

Howard Thurman once wrote *"Community cannot for long feed on itself. It can only flourish with the coming of others from beyond, their unknown and undiscovered brothers."*

It was certainly a culture shock coming to Chincoteague. Coming as a tourist on previous occasions, we hadn't experienced the day-to-day lifestyle. Since I was a foreigner and possibly more exotic than what most people were used to, the locals showed more interest in us than usual. They asked us why we chose to move here, in this land between two waters.

We have a fair number of retired academics living on the island, former professors and presidents of colleges from the mainland. There are also several musicians who add a creative flair and vibrancy to the island art scene.

There is a sort of a hippy undertow to many of these "Come'ere" characters. Many have their own quirks, which makes for some interesting conversations. There now exists many more activities celebrating the arts on the island than when we first visited back in 2004. The Chincoteague Cultural Alliance (CCA) regularly brings in some top outside talent to perform at their monthly coffeehouse events. I have heard that some islanders, however, see this as competition with their local businesses, so they tend to stick to themselves. The event the locals wholeheartedly support is the month-long carnival in July, which is an established tradition.

Mostly "Come'ere's" attend The CCA coffeehouse events so an interesting dilemma exists. The sort of struggle that occurs in many places that have their own strong history. The "Come'ere's" don't know the roots of things that go back a while, whereas the locals do. Still, I quickly came to appreciate that both "Come'ere's" and locals are learning to work together to do what is appropriate for the island.

One thing they both seemed to agree upon is their dislike of the brash developers who seek to build yet another hotel complex on the island. Residents become wary of those visitors who strive to make it more of a party place during the summer. The town regularly issues ordinances to curb unwanted activity from these partygoers, such as not permitting teenagers to ride in the open beds of trucks.

Some Islanders refer to some of the summer visitors as dumb damn tourists or (DDT's.) They are thrilled to make money off them though during the summer, but can't wait for them to go home come the fall. Those who bring their city "all-night-party" mentalities with them are not welcomed, they don't contribute to the island, and should have gone to Ocean City further north instead.

Early on, we received advice about what we said, to be careful, and not offer any opinions about anyone. Friends told us that Islanders got up early for three reasons: hunting, their kids, and church. We liked that people were not about impressing us. We had had plenty of that back in New Jersey where there was a lot of show-and-tell in the areas we lived in. On Chincoteague, people with money live with many who don't, and yet they seem to get on well. They take you as you are, unlike the British class system, which is very stratified. People don't dress fancily. Maybe that's why there is no dry-cleaning service anywhere within a 25-minute drive. I was shocked as I thought the numerous hotels would need this service, but they all have their own laundry facilities. I presume most people simply get an iron out if they need a pressed shirt.

We also noticed that many people smoke, and when we read about the drinking in the local paper, we couldn't help feel transported back into the 1970s again. That may account for the fact that the ambulance passes our house numerous times during the week.

Our house is on a busy corner lot and that means we are sometimes prone to island vehicle noises, especially during the summer months. The traffic isn't just the tourists but also the locals. Some drivers seem to take pride in how much annoying noise their vehicles make as if they are in the final stages of Bronchitis and can't make it to the end of the driveway. Many vehicles sound like they could die any minute. The grinding brakes, souped-up engines or whatever strange sound comes out of their vehicle continues off and on during the summer. A pleasant interlude occurs when the much quieter Island Trolley passes by hardly noticed.

After the roving dinner crowd dies down the break comes later on as the quieter vehicles like the electric rental carts pass by so we can enjoy our summer view with less interruption. Only when we reluctantly turned on the air conditioning on hot humid days did we realize we could isolate ourselves from the noise. We prefer the windows open though, so we simply build the vehicle noises into our summer routine. No wonder we yearn for the less busy months. I thought when we left New Jersey we had left the crazy drivers behind but unfortunately, they show up everywhere these days, even on an island. I could compare this traffic annoyance to being stuck on a 'B' road in rural Wales. Back there, we could be held up for miles by a tractor, a flock of sheep, or one of those annoying caravans that so many people drag around with them for their holidays.

Locals resist change on Chincoteague and in most cases, I agree with them. They prefer life to remain unchanged, so new ways of doing things are sometimes discouraged. When they tore down the once popular Chincoteague Inn, it left islanders with no waterfront "spit and sawdust" bar to congregate after work, a place where one could hang out with no pressure, open the windows to have a smoke or simply watch the sunset.

The Jackspot that replaced the Chincoteague Inn has no such personality. It offers a very opposed ambiance from the Inn it replaced, and that for some is not what they want, so they give it a miss.

We enjoy the ambiance of the Chincoteague Diner where the familiar face of Stephanie always greets us when we enter. If a group of tourists comes in she would of course cheerfully greet them, but if a local enters, Stephanie acknowledges them by name and makes sure they have a good seat. Her enthusiastic smile is always a joy no matter how bad her day might have gone.

When it comes to getting permission to construct or modify a property on the island we have to be very careful. Kenny Lewis is the town code enforcer. It is helpful to be friends with him if you don't want any trouble with home improvements. Woe betide one if going ahead with something, particularly construction, without having run it by him first. He is simply doing his job so like him or hate him, as I heard both sides of people's stories, one had to consult him. There is even a bumper sticker in town that asks "Who told Kenny?" which is funny given the power that Kenny has over decisions in the town.

Before we moved down, we didn't realize how lousy the job market was. We were surprised to discover that most people worked paycheque to paycheque. They didn't put money into retirement, as they couldn't spare it. Also, some people become grandparents in their 40s and often work several jobs to help their kids.

Since most island restaurants open only seasonally, they can't offer full-year employment, so the restaurants have a tough time recruiting chefs because they can't provide a yearly salary. Businesses seem to wash in and out of the town like the tides themselves. A few that have been here for many decades have recently closed. As the owners got older, they didn't have the energy to run a business, some got sick, and others missed their families who were off island.

Opening a business to sell my art was not something I anticipated years ago, but on Chincoteague, there was an opportunity to be a bigger fish in a smaller pond to could carve out my own niche. In New Jersey, a much larger art community had surrounded me.

From 2007 to 2013, whilst in New Jersey, I enjoyed learning about watercolour and pastels, and during this time created a vast amount of work to further my skills. I held numerous solo

237

shows and gained acceptance into many juried exhibits, which gave me tremendous confidence.

Debbie was a huge reason why my art took off, as she believed in me and encouraged me to pursue it at every opportunity. I am not one to boast about my skill level as we British are somewhat self-deprecating, and so telling everyone how wonderful we are at things is unnatural and very uncomfortable. For me, my art talent has been a natural development over the years, with trial and error along the way, and always pushing myself to try out new techniques.

I would hardly have thought that the coloured bird drawings I created when eight years old at Haileybury, and all those pen and ink house drawings I created back in 1977 in Berlin would lead me to opening a gallery.

I named our in-house gallery "Tryfan" after my beloved mountain.

I painted a homemade art sign and erected it on the front lawn. Of course, I consulted Kenny and made sure it conformed to the size and placement laid down by the town code.

My First Art Sign

Using some of my paintings, I created outdoor vinyl banners to hang out on the front porch bannisters, and also purchased a big sandwich board that read "Tryfan Gallery Open," for the front lawn. I was in business! I hoped the Welsh flag hanging on the porch provided an extra enticement for passers-by. Our house is not in the middle of town so people have to make a decision to drive the short distance down Main Street to visit us.

Many people help each other out on the island. We were the recipients of that generosity several times. Whilst not considered part of their 'inner circle,' Teaguers would look after us if we were in trouble.

When I brought my boat down in the first year, I encountered a problem. The boat's cockpit had filled up with ice and it had tipped up on its stern in the backyard. Fortunately, it was still on the trailer. I visited a local garage, Libertino's, and asked them if they had a substantial floor jack. Sure enough, they did, and I was surprised that they allowed me to borrow it without any hesitation. The owner at Libertino's had never met me before and it was the first example of generosity towards us on the island.

Such helpfulness later repeated itself with the loan of some rakes to help me complete our shell driveway. They mysteriously appeared at the back door when I had mentioned to our neighbour Anne Davis that I needed one. We also needed to find a chimney sweep to help us clean our chimneys before we could use them. Debbie asked the ladies at her swimming class and they recommended David Wiedenheft who is married to Barbara Wiedenheft from Leeds in the UK. They both run the very popular Channel Bass B & B in town. David gave generously of his time and came over to climb our steep roof to fix and clean our chimneys.

Chincoteague's community closeness and helpfulness is a lot like the UK village of Sherfield-on-Loddon. Joe, our neighbour two doors up, one evening brought over a bag of fresh tomatoes from his garden. He came over frequently to talk to us in our early days and asked how we were settling in and if we needed anything. Joe invited me over one evening to play pool after I had only been here a short while. He even offered me his truck anytime to put my boat in the water. He gave us some spare gravel to build our front wall. He was a regular guy who helped many people out and not just us. It was the first time in all my years here in the US that a neighbour did something generous like that. Maybe it was unfamiliar to me because I had lived in New Jersey, which was not representative of the rest of the US.

One of the most generous characters we met when we first moved to Chincoteague was Anne Davis next door, who was our only connection with the Bunting past. Many locals affectionately knew her as Queen Anne. One summer evening there was a knock at our back door. I opened it and standing there was Anne's medical aide from next door.

She said, "Anne knew you were on your own so she wanted you to have this."

She was standing there with a covered paper plate.

"Wow, that's so generous of her"

"Well, she knew that Debbie wasn't down here and you probably didn't want to cook for yourself or go out." I uncovered the plate to peek. It was a plate of roast beef with potatoes, carrots, dumplings, and gravy. The aide said,

"I just took Anne out for dinner and she wanted me to bring this over to you afterwards."

I replied gratefully, "Would you please thank her from me and say that I look forward to talking with her again soon."

Anne's worsening condition resulted in her transfer to a nursing home closer to her daughter Bonnie and her family in Delmar. Sadly, she passed away within a year of our moving to the island, so we didn't get to know her well. Anne was too little to know Hattie Bunting, the first owner of our house, but Bonnie shared many photos of the past.

Anne's thoughtfulness was such an unexpected random act of kindness and very appreciated. Again, it reminded me of the small village that my mother lived in where people took meals to each other when they were sick. This was something I had missed when I came over to the US but now I knew it happened here too.

There is also a very friendly older couple named Jim and Virginia who live across the road and two houses down. They had to move into their neighbour's trailer temporarily while their house was elevated above flood level. Virginia is Joe's mother-in-law so Joe is always over there helping them out.

The island is a place with many rumours and plenty of chatter. Some rumours we aren't sure of, but gossip circulates frequently about someone. It amuses us to sometimes read the Chincoteague Locals and Guests Facebook page.

Storytellers abound on the island. People have a lot to say and want to talk. Debbie was standing in line at the bank one afternoon and started chatting with someone. People seemed unashamed to tell us their whole life story in minutes, information one wouldn't think of hearing about back in the UK until one knew them much better. I'm still not sure if this openness is because people sense our interest in their lives, or perhaps it is simply the way people are in Chincoteague. Sometimes the island can be like a magnifying glass. Not only are events exaggerated, but also there is no escaping from the inspection and attention that people give.

27

ISLAND CHARACTERS

Captain Barry's Jeep

Like many small towns, Chincoteague has a cast of interesting characters. They are as eccentric as the village characters I used to know back in Sherfield-on-Loddon, and it is interesting thinking about the comparisons. Why do Brits come across as more eccentric or simply uninhibited? For example, some have no qualms hanging out all their laundry on the washing line whereas Americans seldom air out their "kacks" (an Irish slang term for underwear.) We'd even hang small children out as well, just kidding, but at Haileybury School, I often thought hanging on a line would happen to me.

During our many visits to the island, we stayed at Miss Molly's Inn. Lin Mazza, the owner, always welcomed us and was a great source of advice. She once said:

"You will make lasting friends here. They are always willing to help and they don't look at their watch." How correct she is.

Captain Spider's Sign

Since I owned a sailboat and intended to use it, I investigated the Island Marina and met Capt. Spider, as he likes to be known. When I drove down Main Street, I waved to Capt. Spider most mornings as he strolled with his dog along Main Street. He was not only in charge but a true gentleman and lived near the Marina, where he could watch over the boats. He is different from the other boat captains on the island as he provides a unique service. Since he is a Commonwealth of Virginia marriage celebrant, he can marry you on a cruise or other destination of your choice on the island. He has seen a lot of change on the island since he started his business way back when there weren't as many boat captains as there are now. He is a great source of advice for me about the local waters around Chincoteague and there is always something new to learn from him. For example, Capt. Spider once told me that the way a white plastic pole outside the marina was leaning indicated if the tide was coming in or going out.

I had a similar indicator that I could watch from our family room couch. From there I could look out to see a large green buoy in the channel. As evening came, I noticed a green light on the buoy turn on and flash. Each evening the flashing light seemed to be in a different place on my horizontal plane. Usually, the green buoy was just to the right of a support post under Loraine's house opposite, but sometimes it was way over to the right of that post. At first, I thought the Coast Guard had moved it. Eventually, I realized that the tide was moving the buoy left and right as I viewed it. When the tide was running out the buoy was over to the left and when the tide was coming in it was over to the far right. This was a handy navigation aid to let me know what the tide cycle was, without leaving my couch.

One of the most quirky, fun, unique, and passionate characters we met on the island was Capt. Barry Frishman. He drove around in a black jeep with all manner of paraphernalia hanging off it for conducting his boat tour business. He didn't do "all the pony viewing" as he referred to it, as the number of captains doing that had grown. Instead, Barry carved out his own unique niche with his Back Bay "Get Your Feet Wet" cruises, which he has been running for 27 years, he said.

Now there were the larger 20+ person pontoon cruises on the island. It made the cruises less personal in nature and competed with the smaller operators like Capt. Barry and Capt. Spider. Barry preferred to keep his business small-scale and very personal, rather like a well-known restaurant, where one meets the owner every day. As Debbie pointed out, he was an educator like us, and he ran his trips with such passion that it was hard to forget one of his tours. He compared his environment to a Broadway play, telling us his stage was the landscape and the wildlife were the players for his show.

Capt. Barry loved to have kids on the boat and sometimes he had to tell parents to be quiet when he involved the kids with tour activities. Often the kids were covered in marsh mud and from my point of view, this was the perfect experience for them. Barry believed it was important that kids got dirty and learned about nature. The parents often gave him cursed looks as if he was ruining their children's' lives. CBS News referred to Barry as the "Indiana Jones of Chincoteague." I assume CBS likened him to the outgoing spirit and adventure played by Harrison Ford in the popular Indiana Jones movies. The truth was he could really make a difference in their kids' lives. We saw pictures of kids on his Facebook page who came back 20 years later still affected by one of his trips. Many who had gone into marine biology from the initial spark of interest he generated in them during his boat tours.

He took five trips a day, seven days a week and really didn't have a life from June 1st to September 1st. "You have to love what you do!" he told us. Barry was from New York and didn't suffer fools lightly. It was reassuring to know there was another "tell you how it is" person. In that way, he was similar to Lynne Ballerini, with no frills. We saw him drive by our house many times a day coming and going to take his trips. At the end of the day, Barry still had the energy to talk to us as he sat at the Jackspot bar after a long day's work.

Then there was Diane who was one of our neighbor Anne's medical aides. She loved the local ducks and had names for them all; Lewey, Dewey, Hewey, Blondie, and Crackhead. I couldn't work out which duckling was which, except when Crackhead crossed the yard. Crackhead was noticeable because of a white stripe down the head. Diane often filled a paddling pool with water and set up bricks for them to climb up and enter. They seemed content in there. She also used to call "peep" and they would come running over to her. Diane told us she had all kinds of health issues, but she had a daily motto that stuck with me. Some days she came out of Anne's house and said, "Every day above ground is a good one."

The people we met in that first year were kind and generous. For me, it was the first opportunity to feel I belonged somewhere in the US. It was not just because I could pursue all my interests but also because people had the time to talk and they really cared. Initially, these heartfelt encounters came from the "Come'ere's" but soon we began to meet the locals as well, many of whom we had seen from a distance as they passed our house or visited the grocery store, and some had provided amusing tales for us to hear.

We learned about characters whom we hadn't met, but had seen or heard about. One of the most talked about was "Star" or Star-light/Start-bright as she is known. Stories about her are shrouded in mystery and, depending on whom we talked to, we often got updated versions. She is apparently a middle-aged Native American Indian woman who inherited a multi-coloured house from her husband, Bob Payne. The place is easy to find with its crazy ornaments and shells outside on Ridge Road. She had cemented shells onto her garden wall in an organized pattern, which read, "There is nothing in my world, galaxy, or other dimension, more important … unconditional love." She has a prayer garden in the back and reputedly is into drugs and other weird stuff, which may account for the shell statement. She claimed to have seen UFO's and was sometimes barefooted when people visited her. She apparently also thinks her deceased husband is still alive, but other versions have her believing his soul was in the Viking statue that now lays on its back beside her house.

Our friend Eileen added more to the supposed myths when she came to see us. She said she had seen Star at 1 a.m. in the middle of Ridge Road offering her cat up to the sky as a sacrifice. She didn't kill the cat. It only looked that way. Then another time she saw her dressed in a wedding dress in the middle of the road. A third time someone saw Star eating algae from a pond in Memorial Park.

Jane at Sundial Books told us that 'Star' sauntered into her bookstore one morning with a live pigeon under her arm. When Jane questioned her, Star said she was going to nurse it back to health.

These were all very peculiar sightings and stories, which added some credence to what we had already heard about Star, nonetheless, since I haven't met Star, I must be fair to her and wait to form my own opinion once I have done so, as some islanders embellish tales.

Then there is a man who I refer to as Mr. Wiggle because of his waddling gait when he exercises. I heard that he'd lost massive amounts of weight and seems to walk miles each day for his health. He passes our house every day strolling in rain or shine, even during the hard days of winter when he wears a day-glow orange vest. Mr. Wiggle is not much for words as I have tried to get a conversation going many times but he seems like a pleasant enough fella.

Another man passes our house frequently riding a motorcycle with his dog jammed into a milk crate strapped on the back.

Occasionally we see JJ or "Jamaica John" the name he prefers, riding his bike along Main Street. He is easy to spot as he often smokes a cigar and wears a woollen bobble hat in the Jamaican colours. He introduced himself one evening at AJ's, a local restaurant, and said he was an electrician and actually from Jamaica. He has been here for twenty-three years and is probably the only Jamaican for a hundred miles around these parts. JJ offered to bring some skinned ducks around to our house but we never managed to organize it. He said, "It's best to marinate them in milk for two days to get the gamey smell out."

I thought the porch provided enough interesting characters to watch until I joined the YMCA on the island to maintain my fitness, and started to run into a very active man nicknamed "Thumper" every time after work. I wasn't inclined to say hello since he made such a racket while working out and was oblivious to how annoying he was. I could tell if he had been in the gym the minute I entered through the door as the whole place stank of his body odour. He was referred to by the staff as "Thumper," due to his peculiar way of running that involved slamming his foot on the treadmill making a loud stamping noise as if he was wearing lead shoes. Occasionally he broke into a skip and then came down on the belt with a loud thump. The staff told me he had already broken one machine and they advised him to run properly. I wore my headphones to block out the noise. The members had to put up with him because the YMCA management hadn't done anything about him. People even asked when they called the YMCA what the banging noise was is in the background thinking there was construction going on.

We got used to hearing the Teaguer language, which was familiar to me. Many years ago, we visited Smith Island in the Chesapeake and immediately I recognized the distinctive way in which the locals spoke. It was a sort of out of date Elizabethan dialect or engrained West Country accent from the UK. It wasn't entirely foreign to me, as I was used to this way of speaking. Whilst the Teaguers didn't quite roll their r's so much, they did speak with a slur of their own. Their language is a broth, many years in the brewing, impenetrable, with inflections, and words join together. When they built the bridge over to the island in 1925 people could easily visit Chincoteague and as a result, the island wasn't as insulated, so over time, the accent became diluted. Now it's mostly the older generation who speak with a Teaguer accent.

From our various encounters, we started to understand how Teaguers pronounced their words. What we learned so far is that with 'R' controlled vowels like "fire" or "tire", Teaguers didn't pronounce the 'R'. They didn't say 'ing' either. It wasn't Bunting Road, it was Buntin Road, as words shortened. We lived on Chincotigg, not Chincoteague. We had seen a man wearing a T-shirt that read "Shinkatig," which was the pho-netic way of saying it. Some words like bar were pronounced as "baar", stressing the longer "a." Locals pronounced house as "howse" and boat as "bowt." The best way to listen to some of the old time Teaguers speak was on the island library oral history files. These files captured many locals speaking about the past and what their life was like back in the day. Some people said it was a lazy way of speaking using the back of your tongue and lowering your jaw. Some days it seemed the island was 20 years behind present-day life, which was quaint. On the other hand, the old timers were dying off so there was a lot of change going on.

In only one short year I had begun to sense the acceptance into a new community. I was determined to respect their ways of doing things. I listened a lot and was appreciative of so many strangers' help. It was a new experience for both of us. Living in a place for a length of time where I could develop relationships and experience a sense of community was a lifetime wish and now it might be possible.

28

THE OYSTERMAN'S SHACK

The Bivalve Trail

Each year a rebirth of the marsh takes place. The dull, murky brown stalks lying flattened from winter's high tides and winds are pushed aside from beneath, or float away on a spring tide. Our first year on Chincoteague we saw the emergence of bright, light yellow shoots coming from the bases of the reeds, which turned into a gentle greening of the marsh. At first, it was simply flickers of life here and there, but it started to rise as a curtain of green from the raw umber darkness. A great transformation occurred, blossoming into an emerald green carpet, which when caught in the sun displayed a shimmering multitude of greens and gold hues across the entire landscape as far as one could see. As our year unfolded we learnt how to tune into the distinct seasons and the changes that occurred all around us.

As well as changes in the landscape in May, we could sense a noticeable change in the number of people on the island. It was the build-up to the first major holiday, a time when the tourists came back. Most tourists were just regular people who loved the island as we did, but some chose to bring some unwelcome behaviour to the island way of life.

It was the Friday evening of Memorial Day weekend and as the day had progressed the traffic had increased. Huge RVs thundered past our house along with a fleet of SUVs loaded with bikes, canoes, and children. Some of the RVs were bigger than some of the trailers people lived in on the island. On they came and how busy it suddenly was. I could see tourists weighed down on the causeway bridge in monstrous rumbling trucks, decked out with window and bumper stickers commemorating past visits. A plethora of images kept streaming by: a swaying convoy on Maddox Boulevard, the trailer tide streaming onto the island, adolescent girls in bathing suits screaming out the back of pickup trucks. Most of the incomers passed by us to go south to the Inlet View campground or they made a left towards the Toms Cove campground. It was easy to spot the newcomers with their spotless cars, untanned skins, and perfect hairdos. The party house catty-corner to us and the house to the left of us erupted into life. Numerous families arrived with teenagers, who hung out on the porch with their iPhones.

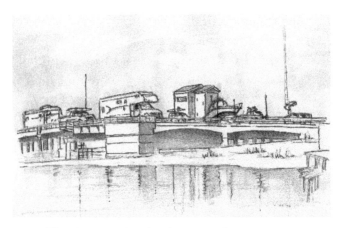

Tourists coming back across the causeway

As I looked out, it was getting dark but I still heard hundreds of Laughing Gulls way out in the marsh. Maybe they were having the last laugh to welcome the incoming tourists. One thing was for sure, many gulls became road-kill victims from the speeding vehicles on the causeway in the coming weeks. Bright white car headlights streamed across the causeway, evenly spaced, like the steady rhythm on a heart monitor. The island trolley and open-sided electric cars passed our house with minimal sound, however, the occasional lines of scooter renters sharply interrupted our peaceful world. Lights switched on in all the formerly dormant houses that had been unoccupied for the winter. The island had come to life and it was time for the local businesses to make their money. The window of opportunity was here and now, everyone had their chance. I was amazed at how often people stopped to say hi on the corner or waved as they drove past our house. It happened all day. An endless display of pleasantness, mostly from the locals and repeat family visitors.

It was 2:00 p.m. on Sunday during the Memorial Day weekend. I had been working hard for three days on our new shell driveway, as well as installing our mailbox when I decided it was time to take a break and walk alone on the refuge. Debbie wasn't with me as she was back in New Jersey. I wanted to find the Bivalve Trail that had recently opened.

I grabbed our trusty homemade Witch Hazel bug spray that had worked well so far and set off in the car. On crossing the bridge over to the refuge I noticed a line of cars leading to the entrance booths. I had not seen this before, having always had the opportunity to drive straight through the booths, generally only manned on winter holidays. No problem I thought, as I probably owed my fair share of entry money. Debbie and I hadn't purchased a $30 yearly pass yet which was something very worthwhile for residents like us, who visited the refuge often. The booth attendant had to ask a colleague in the adjacent booth how I could get to the trail.

I parked and headed to the Woodland Trail, which was in the shape of a loop. The Bivalve Trail cut off sharply from it once one was about halfway around. As I strolled alone through the woods, I felt the silence engulf me. All I could hear was the wind rustling through the tree canopy above and the chatter of birds further down the trail. A hot early summer's day in the pine forest brought out the rich spicy smell of pine. It was a sharp intense resinous scent, and with the enjoyment of the fresh fragrances in my nose, I walked and listened to the gentle breeze making the pine needles "rush," which was instantly refreshing and soothing.

While I ambled along the silent path in this vibrant woodland, loads of cars noisily poured in through the Refuge entrance gates and mostly headed straight for the pristine ocean beach. Then a sudden noise interrupted my silent world like an express train about to pass, as loud chattering reverberated through the woods, and a group of people hiked the trail without seeming to notice what was around them. When they passed me I didn't see them savouring this tremendous environment, but instead, they strode noisily with their iPhones out and earbuds in, chatting loudly. Gratefully I heard their voices fade away as they continued further up the path.

Tall Loblolly pines were engulfed here and there with Poison Ivy growing up their trunks, interspersed between deep thickets, from which numerous birds flitted. Some pines had huge trunks that were notched, thick, with chunky plate-like scales or irregular tiling that stretched all the way up into the canopy. They resembled the formidable breastplates of Roman armour ready to defend the tree against the voracious Pine Bark beetle. Some trees were snapped in half and stood splintered like those from a World War One landscape, a few with a beautiful semicircular orange fungus growing up the trunk like embedded gold coins called a "mock oyster." The Loblolly pines formed a crown shape at their tops, rather like an impressive head of broccoli. Some of this broccoli was not green, however, as the Pine Bark beetle had ravaged substantial stands of trees, turning everything a rusty brown colour.

I rounded a corner and saw a small clearing to my right, with a single tree in the centre. A melodious song came from the tree, and I caught sight of a male Rose Breasted Grosbeak going about its business as if he didn't notice me. Close by, the female did her own thing while the male sang his heart out. The sweet song was the only sound heard combined with the wind symphony from the pines above.

Then came another sudden interruption from a family of kids on bikes asking their mother if dinosaurs lived in the woods. Despite my feeling of annoyance, I couldn't blame them for shouting and being slightly scared as any kid might be. At least they were outside and not in front of a computer at home.

I sauntered further and nearly missed the Bivalve Trail off to my left as no sign marked it. With no sign for the moment, this thwarted the casual walker lest they be drawn down the dark tunnel of pines. Tiny white shell fragments lined the secret path, decidedly narrower than the asphalt trail I had been on, and led me into a silent wood of closely planted pine trees. I didn't hear my footsteps anymore as the sound of gravel was gone from my feet walking deftly on soft pine needles lying on top of the white shells. The path twisted up and down and was dark, somewhat claustrophobic, and yet strangely comforting as the mysterious tunnel through the trees was leading me somewhere.

As the silence once again engulfed me, my mind began to wander. Where had I experienced a similar path like this before? I felt a sense of déjà vu, as though this path took me back to somewhere from my past. I remembered another quiet place where I was equally enthralled as I walked through an alley of trees. Then it came to me, I was back in the alleyway that led up Park Hill behind the church in East Meon, when I was just eighteen, and taking a break from my summer job of baling hay. The alleyway up Park Hill was an escape path for me temporarily to forget the pain of learning about my birth father. I took those walks to console myself and regenerate with nature.

Conversely, I strolled along this path in complete calm and contentment. I felt jolted from my current existence and savoured a connection to something more immense than the mundane elements of my life. The silence and warm ocean breeze soothed me and lulled me into a sense of wonder of the raw connection to the living, breathing world around me. I felt suspended in a weird calm void as if I had left the world behind and entered a "thin space."

Experiencing a thin space is supposed to disorient us, make us confused and lose our bearings. The veil that separates heaven and earth lifts, and one is reputedly able to receive a glimpse of the glory of God. It wasn't like that for me but it was a unique spiritual quietness.

It is no wonder that thin places are most often associated with wild landscapes and islands, which often means travelling to a place where we have less control and where the unpredictable becomes the means of discovery.

A warm breeze gently caressed my face, similar to the warm air that used to greet me as I rose to climb above the village on those hot summer days in East Meon many years ago. I remembered Shelley's poem again. A Skylark was free from all that gave pain to man. It was higher up than we were, spreading joy and hope, and not affected by all that happened below. When I was eighteen, hearing his song high in the sky eased my worries. The Skylark was missing from this walk, but I didn't need him now.

Instead, I heard the faint roar of the ocean waves a mile away, crashing on the Assateague shoreline. I focused on the tunnel of trees in front of me that twisted, rose up and turned, leading out to Tom's Cove. I looked up through a space in the canopy above and caught sight of an enormous Bald Eagle, his bright white head illuminated in the afternoon sun as he glided with straight flat wings over the treetops. This wasn't the Sparrow Hawk that I looked for on Park Hill, hovering in place; here was a bigger bird, more majestic and powerful in his flight. There was no steep hill for this walk as I had had before, but the soft dark pathway intrigued me, a silent walk leading me to a much-anticipated view. I felt a peace that allowed me to contemplate the real meaning and purpose of life as an adult, whereas back in East Meon, I didn't know myself and worry plagued me setting out into the world with so many questions and concerns. Now I was grown and could reflect back on what I knew about the world and what was important.

I liked that this trail was hard to find since it made it more special and secretive like I was going to my own enchanted place. Since the pines were so close together they became a dark sound trap with bird songs amplified. I heard the distinct 'sip' of a cardinal as he called from somewhere in the understory.

The light appeared ahead in the tunnel of trees, which I assumed was Tom's Cove. Dappled sunlight shone on the shell pathway when suddenly I broke through the trees to see a classic oysterman's shack standing firm in an idyllic setting. I felt I was viewing a landscape painting from an old master.

The woodland curtain had been pulled back to reveal a glimpse of the past, a very real working past, where men gone before had pulled up their boats to maybe take a short rest from the water, sort their catch, or simply hang out. The reality was that someone had stayed out there to watch over the oyster beds. The owner was Tommy Clark of Don's Seafood in town. He reputedly used to pay someone to stay in the shack and sit with a gun to watch over the oyster beds, but that was many years ago. Beyond the sand of this remote beach, the shack stood as a major feature out in the bay. A line of dark weathered posts led out from the shore, evenly spaced, towards it.

The shack's roof had an enormous Osprey nest perched on it, with the two birds perched on the gable at the far end. The roof had modern shingles and looked well maintained. The shack was a typical rectangular house shape but didn't look that old, unless the pale blue vinyl siding covered the older part. It had windows on all sides and a small extension off to the side. I questioned the angled supports beneath it, however, that were dark and twisted. Some posts leaned at a precarious angle, and I wondered how stable the building really was.

I emerged onto a silent deserted shoreline by the cove and as I strolled out on the short beach, I looked left and saw hundreds of cars maybe a mile away parked on the visitor beaches facing the ocean. All I could think of was how lucky I was to have my own quiet beach to myself with no one around. It was just as I remembered having Park Hill all to myself back in East Meon.

Sun-bleached and bruised driftwood lay randomly cast up on the shoreline, alone and without purpose. The driftwood had weather-beaten ridges and grooves, the hallmarks of its resistance against the forces of water. Most pieces were a subdued grey colour, twisted and gnarled as if years adrift in the salty brine had washed the very colour from them. Some looked like a well-loved T-shirt that had been in the machine a few times too often. Maybe some fragments would tell me the tales from storms and giant waves they had been through. I picked up and examined each piece of wood, hoping it might have come from some ancient shipwreck or it might contain a few nails or inscriptions etched into it.

I knelt down and slowly dipped my hands into the still waters of the cove. The water swirled slowly and lazily near the shore, like the cream in morning coffee that curls on the top as one pours it. When I lifted my hands up again, a gust of air made them feel cold, yet the afternoon sun warmed my back. When the ocean breezes momentarily stopped, it was hot and still, reminiscent of opening an oven on baking day. When I looked over to my far right across Toms Cove, I could see the Wallops Flight Facility buildings in the distance. It was possible to see mirror images of the Wallops base shimmering in the heat out on the water. Here I could have sat all day were it not for the rumbling of my stomach and the need to get back to my chores at home.

I noticed piles of Cordgrass washed up on the shoreline from previous high tides. The bay was not very deep, maybe six feet at the most, but it looked deep enough from where I viewed it. To the left of the shack, I noticed the obsolete Toms Cove Lifesaving Station on the far shoreline. It stood out with its brick-coloured red roof, white façade, and various rusted antennae. The aerials used to be in service many years back to save those shipwrecked on the shore.

The gentle salty ocean breeze picked up again, and I listened to the steady rhythmic sloshing of short waves lapping up gently onto the sand. I knew that others would find my secret place soon as the trail became better known, but for now, this had been my special find on a glorious early summer's day. It provided the perfect peace to end my few days alone on the island. I took many photos of contrasting views of the shack and planned to create some watercolours. A camera would become necessary every time I took drives on the refuge.

As I was about to leave, I heard other people who had also discovered this trail. Noise travelled quickly on the breeze so I could hear them—a family of four on their bikes, parents and two teenagers—chatting loudly as they got closer. A reminder of the real world again, the busy world of people and cars. The teenagers decided to sit on the beach unsurprisingly with their iPhones. I doubt they noticed much about the shack or the view beyond. It was time for me to go. If only I could preserve this beautiful scene and freeze it in time, like roses that kept their scent for a week.

As I trekked back through the wake of many voices, I held that time and place in my mind, just as I had held Park Hill in my memory for so many years. Such places are private respites where one can go to retreat, to re-energize and gain a different perspective on life: a place to renew the spirit on an early summer day. I felt blissfully reinvigorated, rejuvenated and delighted, having celebrated the wonder of this special time and place.

The English landscape expert W.G. Hoskins once wrote:

"Few people in this overcrowded country have not some favourite heath or common or moor to which they retire when they need solitude, or unpolluted air, the glimpse of wildlife, or the sound of water falling over stones."

Hoskins understood that humans will always need special places where they are able to contemplate the natural world. I had had one of those days, with an added bonus of a memory of another place further back in my past. How ironic that on that day a simple tunnel of evergreen trees could evoke such a special treasured memory.

29

RHIANNON

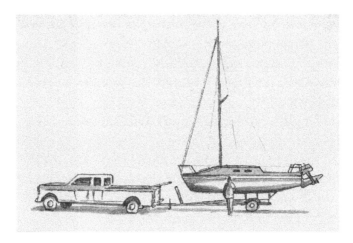

Rhiannon hitched up to Captain Doug's truck

Whilst my walk along the Bivalve Trail to see the Oysterman's shack reminded me of East Meon, my sailboat sitting on its trailer in our backyard reminded me of my earlier childhood. It called out to me to sail it.

I remember as a child looking down into a small cove below our house in Borth-y-Gest, North Wales, gazing at the sailboats bobbing up and down as the tide came in, and then resting awkwardly on their sides in the mud later. I always wondered what it was like to sail a boat and wanted to try it one day.

Much later on in life, during my army training, my platoon visited the coast in Devon where we paired up and had to figure out how to sail some puny wooden boats lying on the beach.

The rudimentary boats looked rather boxlike but at least they had a simple sail setup so we got used to them. My partner, Hargreaves, was very heavy, so we didn't sail much as he capsized the boat several times whenever he clumsily moved around.

Later on, I experienced more sailing by renting sailboats down at the shore in New Jersey. I thought of owning my own boat down the road, but really couldn't see it happening. Just as our island house presented itself by luck and perfect timing, so, in 2013, did the boat. A retired doctor advertised for sale a sailboat in great condition that he had lovingly cared for and maintained for many years. The Precision 21 had a shallow draft of just one foot nine inches, making it ideal for the waters around Chincoteague.

We had towed it down in the fall, and when spring arrived, I felt it calling me.

Now I could finally sail off into the bay in my own "pea green boat," as I had dreamed of when young, reading the owl and pussycat story, except my boat was blue. I had a vast horizon dotted with tiny islands that really existed around Chincoteague. It wasn't overlooking black rock sands like the view in North Wales, but there were similar shifting sands to deal with around Chincoteague Bay for sure.

I looked forward to the relaxing combination of fresh air, open water, and warm sunshine that one simply can't find on land and knew that the first time I headed out into the bay it would feel like another place.

Before venturing out, Debbie insisted I take a course on how to sail and navigate, even though I (naively) felt quite accomplished. I signed up for a weekend course at an excellent sailing school in Norfolk run by the American Sailing Association. It was an interesting experience, not least because it took place in the bay alongside the US naval carriers and battleships. We sailed far enough away not to cause a security risk, but we could see the naval battleships moored up just around the corner from the school. I took the course with Jack, a naval commander of one of the very ships in the bay. Jim, the instructor, thought it amusing that the captain of one of the most high-tech ships in the fleet who commanded three hundred men was learning to sail on a twenty-two-foot sailboat around the corner from his frigate.

When Jim asked Jack why he wanted to learn, he replied, "In my job, I am so far removed from the real sensation of a boat and how I can make it react. Getting real "hands-on" experience with a sailboat will be exciting."

Jack was cocky, but that came with his rank, I suppose. After a few manoeuvres in the slip, Jim let Jack take the boat out of the marina for our first trip. We were to take it in turns taking her out and in, completing various exercises after Jim had shown us first how to perform them, such as the correct way to sail up to and then stop at a mooring buoy, as well as the man overboard rescue process.

Jack, Jim, and I set off along a narrow channel of boats. Jim warned Jack that as he neared the end of the marina to exit, the current might take the bow round to starboard and swing her leeward close to the walls of the marina. He warned Jack to be careful and not to crank the engine up too much.

Sure enough, as we hit the end of the docks there was a change in the current; the water became choppy and the wind direction changed. The wall of the marina had protected us up until that point but now all of a sudden the bow swung around, and Jim yelled to Jack, "Ease up on the engine and push the tiller over to port and head up into the wind." Unfortunately, Jack got confused with Jim's directions and instead, turned the tiller to starboard and gassed the engine. Now Jack, Jim, and I were headed directly at pace towards the concrete wall of the marina with hardly any room for turning.

"*Yeeks*," I thought. "*This isn't going to turn out well*," but didn't dare say a word, not knowing what to do myself, so I grabbed the boat hook and braced for the smash that was about to occur, knowing full well that the boathook was of no use against a 2,000 pound sailboat travelling at speed. Jim stopped the engine, leapt quickly over to the tiller and pushed Jack out of the way but I could see he wasn't going to avert the crisis. The boat's momentum, combined with the wind and current, was too much to handle so we braced ourselves for impact against the solid concrete marina wall.

The crunching sound that followed was very painful to hear as the bowsprit rode up the wall and gave way at the base where the screws popped out of their plates. The fiberglass bow buckled in; it was shattered in a tangled mess. All I could hear was the intense crunching and scraping sound of the steel bowsprit on the concrete. Jack had said he was confident of getting the boat out as he was the commander of a massive Frigate. I simply hoped for his sake that his naval crew wasn't watching off the bridge of their ship in the harbour.

There was total silence between us, as Jim valiantly ordered commands to both of us about what to do. He immediately used his radio to call back to the harbourmaster for assistance. We weren't sinking, but we had a damaged bow and part of it had been lost overboard. Jim restarted the engine as we pushed the boat off the wall using the boathook. Luckily we could slowly motor her back into her slip.

Once moored up, Jim asked us to go back to the clubhouse and take a break so the instructors could sort out what to do next. We could see Jim talking at length with the harbourmaster, while another instructor surveyed the damage. Jack and I didn't speak. After half an hour, the instructors decided we would take the other boat out. This time, Jim manned the helm and we safely made it out into the bay in complete silence. Jim struck up the first words between us in ages and made light of it by stating this was the first time anyone had mangled a boat, and the insurance would cover the damage. Jack complained about the conditions, but it was Captain's error in my view as Jack received clear instructions about what to do and when. So much for the cocky commander. Jack remained quiet for the rest of our course. He took some pictures of us sailing as I didn't have my camera, but he never emailed them to me.

In early July, Debbie and I launched "Rhiannon," the longer version of my mother's Welsh name. Mum would have been teary-eyed had she been alive to see it. The only other sailboat owner on the island, Capt. Doug and his wife Nancy gave generously of their time to set up and launch the boat. Doug was a "Come'ere" like me and provided me with valuable lessons. The first task was raising her mast. When I showed Doug my homemade 'A' Frame[35] set up for the mast he didn't poo-poo it, but simply said, "Let's give it a try and see how it goes." He made some suggestions on how to improve it and told me about his method for raising the mast, which seemed so much easier to use, a design I put away in my mind for next year. We got the mast up and lowered her down the ramp. It was thrilling as she hit the water.

We moored Rhiannon temporarily at a floating dock not far from the launch ramp so we could rig her sails. The plan was to then motor her around to the Island Marina to her slip. Capt. Doug was having trouble attaching the Genoa[36] (a large sail in the front), as the shackle was tight for the fitting, when a chatty commercial fisherman, Chip, wearing a fluorescent shirt, pulled up alongside and started talking to us. Chip managed his own business "I clam 4 U 2," and recommended that I take Debbie with me sailing at all times, as the Coastguard would be less inclined to inspect me if a woman accompanied me. Chip said, "I was boarded by the Coastguard so many times that I became sick of it, until the day I had three women aboard to go clamming and they didn't bother me anymore. If I am stopped again now I have all manner of required navigational lights on board in a bucket."

The topic somehow ventured on to the rules and politics on the island whereby Capt. Doug gave me advice about living here. He said, "Don't offer any opinions. You are not from here and Teaguers have their own way of doing things, so don't

---

[35]   A basic structure designed to bear the load of raising a mast.
[36]   A type of large jib or staysail that overlaps the mainsail.

interfere." It seemed like solid advice to me. I think Doug didn't want me to get in trouble, as there had been other sailors before us who angered the harbourmaster, including one who didn't pay his slip fees. Doug told me about the wealthy person with limited sailing experience who once brought a 30' Bristol sailboat with a fixed keel into Merritt Harbour. It weighed an enormous 13,000 pounds, so when the owner didn't moor it properly, and the tides came in higher than normal, the boat dragged under water and sank in the harbour. Needless to say, the harbourmaster hasn't liked sailboat owners much after that incident.

Once the boat was ready, I took the tiller for the first time and headed out of Merritt Harbour for our short sail around to the Island Marina. Turning briefly to my port side the breakers in the distance signalled the Atlantic Ocean where I would sail one day when more comfortable with the area.

For now, I concentrated on keeping the red channel markers to my right, or as they say in the navigation world, "Red, Right, Returning." Capt. Doug pointed out the shoals that appeared with their rippled slacker water and some submerged rocks on one side of a buoy. We headed north, keeping Main Street to our right and staying well clear of the docks that protruded into the channel. Capt. Doug told me we had about seventeen feet of water and not to venture much beyond the green buoys to the left as one could be in two feet of water very quickly.

"Stay in the channel and you'll be fine," he said. Capt. Doug was an amazing guy, full of knowledge and with a gentle disposition. Formerly a PE teacher, he had an encouraging and yet not overly instructional way about him. I could tell he must have been excellent with students.

Capt. Doug and I shared sailing stories while he provided me with a ton of advice as we motored. He advised me to keep the jib sheet taut when I unrolled the furler, as it would fold up much easier. Also when I tacked, he suggested I bring the boom to the centre in a controlled manner so that it didn't swing wildly around.

"Think about how you can lead the lines back from the furler so they don't interfere with the shrouds or jib halyard," said Capt. Doug.

We eventually sailed around the island to arrive directly opposite our house. Even though I could see our second floor, it seemed our house was so tiny, insignificant and far away. The view from the house suggested I could sail closer, but we had to stay well off the docks for deeper water.

We neared the Island Marina and Doug pointed out a series of buoys that I could use to create my own practise course. "You see there are five in total," he said. "They form an oval shape and provide ample opportunity for you to sharpen your tacking and jibing skills." Doug suggested I potter about with this configuration before venturing out to explore any further.

There was a contented gurgle of water as we sailed along peacefully. The rudder clunked on the pintles[37] as a swell passed under her. The wind was singing through the rigging as the mainsail fluttered. The chop of the bay steadily hitting the boat was a form of poetry.

Sailing requires attentiveness, but it also encourages day-dreaming. The two, combined, put me in a state of alertness that was both stimulating and relaxing. I surrendered the tendency to plan and organize my time and instead savoured the moments when out on the water. We are always subject to the weather, which can change very quickly here so I keep reminding myself that sailing is a skill. One just doesn't jump on board and turn a key like other boat owners. I have to sense everything around me to control how my boat gets somewhere, rather than merely driving a throttle forward.

As we neared the Marina entrance, I heard a familiar sound. Debbie was playing the "Marines Hymn" on her bagpipes to welcome us in. It was a very special moment, which Capt. Doug liked as well and found amusing. Not many boats have that kind

---

[37] One of the pins on the forward edge of a rudder.

266

of welcome down here. As we cruised in, Capt. Doug asked me to check the centreboard and see if it was down.

"Yes, partially," I said.

"If you clear the marina entrance without it kicking up, you can place a piece of red electrical tape on the line as a marker for the following time," he said.

Once Rhiannon was in her slip, Doug showed me how to mark and arrange the docking lines so they were flexible to account for the rising and falling of tides. He suggested I mark the lines with tape so that I knew where to tie them the next time for ease. In addition, he suggested that I keep the stern protruding slightly out of the pylons so that the engine and rudder avoided any damage.

Debbie took a wonderful photo of us to mark my maiden voyage in Rhiannon. Capt. Doug kindly said that he would check on Rhiannon when he was next at the marina to make sure her lines hadn't moved, and then took me over to his boat to show me how his boat was rigged. I picked up a few ideas to add to mine, such as a cover to protect the tiller and some cup holders. He also had an engine mount that was easier to raise and lower which was something I had to address on my boat. As Capt. Doug waved good-bye and turned out of the Marina, I stood by Rhiannon for a moment in silence. There was my boat looking great in her slip. I realized another wonderful dream. I then looked skyward for a few moments and wondered if my mother was looking down on her son, fully grown now with his own boat in a faraway land. Our lives take many turns and some days are not fair sailing. This day was perfect, however, from start to finish, and as they say, some memories can come full circle. I looked forward to being at one with the open expanse of the bay.

On July 11th Debbie and I took our first sail in front of the house to cruise around the buoys. I managed to leave the dock and return without incident, which was an achievement, given how tricky it was. I made a note of some adjustments for the following time, and put the flares and safety equipment on board and installed the cotter pins into the shroud turnbuckles for extra safety. We got back to our porch and all of a sudden saw dolphin out in the bay where we had just been sailing.

Sailing Rhiannon off Merritt Harbour

We enjoyed many sails with family during the summer. The ritual of hoisting up Rhiannon's mainsail and seeing it filled with air became a resurrection every time I took her out.

The most memorable outing was my last sail of the season towards the end of October. The weather was still warm enough and reached 70 degrees with a wind that fluctuated between 3 and 8mph. There were no bugs at all, especially the hard biting green flies and even better, no boats cranking their motors up and whooshing by me at high speeds or sport fishing boats with six people on board shouting and hollering. Even the shorebirds were unusually quiet for a change; mind you, the worst offenders the Laughing Gulls had mostly left.

The wind was out of the East again like my previous adventures and so the perfect time for me to sail up and down the bay on a beam reach. The sky was full of Mares tails, those wispy high cirrus clouds that looked like the ribs from a human skeleton or the markings on a Mackerel. In places, the blue looked like someone had taken a fine-toothed comb and gently scraped in some white streaks like that of a ponytail. As the old proverb goes,

"Mares' tails and mackerel scales make lofty ships to carry low sails."

Together, wispy cirrus clouds resembling horsetails and patchy cirrocumulus signal that a rainstorm is on its way. How ironic these were in the sky with the Chincoteague ponies all around us.

After I hoisted the mainsheet and jib, all I could hear was the steady gurgle of water under Rhiannon's hull, which sloshed more when the breeze picked up. There was total silence except for the birds and soft gurgles. It was great to feel Rhiannon respond to the wind and move under her own power. When I sailed her she came alive, compared to the inanimate object that simply floated in the dock.

I liked sitting high up in the pulpit at the stern, where I held both jib sheets and steadied the tiller with my leg. The slightest move of the tiller altered my course. Sometimes the rudder would clank rhythmically after the wake from a boat passed under her. I had to concentrate on juggling the sheets and tiller from the pulpit and when the wind blew up, I wished I had gloves, as the jib sheets gave a slight burn to my palms from holding on so firmly.

Perched nearly at the same level of the boom I felt at one with the wind as it conformed to the shape of the boat. Its rustling forced the sheets to crinkle and then stretch out as they filled with air. Everything was in perfect harmony on a gorgeous October day. I felt as if an electric current, the called up energy in the bay, flew down along the tiller into my arm. My connection to the water was powerful. The telltale signs (lengths of string tied onto the sail to indicate the direction and speed of the wind) dangled and then when I picked up speed they flickered sideways against the genoa. I sat back and savoured the time with great satisfaction, one hand on the tiller and the other on my cup of British tea, making occasional corrections to the sail trim and sensing how she handled in a light wind. At one point I stretched out in the cockpit resting my back against the pulpit, with my long legs flat out. I remembered the perfect music to accompany me, the Adagio of Spartacus and Phrygia from the ballet Spartacus by Aram Khachaturian. It's a haunting piece that is perfect for going to sea and I imagined it played as I sailed down the bay.

For a moment I felt transported back to the tiny cove in Borth-y-Gest, remembering all the stocky colourful wooden boats resting awkwardly on their keels at low tide. Here boats don't lie on their sides and then dance and loll about on their anchor chains when the tide comes in. The Chincoteague tides are not nearly as extreme as North Wales.

My body completely relaxed as I glided off into a trance-like state with the quiet gentle movement of the boat and soft breeze. The conditions were so ideal that dropping both sails at the end was easy, unlike previous occasions when I got myself into all sorts of trouble. I reluctantly pulled the cord to start the outboard and slowly cruised back into the marina. The sailing year ended with a great last day to remember.

30

FROM THE FRYING PAN INTO THE FIRE

"Chatham"   "Arcadia"

The changes had been dramatic since I decided to move to the US. I first moved to the affluence and fast pace of New Jersey, then to a more working class and slower pace of life amongst Teaguers on Chincoteague. Now I was embarking on a third cultural immersion, this time into the poverty of Accomack County in Virginia on the Eastern Shore.

Having enjoyed the summer, it was time to focus on working again. I summoned the courage to start over in teaching despite my treatment in New Jersey. I felt I still had a lot to give, and my talents would be wasted if I didn't help students less fortunate in our county. I was lucky and was offered a position teaching Personal Finance at Arcadia High School on the mainland. The school mascot was the Firebird because the school had burnt down many years ago and only a tiny part of the original building remained. The school logo resembled a cardinal crossed with an eagle with yellow trim. The Firebird name was very appropriate since I had jumped from the very high standards of a leading high school in New Jersey to the very diverse standards in Accomack County. In effect I was about to dive from the frying pan into the fire, teaching in a county where the teachers were paid some of the lowest in the state, while the administrators were paid significantly more.

At my last school in New Jersey, the student population was ninety-eight percent white, befitting a very homogeneous affluent area where most students moved on to a four-year college after high school. At Arcadia, around seventy percent of the students went on to a two or four-year college. Even this figure was not accurate, as there was no way of knowing once they left if they had actually attended a community college or not. In contrast to New Jersey, seventy percent of the students here got a free lunch and came from a totally diverse socio-economic group.

Up north, parents were heavily involved in their students' lives, motivating them and driving them to do well. Consequently, "Back to School" night meant one had a classroom full of parents, many standing in the hallway. At Arcadia, I was about to find out that only six or seven parents stopped by if I was lucky at back to school night.

The week of New Teacher Institute prepared us for teaching in the district. They taught us what to expect when we met our new students and the administrators spent a lot of time discussing what it meant to be teaching amongst poverty.

One of the speakers at our training was Ms. Tankard, a teacher who had been in the district for 25 years. She came from a trailer herself, and I recall her saying:

"Kids will come to school with their own baggage. You may not recognize the same kid's behavior from one day to the next. Some days they will not have eaten or slept. Some kids look after parents or grandparents. Some work nights and some have depression with mood swings. Parents often work at the Perdue or Tyson chicken plants on shifts, and if they get too many calls at work it could lead to a firing. You therefore have to be careful choosing an appropriate time to call parents."

"Kids sometimes hit their siblings at home but have to be taught not to do it in school, where it is not allowed. Kids often bring themselves up and sometimes a sibling as well. Our question to the students was often not "*where do you live?*" but "*where do you stay?*" Students are more concerned about how much food they can eat as opposed to how nicely it is served. They are used to bartering for stuff and will use that tactic in school. They will ask for a reward if well behaved in class. Landlords in the area sometimes charged rent not by the building but by the number of people living in the trailer."

Ms. Tankard told us that often her meals as a child depended on what they picked in the fields that day.

"*We was poor but we was rich,*" she said.

This meant that in poverty you had your family and that mattered a lot. The middle class aspired more to having material belongings, more so than poor people did. She told us, "In some places if you leave your clothes out to dry for too long they will get stolen off the clothesline. Families can't afford pets here because they don't have the money to feed them. These students are only motivated to get through school as painlessly as they can."

It was shocking and depressing to hear this, but it made me even more determined to help these kids.

One of the Special Education teachers told me that students on disability could get as much as seven hundred dollars a month. That meant in some cases they supported their parents and felt tied to home. Most parents worked at the chicken plant, spent their day out on the water, or operated local small businesses. They also worked at the local convenience stores along Route 13.

Just a handful of the NASA Wallops folks sent their kids to the public school system. Many preferred instead to send them to the private schools, like Broadwater and Christian Academy further down the peninsula. The Arcadia student worlds and what they related to were very small. What they saw of the world was through their TVs, and our instructors told us that some even believed that reality TV was real. Often these kids defined themselves through the movies they watched.

The reality for these kids and their values was at odds with what I knew. Some students prided themselves on the shoes they wore. It was all about the shoes, the car rims, or how high their truck was off the road. To them, 22" rims on their car or $250 Jordan sneakers were the real thing. The new teacher instructors warned us they weren't full of ambition or drive as there was nothing to inspire them. The creative instruction I had taught up north wouldn't fly here, as much of the teaching was textbook-driven, with many worksheets. Teachers had to strive to teach to the higher levels of learning such as creating and evaluating, but in reality, the students weren't ready for this.

As I drove south to the board office to take my teaching institute classes, I couldn't help notice the sign for a trailer park off to my left. It read *"Dreamland"* and then below that *"A touch of class."* On looking at the state of some of the trailers in there, I couldn't help but feel sorry for them. I later learned that Accomack County had the highest number of homes in the state without indoor toilets. From where I had come, this was definitely the lowest class of accommodation, but for many, this was all they could afford. I had been forewarned that some of my students would be coming to school not having taken a shower for days, with dirty fingernails, and may have slept in a drafty trailer. Some didn't even have a regular stable home and some slept in an unrelated place every night.

Ms. Tankard continued to tell us more at our training.

"These poor kids live day-to-day and not for the future. They are not proud of where they live and feel trapped here. Many haven't even been over the Chesapeake Bay Bridge, let alone north, or on a plane. They aren't encouraged to leave home to see the world and feel obligated to stay here in Accomack County."

It was a stark awakening for me to a very different world, but I felt confident I brought a lot to the table and could help these students believe in themselves.

I visited Arcadia High School to get acquainted and to prepare my classroom. It was located beside the main highway. The building from the outside looked just like any other modern high school: flat-roofed, devoid of architectural features, and with very few windows. It did not look like the gothic monstrosity I attended when I was a child, but its modern looks were deceiving, for inside I was about to find out about its structural decay. I found my classroom, an inner room with no windows, unfortunately. I had hoped I might have something to look out at each day, even if it was the highway. Locked up for the summer months, the building smelled of musty roasted stale air. To place posters on my wall I had to use special magnetic tape as they disallowed normal tape. This made it difficult to decorate my room.

I quickly realized how teachers made do with a scarcity of resources in a district that had very little money. Toner cartridges were cheaper to buy if refilled and repurposed, but as a result, some didn't work. They rationed paper to two boxes each, which many teachers locked away. If left unattended, other teachers stole it. We took whatever paper we needed to the copier, used it, and then brought the unused paper back to our classrooms for use next time. You had to make do with what was available and make it last. The copiers ran so slow in the school that I could go out for breakfast, come back, and the job would still be running. Some of the copier machines sounded like a tiny animal squashed in pain when you used them.

Another challenge to contend with was the physical amenities at the high school, the crummy plumbing, lead-contaminated water, insects and mould, and I haven't even got to the black snakes yet. The men's faculty bathroom reminded me of the icy cold toilets back in my Haileybury school days. They were cold and dank, dimly lit and with only the cold tap working that sprayed out a random jet of water in all directions. At least they had doors on the stalls. Getting hot water was a risky prospect as you either scalded yourself with its sudden emergence in the main office bathroom or waited forever for the warm water to arrive in the boys' bathroom. I guessed it went with the territory. The authorities had shut off the drinking water because of lead contamination in the school pipes so instead there were bottled water coolers stationed around the building.

Other teachers warned me that roaches lived in our computers. They came out when the lights switched off for a while, so we had to be careful when we watched a movie in class. The sudden appearance of nasty black snakes in certain classrooms was rather like a nightmarish horror movie unfolding while learning. Apparently, one snake had dropped down from the ceiling air conditioning vent during a final year exam. It had dangled helplessly for a minute above one student, then landed with a plop directly on their desk, scattering the screaming students in the process. I just hoped I didn't have those in my room. The last and maybe most disturbing news from a health point of view was the presence of mould in the school. The administrators told us it was not airborne and that it was limited to certain areas of the school. They had it under control, they said but needed to keep on top of it.

When I asked about a textbook for every student, my colleague next door replied the school couldn't order any more, so I had to make do and have them share. Many of my books were in such poor condition I had to glue them back together again. A gallon of Book Saver glue left on my cabinet for me to use! A colleague told me not to let the students take the books home, as many wouldn't come back, given the way the kids lived and moved around. This meant I was in for an inordinate amount of copying on the 'squashed dying animal' copier machines.

In addition to the week of new teacher training, we had to be in school two weeks before the students. The only more boring thing I could think of was waiting for an English bus in the rain, or queuing in line at the unemployment centre.

Maybe some teachers really needed two weeks to find their classroom. It only took me a day or two to set up my room. The administration gave out a smattering of gifts during this time, school branded items such as coffee mugs, scarves, ID card holders and Arcadia binders, no doubt to make us feel happier and valued, whilst also trying to instil some school pride.

I was pleased to learn that the school had a technical division where the students could learn welding and automotive skills. This meant I could get my car fixed with a member of staff watching over the students. They weren't able to tackle anything complicated, but they solved most of the routine service fixes. The cosmetology teacher could give you a cheap haircut, and the home economics teacher had the kids prepare a tasty teacher lunch every month. Not bad for a school that didn't have much. These were trades and professions the students could learn to prepare for jobs when they graduated, rather than simply working in fast food restaurants.

Ms. Bell was my mentor and department chair and taught in the class next to me. She was a class act. She dressed professionally and had a very welcoming manner about her. I liked her from the moment I met her. She had been at the school for a number of years and had seen it go from bad to worse. She told me not to be too generous and obliging at the beginning, as the students would take advantage of me.

At the first full faculty meeting, I was surprised to find the faculty white and mixed in age. I knew that many of my students were black, so I narrowly assumed that several of the faculty were too. One of the older teachers told us, new teachers, that the best way to get through the day was taking a Valium and a shot of Jack Daniels; everyone whooped with laughter. Seven weeks later I felt I needed this kind of medication. They could fire us for four reasons; failure to pass students according to the SOL's (Standards of Learning), a sexual matter, drinking on the job, or anything inappropriate we did with money.

Sixteen teachers joined Arcadia the year I did. During the last four years, Arcadia had lost forty-one teachers, which was a poor record. The principal explained the turnover as individuals missing home, but I didn't believe that.

After the faculty meeting and before the students arrived, I had a chance to get to know my fellow teachers, some of whom appeared to be interesting characters. They didn't wear floor-length black robes like my teachers at Haileybury, but some had intimidating personalities. The highly strung Special Ed teacher, Ms. Edwards, started imitating a British accent after she met me and whenever I saw her in the hallway. Other teachers said she was nuts and did this often when she met someone from a unique place.

Then there was Mr. Stiles, who came into my room to introduce himself. One of his first questions was "What do you think we should do with the Middle East?" He was very liberal and had some drastically non politically correct solutions to the Middle East problems. I was seldom sure if he was looking at me, as one of his eyes stared to the side. It turned out he was a re-enactor and enjoyed reminding me about how the Americans beat up the British some time ago. He loved to discuss history and many times I saw him smoking his pipe in his truck before he entered school and later afterwards. He reminded me of Mr. Fiori, my scary Bloxham math teacher. Mr. Fiori smelt of tobacco and had the habit of leaning over me to see what I was working on. Then his yellow stained hand dropped onto my worksheet combined with his nicotine breath. It is no wonder I hated math.

Mr. Mack, the biology teacher, was fondly known as the amusing sage in the school. He reminded me of Jack Nicholson the actor and had a sharp sense of humour that I liked. He didn't suffer fools gladly and was the first to point out stupidity in a faculty meeting, especially when the administration asked us to do something that didn't make sense.

I soon realized that properly pronouncing student's names by learning where the apostrophe went was going to be a challenge. The Special Ed department brought around individual sheets for those students who had medical or emotional issues.

There were quite a number of them, so we had to sign the sheets to acknowledge we knew.

A fairly comprehensive handbook for students covered much, especially policies regarding cell phone use and dress code. The school in many cases provided the only structure some students received to learn certain life skills. How many of these would be enforced I was about to find out. I was surprised to learn that students who took advanced placement courses worked behind screens in the media centre as a separate group. I didn't think this was the way to handle AP courses and it certainly didn't provide them with much silence.

My treatment at Haileybury and Bloxham was incomparable. For one, teachers could count on discipline at home, and being a son of someone in the army meant I had way more respect than anyone else did. Here the students had the discipline laid down by the handbook but because they weren't used to any discipline at home, I didn't think they conformed much in school. I was about to find out.

I put in place a rigorous classroom management plan for the year and waited to try it out. On August 29th I met my first kids at Open House. The first student into my classroom had two rings through her lower lip, one through her nose, and a severely cropped hairstyle. I quickly realized from my printed-out class list that she was the cutter kid (someone who self-injures) the guidance counsellor had warned me about. She had an advanced medical directive, which I had signed, so I knew I had to be careful with her. Following her came a boisterous black kid who seemed to like himself a lot and wore some expensive looking sneakers. Then a white kid with long hair wearing a yellow Nascar T-shirt. He was a younger version of Steven Tyler from Aerosmith. Then some girls came in who wouldn't stop talking and liked my accent, followed by a Hispanic girl who was very polite and quiet.

One parent came with their daughter who immediately stuck out from the rest. Her name was Brianna, she was very chatty and confident from the moment she stepped into my room. She had shoulder length blonde hair, piercing blue eyes with a great smile, and started to tell me I shouldn't be overly welcoming to the students or they would take advantage of me. I could tell she was a tough cookie and didn't suffer "the stupid boys," as she referred to them. She said she loved the theatre, animals and dressing up with fake blood on Halloween. I could tell she was going to be a major contributor to my class. She gave me a warm smile as she waved goodbye.

Then some parents came into my classroom still dressed in their assembly-line work clothes with the odd chicken feathers stuck on their uniforms, They just came from their shift at the local chicken plant. One naval dad from Wallops introduced himself and said his son was into science and space. I noticed every student and parent came from an unrelated place and each had a unique story. There were none of the homogeneous well-dressed parents and students of New Jersey here. It was a pleasant surprise and a taste of the real world, albeit in a rough way. No doubt this new classroom setting had its own challenges and maybe its own rewards.

My first day of school at last arrived, and I waited for the students to enter my classroom. I remembered a scene at the beginning of the movie Gladiator when the Roman army faced the Barbarian horde ready to attack. I felt nervous as the student horde burst into my room that first day.

I also remembered Russell Crowe's line from Gladiator when he was in the amphitheatre and about to fight for his life. He said to his fellow soldiers, "*Whatever comes out of those gates, we must stick together,*" I felt the same way that first day of school when I was faced with twenty pairs of eyes staring at me. I knew not what to do or say next. An eclectic mix of youth clad in camo and dishevelled clothing, fiddling with their I-Phones, waited for me to say something.

I jokingly thought, *Why not write on the board the course title is "How to get off the Eastern Shore"?* Then I gave the students six tasks they had to do before they graduated to help them achieve this, get a bank account, savings account, get a driving license, work a summer job, get on their parent's credit card, and create a well laid out resume. I also discussed their need to do more than get a high school diploma and to eventually find a salaried job and not one that was hourly. They could go to the Eastern Shore Community College or if they could afford it, a four-year university. I purchased five giant colour posters of Welsh castles and put them up on the back wall of my classroom. Above each poster, I placed a contrastive word. The line when read said, "Budget And See The World." I also showed a video titled "Knock Knock" during my first class, which explained that they were not their mums' and dads' choices. They have their own lives to live and should make their own choices about how they want to live.

I knew I "wasn't in Kansas anymore" when I was asked to cover a class for an absent teacher. A student named Autumn asked me if I could throw away her candy wrapper.

I said, "No, you can get up and do it yourself."

Autumn replied, "But I can't get up, Mister, I have been shot and this is my first day back in school."

I replied, "Yeah right, that's a great excuse."

Then the other students at her table told me that she really was telling me the truth. Someone had shot her.

She then told me what happened.

"I was dying for a pee late at night so I rambled into a field by the road. As I squatted, I felt a sharp pinch in my hip and then I couldn't get up. Somebody done hit me with something. I had to call my friends to come and carry me over to the car. Then I noticed blood on my clothes and then the pain started. I still have the bullet in me as it's too close to a nerve for them to remove it. The police are investigating it."

The week of New Teacher Institute hadn't prepared me for a story like that, or the time one of my students rolled his pants up and proudly showed me his court-mandated ankle bracelet that he had to wear 24/7. I never knew what he had done, but at sixteen he was already in the courts. I was totally unprepared for what I was about to experience.

During those first few days, the students were curious about why I had come to Arcadia High School. Who was this tall white teacher from England (really Wales) who seemed out of place? Some thought (and still think to this day) that I am in the witness protection program hidden away on the Eastern Shore for some criminal act. They asked me why I came here when there was nothing to do down here. Brianna piped up and said, "Animals have more to do in zoos than we do, Mister."

The students told me they were desperately trying to get off the Eastern Shore; Why did I want to come here? I replied by telling them I liked the outdoor life, which they didn't believe. Some of them ventured to say all they did was shoot wildlife. Despite their loathing of the area, I noticed one of my students wearing a distinctive T-shirt. The headline read, "It's an Eastern Shore Thing." with an image below of a pair of white rubber boots on a dock. The payoff line beneath the boots read, "You wouldn't understand."

"What is it with the white boots"? I asked Chelsea. "Why white, rather than green or black"?

"It's what watermen wear here, Mister," she replied.

She didn't really know so I said, "You know that for all the moaning I hear from you, you sure are proud to wear the T-shirt.

Later I did some research about the T-shirt and found out that some people call the white boots 'shrimpers,' and some 'hospital boots.' Not only are the white boots cheaper, but the main reason for wearing them is they are non-marking on the boat decks. They are also cooler to wear as they reflect the hot sun much better than the darker colours.

Viewing the student body during my first weeks at Arcadia, I never knew that so many shades of camouflage existed, other than the plain green and brown army looking colours I knew. Here I saw pink and blue shades as well as variant patterns. Students had camo backpacks, camo shoes, camo-coloured pens, and notebooks. I was waiting to see my first camo head bow, which seemed to be the norm for dressing up. I even saw my first camo iPhone cover.

Sarah wore seven-inch heels to school every day. She had nine contrasting pairs of shoes, she told me. The boys gave her some stick[38] for it but she brushed them off. One morning in class she made a comment I particularly remembered. She had had enough with one boy who was annoying her about the shoes. So she told him, "At least they are bigger than your dick." She never heard a word from him again.

A hefty white student with glasses named Josh sat at the back of my class playing a video game, which I kept trying to block. He was antagonistic and combative towards me and the other students. On one occasion he told us, "I sleep with a pistol under my pillow Mister. The trailer me and my family live in has been broken into before. One time a man came through our window and I told him I had a gun. I have the right to defend myself."

When I was grading what the students had learned from my first class lecture, I read some disturbing notes from one of my students. Dave was venting about his life and said that he was tired of his dad buying cheap wine to get drunk and then beating him. I spoke with him later in the day and told him he could talk to me if he needed help. I also needed to mention this issue to his counsellor as well. I was sure it wouldn't be the first time I heard stories such as these.

Some of the black kids told me more about the hierarchy of "hoods" on the Eastern Shore. They told me there's the "Real Hood" itself in Rolling Acres. There are plenty of shootings and scary stuff down there, they said. They even put gunpowder on the Pit bulls' gums to make them angry so when the cops come for a raid they are afraid to go into the trailers. The kids then told me there was "the country-hood," pretender hoods that tried to be "wannabe's." Then they made me laugh when they said there's the "never-will-be-hood," which comprised

---

38   To give someone some stick is to criticise or punish.

the Latinos and Mexicans. The last group was the "whites" in Chincoteague, Onancock, and Parksley who had their own hood.

The students had very low self-esteem and these pretenders impressed them. The system did them no favours. The intelligent ones who might go somewhere had no fast track or any opportunity to do advanced placement courses for a whole year. They just joined regular classes like everyone else. They had nothing to aim for, which was a terrible shame.

My students called me "Mister" or "Sir," which made me uncomfortable since in the past slaves called their masters in a similar way. When I was training in the army, they treated me with no respect and called me all sorts of low life things until I completed training. Only at that time did the other ranks who trained me refer to me as "Sir."

Students had their own way with words. A few referred to me as "What's up dawg", "Bro" or "dude," which I reminded them not to say. They used the two letters "Ha" to reply to anything I asked them that they didn't hear or understand. When they wanted me to stop speaking or explain something, they sometimes said, "Hold up, Mister." They also said, "I would have done hit you by now." Another new word cropped up during one of my lessons. If something was "clutch", it meant it was very cool amongst the black students.

I learned more about the students' way of speaking as the months ticked by. We occasionally got off topic and I picked up on a word they used to describe something. One time that word was "booty," so I asked them to explain what the difference was between a "butt and booty." They told me that most white people just had butts but black people had booty, a more pronounced bottom shape, which they explained by pulling up a few celebrity examples on the in-class computers. Then they told me about the subsequent level up, which was "ass" or "colossal." The girls particularly liked the football players, who they said had some great ass. The discussion moved on to why the girls coloured their hair, something I hadn't seen back in Chatham. The only explanation I got was they needed a change and that was quite a popular thing to do.

Just to illustrate how words are different here, I had an unexpected experience. I was telling my students how in New Jersey when it snowed we got someone to come and "plough" us out. The whole class suddenly burst into laughter when I said this. It transpired that in the urban dictionary, the term "ploughing someone out" was to have rough sex. Go figure! Another phrase I learned was "coochie cutters." These were apparently short pants that cut into the vulva.

After a few weeks, the honeymoon was over. A few students persisted in being chatty and disruptive so I moved them to the back of the class. I moved the engaged and motivated students like Brianna to the front of the classroom.

Then I asked them each to keep a budget for a week to see how they spent their money or their parent's money in most cases. Unlike New Jersey, where students got allowances, I saw none of that here. In fact, what I didn't expect to find was bullets on their budgets. This was a surprise; so was the fact that the local Walmart had bullets on sale in the middle of the aisle. Many of my students worked after school in jobs that my previous New Jersey kids wouldn't go near, places like fast food drive-throughs, kitchen help, and farm jobs early in the morning.

They also had jobs after school where they worked late, then came in the following day. John worked at washing dishes at the Blarney Stone Pub. Jenn and Caitlin worked the drive-through at Wendy's, and Sam had to get up every morning at 5 am on her parent's farm to feed all the animals. Some of the heftier kids worked as volunteer firefighters; it was cool when they had to excuse themselves from class to get to a fire.

These kids worked hard and weren't soft. Often they helped with bringing in income for the family so it was not an easy life for them. Seeing their way beyond the Eastern Shore was hard to contemplate for many. They couldn't see a way out and felt compelled to stay by their families and therefore stuck here. A guidance counsellor told me that those who made it into a four-year college often stayed only a semester and very few graduated. They couldn't keep to a schedule and missed the comforts, albeit rough, of home.

It was heavenly driving back across the causeway to the island after a stressful day. I turned on a local classical radio station and entered another world. Staring across an endless vista on either side of me while listening to some heavenly music allowed me to unwind. It was as if I was leaving on vacation every day to kick back on my own porch facing the bay. To relieve my stress I could take a quick sail anytime I wanted, as "Rhiannon" floated two minutes away in the Marina.

Quite early in my first year, a number of teachers were fired, some for quite unusual reasons. One got drunk after purchasing liquor on the way to school and storing it in her desk. She also had her students doing yoga on the floor in the dark that was inappropriate. Another teacher was led out in handcuffs, accused of robbing a local Dunkin Donuts. The psychology teacher threatened to commit suicide (apparently by jumping out a first-floor window), and left promptly. Perhaps the most shocking episode though was the teacher who apparently unbuttoned her blouse in class, revealing herself to the students. She then suggested a threesome with two of them. Nothing surprised me about what might happen at Arcadia.

On a more light-hearted and fun note, I was asked in October to participate in a school basketball game. The vice principal approached me in the hall and asked me to join the faculty team that played the students. Since I was tall, she assumed I knew the game and might be a great asset. Because it was my first year, I couldn't say no, and so entered into the spirit of the occasion.

My students got wind of it and were curious if I could play, so I simply piqued their interest by suggesting I had a surprise in store for them. Many didn't think I knew anything about basketball as I was used to UK sports, which were so night and day. For fun, I did some research on the NCAA and managed to find a player named Daniel Thomas, a star player for Kentucky around the same time I was twenty-two. On my computer, I pulled up his stats without a picture. I asked one of my students on the student varsity team to come up to my computer screen, and I casually showed him my fake stats. I impressed him and word quickly then spread around that I was an ex-NCAA all-star.

Soon the ill-fated day was upon me. The teachers kept me out for quite a bit of the game but the students on the benches started to call my name to go on the court. "We want Mister Thomas!" they shouted. I entered the play when we had a twelve-point lead. Maybe they knew what was coming because my contribution was a disaster. They threw me the ball early on but I froze near the basket with everyone shouting "Just shoot it!" A shorter player stole the ball, dribbled around me despite my size, and laid it up to take the basket. Before I knew it, we had conceded ten points and they pulled me out, complete with a tiny gash above my eye from an elbow and a very sore ego.

If only I had grown up here, I might have amounted to something. The following days I faced questions and comments from students and teachers like "what happened?" and "we expected more!" Some of my students told me they intended to train me up for the following year. I had brought this embarrassment on myself, but I enjoyed it, and I think it made me more approachable with the kids.

I continued with my revised classroom strategy that I would never have used in New Jersey. I put those who wanted to learn near the front and those who were disruptive near the back. I also only rewarded those who behaved. I taught to the interested kids and those who wanted to learn and pass. On some days, I commented to the kids concentrating up front that I heard some voices in the back but couldn't understand them. I handed worksheets to those at the back telling them that I didn't expect them to complete them. What I found out was that the uninterested kids suddenly didn't like sitting back where I ignored them, so they started to behave better. I guess one calls it reverse psychology, but there was a marked improvement in their behaviour as the semester moved along. I kept going with my instruction no matter how many disruptions I got and told the students in the back they could get copies of notes from their friends.

I had also assigned roles in my classroom to help with student engagement. I appointed one student as my tech person to fix anything that happened with the equipment and one to run errands down to the main office. The last role I specifically offered to the uninterested students in the back. They could select the music we listened to in class. Of course, I had to listen to it first to omit the profanity. All of a sudden, the uninterested students competed for this role, and I had them engaged. Jaquan headed up the music role. He was way too chatty, unfocused and not willing to do any work, but when it came to music he knew even 60s bands.

To pass my course I told my students they either joined the train to the destination or not. In other words, they had a choice to join the course or stay behind. I didn't have time to provide make-up work so the students had to be in class to progress with their grades.

When I tired of students hurling their wheeled chairs across my computer lab, I exchanged the comfortable swivelly ones for uncomfortable stationary metal chairs. Brianna liked my sadistic idea and enjoyed seeing everyone squirm on the uncomfortable metal ones. The students asked me why I replaced the chairs. I merely threw an imaginary student under the bus and told them that a student had fallen and cracked his head, so we had changed the chairs in case the district had a lawsuit on its hands. Brianna immediately chimed in, stating that it had been an awful accident with lots of blood.

The administration attempted to direct the students firmly, by yelling at them over the intercom to get into their classes on time, which I did not like, as I was sure plenty of yelling occurred at home. When they entered the building, I heard one administrator say, "Hoodies off or I'll have your A.S.S in I.S.S (the in-school suspension office). The administrators tried to get them into classrooms efficiently, but that was like trying to herd cats. The administrators told teachers to lock their doors on the second bell and send all those who turned up late to ISS. When that overflowed, students occupied another classroom. During the day I experienced numerous rude interruptions over the intercom. There was no polite etiquette announcing who was speaking, only an order blurted out over the intercom.

Most school days and often several times a day we heard the familiar words, "Please excuse the interruption". By limiting the amount of centralized invasive notices, it would make for a more learning-conducive environment and teachers could do their jobs.

At least there was no physical punishment. Here a student was sent to a separate room to work on extra assignments provided by their teacher. In my day, we had masters with canes in their hands waiting to exercise them, or in the case of my math teacher, a metal ruler that struck my knuckles at any point during the lesson.

Arcadia administrators did not proactively address bullying but ignored it until a fight occurred in school. They compounded the problem with favouritism, which was not lost on the students.

I had the more active and recalcitrant students in one block at the end of the day. Because they had required classes earlier, they all came together at the end. Trying to calm down a post-lunch class of students became quite a challenge.

After seven weeks, the constant need for student discipline (or lack of it) was really wearing on me. My end of day fourth block class had become disrespectful and annoying, but knowing I could retire back to my porch each day was something I looked forward to. No matter what the weather, every day I left the building to sit in my car in the parking lot for a 25-minute lunch. There I could enjoy the quiet sanctity of my car in peace, enjoy some fresh air, and have my own space to relax and regroup. It really helped me prepare for the crazy fourth block at the end of the day.

The uninspiring view from my car in the school parking lot

Occasionally I listened to some classical music on the radio or caught the news. In a daze, I gazed at the rundown homes in front of me through the front windscreen. On some days I asked myself, "Am I really here?" My classroom strategies had not worked that well, so I had to rethink my approach to create a better classroom.

I talked to Ms. Bell about her methods. She said, "I simply listen to Joel's advice on the radio. He's a minister, takes stories from the Bible, and relates them to how we live our lives today. Joel advises me to hold my tongue when I feel like cussing."

"One day the Lord didn't hold my tongue," she said, "And some unacceptable words came out of my mouth to a student. That day I forgot to listen to Joel on the way to work."

Just before Thanksgiving, parent conferences took place one evening from 5-7pm. I was optimistic that some might show up but I had more roaches in attendance than parents.

One section of my course covered housing, so I decided to ask my students where they thought was the best place to live on the Eastern Shore. They said Captain's Cove and Chincoteague. Their idea of the perfect house was a doublewide trailer where many were used to using only one bathroom. The black students said they didn't go over to Chincoteague because it was white, the taxes were high, and they didn't feel welcomed. I was surprised at the unofficial demarcation line that still existed on the mainland between the black and white communities. Brianna told me she lived in Atlantic and informed me about how divided things were. The community of Atlantic was mainly white but places like Parksley and Onancock had clear divides between the whites and blacks. Often one side of the street was white and the other black.

I liked that there was far less pretence here than among the kids from New Jersey. Students hadn't had much positive reinforcement, so when I gave them praise it seemed to mean more to them.

At last, the Christmas break arrived with much-needed relief. The teachers were exhausted and tired of trying to keep the kids focused. During the holiday I stayed on the island for the whole two weeks and didn't go anywhere. I needed to veg out after teaching nonstop without a real break for weeks.

It was brutally cold when we returned to school. My car's heating system was broken, so I wasn't able to escape to my car for lunch. This meant I was cooped up for the whole day in my windowless classroom, but at least it was warm. Many of my students told me they only had one room heated in their house. Some had burst pipes, and some had no heat at all. Given these conditions, many felt much safer and warmer in school. It also meant they received two meals a day—more than many received at home.

Early on I took the behaviour of the kids personally and allowed myself to get upset with my lack of control. Now that I was more relaxed and accepting of who they were, my classroom environment improved. I taught to the kids who wanted to learn and had come to terms with those who didn't care. It was not like me to leave kids behind, but I couldn't keep going back to encourage them when they refused to become engaged despite every method I had tried. They chose to fail, and it was a shame that I couldn't help them. I reminded them they were either on the train to the final destination or not. Some got off on the way and lingered in ISS (in-school suspension) or "the platform waiting room," as I referred to it. My course was not hard to pass, and it taught them valuable life skills. All the content was useful when they got out and started their own lives. It was a shame that some wasted this opportunity, but trying to force these "checked out" students to learn was not possible.

In early January I turned down a teaching job at Chincoteague High School on the island where I lived. It would have been an easy transfer and a five-minute commute. Some of my co-workers thought I was crazy, but they didn't know about the nature of the island school, which was stricter and less flexible for teachers, and that I had to teach keyboarding if I moved there. I felt committed to helping the Arcadia students, where I could have a more positive effect.

I asked the students if they wanted to review for a big test. None did, which surprised me. Was it because they didn't care, or were they so tired having gone through all the state required standards of learning? I did not ask why.

I felt sorry for the students, as they had no voice or privileges in school. Their time was rigorously controlled, and so was ours. We were constantly reminded over the intercom to sign in, told exactly how much time we had for lunch, and not to leave the campus during school. If we wanted to get coverage for our class to leave early for a field trip, we had to walk around the building and ask if any teachers were available, as the school secretary and principal offered no assistance. On one occasion, I needed coverage for one hour for my last class of the day. I couldn't get help, so I missed the field trip.

It was such a far cry from the respect and support teachers received at Chatham where the staff and seniors could leave the campus for a 45-minute lunch. Mind you, that culture of mutual respect and trust had taken years to create.

The fourth-block chaos started again. On thinking about why this occurred, I figured out three main reasons. First, the students came straight from lunch all sugared up. Second, they were more awake, and third, they were hyped up after socializing with their friends in the hallway. The students persisted in trying to get on their phones in class so I asked a few of them if they had heard about the new app "I don't look down at my crotch." They asked me what that was. I calmly reply, "You don't look down at your crotch at your age unless you are on your phone, so stay off it, because I know when you are on it."

In my classroom, Josh wound up Brianna to the point where she was ready to punch him. Luckily I had a huge student in class named Lucas who always volunteered to go over and scare Josh in a friendly way if he acted up. Lucas, who we referred to as Shrek, was a gigantic softie and didn't do any harm, but if he got up out of his chair, you knew to be quiet. "I got you, Mr. Thomas," Lucas would say.

I provided more structure for my fourth block class. I limited their free talk time and got them onto worksheets and "do-now's" immediately when they entered my classroom. This improved things quite a bit.

The students noticed my tall metal stool, the seat signed with a few signatures. They asked if they could sign it as well and write a message. I said that one student who in my opinion had contributed the most to my class would be able to do so at the end of the year.

The days thankfully became warm enough for visits to my car, where I rolled down the window, listened to classical music, and relaxed for a short while during my short lunch break.

I came up for air again when I escaped outside for lunch. Swallows had arrived and dove close to my head as I stepped out of school. They had mud in their beaks and were building a nest-cup above the teacher entrance door. The fresh wet mud was darker around the nest rim and was a reminder of a contrasting world that lay outside the school walls and a welcome distraction from all the craziness inside. A world that we were ready to embrace as the school year wound down.

31

A DISTINCTIVE WORLD

A Typical Rundown Trailer

I don't why it had taken me a few months to realize more than ever that I lived in two contrasting worlds: school and the island. Maybe it was because the weather was now much warmer, the marsh was colourful, and the stark difference between my two worlds was more noticeable. Fourteen miles of roadway, including the four-and-a-half mile causeway, separated my daily back and forth routine. Each day as I drove to school I traveled from one world to the other. I started the day with bright sunshine on a beautiful spring morning. As soon as I left the island on the raised part of the causeway, the classical radio station I listened to became clearer; a beautiful Mozart concerto played while I cruised along in my peaceful trance viewing the ducks and seagulls going about their business in the channels below. I looked to my right and saw the elegantly dressed Black-necked Stilts feeding in the shallow pools. I noticed everything as I drove over the causeway, with its vast drum flat surface stretching out on both sides of the car, where glasslike pools dotted the landscape amongst the spartina grasses, reflecting the pale cerulean skies above. I noticed the white gantry towers of the Wallops Island Flight Facility looming in the distance. Sometimes I saw a lone waterman aboard his Skiff[39], dressed in bright yellow oilskins. The sun picked him out and his bright white boat against a cobalt blue backdrop. It was a perfect scene for a watercolour with great contrasting colours. Four inches of bright green shoots slowly emerged from the bases of the marsh grasses. The scouring of fiddler crabs agitated the dark mud below. The Laughing Gull colony was busy claiming their places for the breeding season. Snowy Egrets were sprinkled everywhere like miniature blobs of white meringue that had been piped along the channels. Every day I scanned the Wallops fence for the odd Meadow Lark or Kestrel. One morning a single, enormous wild turkey flew against the Wallops fence, running alongside the traffic in some distress.

I made a left turn towards Atlantic. I drove through open countryside with assorted barns and outbuildings where corn was beginning to grow in the fields around them. I passed one of the trailers that had always had some colourful whirligigs outside, and noticed it, too, was now devoid of life; it sat, empty, dark and foreboding. A misshaped and broken water heater was hanging precariously through one of its windows. Once again I wondered what had happened to this family. It should not have bothered me since it was commonplace for the trailer landscape to alter, as I had witnessed it many times. At least everything was perfect with my world as I began my final day with the students.

---

[39]   A shallow, flat-bottomed open boat.

As I turned the corner in Atlantic to head for the school I glanced to my right into a wheat field. Perched on a stalk close to the road the brilliant blue of an Indigo Bunting caught in the morning sun and perfectly positioned against the golden hues of the wheat field. I passed the rustic Marshall Manufacturing Plant, which made crab pots and other animal traps, then out across open farmland again, where the road passed some well-kept single-family homes set back on their beautifully landscaped properties. Two homeowners proudly flew their Confederate flags, the subject of much controversy.

The scenery then started to go downhill, as the landscape became more wooded and dotted with damp algae-ridden buildings that had seen better days. Perfectly cut lawns with manicured flower borders gave way to overgrown yards with a mishmash of broken machinery strewn around outside. I passed a decaying oyster packing business off to my left with its abandoned and overgrown loading bays; an abandoned black and white crooked house stood precariously nearby, sinking into the landscape around it at odd angles. The remnants of a recent house fire stood out, the family now living in a trailer alongside the burnt-out house; then came the smouldering smoke of another house fire with the blackened chimney stacks all that remained. I couldn't help wonder why so many house fires occurred in the area. Was it carelessness or something more sinister?

Then I passed a small house surrounded by rusted tractors and other farm machinery lying around the yard. It was odd to see a sparkling Cadillac parked on the grass outside, and then past another grand substantial house abandoned out in the open that could have housed a massive family at one time. I was sure it held many memories, although, for some reason, I had a sense they weren't all joyous ones. I saw a forensic team with white gloves at that house one afternoon taking away samples, which made me think something untoward had happened. On the rickety brick chimneys perched a few bedraggled, motionless

Turkey Vultures; gaudy black adornments added a haunted look to the place.

Then I drove past a few trailers and one, in particular, I always noticed. It was a pitiful sight. The yellow paint was peeling off it and brown rags hung as flimsy curtains in the massive end window. A rusty bent TV aerial was hanging precariously off the side of the roof. The entrance door had a hole in the bottom section and numerous scrawny cats waited for food outside.

Blackened oil drums still had a pall of smoke coming out of them and wet clothing still hung on the washing line from a few days back. The drab clothing spoke of poverty. In fact, it seemed there was more stuff outside the trailer than maybe in it. A washing machine lay on its side, some bikes were strewn along the muddy drive, and various potted plants and defunct pieces of machinery lay helter-skelter around the property. The family who lived there had not been at home for a while, as I hadn't seen their rusted minivan parked outside. When home, they often waved at me most days as I drove past. I wondered what had happened to them. Poverty preserves nothing.

It seemed that houses I passed like this during the school year suddenly seemed abandoned. In the period of one year, I had seen so much dereliction, with no signs of life around houses, the outside world beginning to grow over them. I wondered what happened to these families. Where did they go and what misfortune had taken place?

Some days outside another home, an emaciated man sat in a cheap torn deck chair on the front porch of a run-down trailer with ripped filthy curtains. His car, like many, lay rusted with flat tires behind the trailer. Sometimes I noticed what looked like a drivable car in front of a house but parked in the same place for months, and I wondered if someone ever used it.

Modern satellite dishes dominated roofs that could hardly support them, yet so important to those inside, a link to the outside world with lifestyles they maybe yearned for through their sixty-inch TV screens. Some had a Pit Bull Terrier for protection tethered on a leash close to a dog hut, a poor man's alarm system.

How people lived in these places, I didn't know. Many trailers had tarps for roofs that looked ready to collapse. Others had dilapidated weathered wooden siding covered in green algae that was falling off the building. Cracks appeared everywhere especially near the ground where animals and the cold could get in.

Some homes looked abandoned with no sign of life except a beautiful patch of flowers blooming in the shade, where once a human hand had planted them with care. I thought it ironic that someone had taken the trouble to conceal an oil tank with an attractive fence yet their house was a complete wreck.

A tall thin man with sharp white eyes that stood out against his mournful face, born of hardship, became a common sight most days walking alongside the road. He always carried a short metal pole that he slowly twirled. I sensed he used it for protection. He always gave me a friendly wave as I drove past him.

Another time I saw a hefty, frail, aged woman teetering unsteadily, struggling to hold her walker outside her home. Her rusted-up car protruded out of a bush in the back.

Some of the school homebound teachers told me they had to step over holes in the entranceway floors of the trailers they visited. Once inside, however, they found the latest TVs and gadgets, which were far more important than fixing a gaping hole in the floor.

I felt like I had driven through a third world country just before I crossed the highway and came to the school.

I paused to cross over Route 13 while the traffic passed. The passing trucks were stacked with chicken cages in neat tall blocks and chickens sandwiched into cramped wire cages for their brief ride to the killing plant. Cream feathers flew out of the back as they whizzed by. Many chickens lay dead already with their necks hanging bedraggled from the cages. The trucks headed south were always full, whereas the ones coming back were empty save a few leftover feathers flying out of the backs along the highway.

Entering the school parking lot was like entering another world. Before I parked, I had to remember which cars the smokers owned so I could park my car away from them as they sometimes ventured out for lunch later at the same time as me. I parked in my familiar spot facing out towards an assortment of ramshackle homes where later I would eat my lunch. For a moment I paused in my car listening to the first part of Handel's Water Music and thought about the diverse worlds I had come from. First from the UK to the busy tri-state area up north, then to the very divergent culture of Chincoteague, and now over the causeway to a very distinctive world altogether.

I left my car, punched in my code to enter the school, and immediately breathed in the musty stale air trapped inside. I made my way to my inner windowless bunker to be bathed once again by the pallid blue glow from numerous computer screens and start my day.

On May 27th the dreaded SOL (standards of learning) exam period started again, so it was back to classes half full for 13 days, constant room changes, and general interruptions to the usual routine. On June 1st Ms. Bell warned me about what she termed the "ghetto" graduation I was about to witness. Ms. Bell said parents acted out of control and wouldn't wear appropriate clothing to the event. She wasn't wrong, but it wasn't as awful as I had imagined and was a short ceremony at least. Unfortunately, there was no inspirational guest speaker, and no "chicken house fans," as Ms. Bell called them, to keep us cool.

On June 2nd I came back into school after lunch in my car and gazed up at the abandoned swallow's nest above the entranceway. Even the birds had given up nesting there. Maybe they knew what it was like at Arcadia and had moved on. I focused on those students who had been pleasant and appreciative of what I had done. I reminded myself that life had already dealt these kids a set of rough cards. No matter how much I tried to point them in a positive direction and give them the tools to be successful, they often had tougher battles to face. I had tried to open their eyes to a larger world and to dream big. I had shared stories from my own life when I left home for London. These students owed it to themselves to move away from the Eastern Shore for a while at least and see the world. I would be pleased to hear in future years that some did this.

I looked forward to the end of the school year and pondered how I was going to enjoy the summer. I looked forward to sailing Rhiannon out in the bay as opposed to being stuck in a stuffy classroom with teenagers. My mind wandered back to that incredible sensation I used to have as a child when I flew from school in England back home to Germany to enjoy the holidays. I re-lived the enormous sense of release and freedom when I used to depart the straightjacket system of the boarding school.

On the last day of school, I brought a special item to show my students that I hoped might make them think. It was a trusted friend from my childhood, something that I too had carried to every place that I had lived, just like the brown suitcase my mother had hauled around during her life. I took a large cardboard box into my classroom and placed it on the front desk. The students were curious and immediately asked if I had brought them food. Towards the end of the lesson, I opened the top of the box and pulled out my antiquated tuckbox from school when I was eight. The students stopped talking and waited for me to say something.

"Does anyone know what this box is?" I asked.

"Are those your initials on the top, Mister?" one asked.

"Yes, they are."

"Why do you have four initials? Are you fancy or something?" asked another.

"It's a long story."

"What's in the box, then?"

I started to tell my story. "Well, when I was a child my school allowed me to bring this 'tuckbox' as it was called to keep all my prized possessions in. It was the only safe place we each had to store special belongings. It had to be a certain size so it could fit under our desks. Similar to the ones you may have seen in the Harry Potter movies, right? This is a "tuckbox" because "tuck" is another name for sweets or candy. It often contained special candies and foods we brought from home.

"Some students brought a photo of their parents to remind them of home since we were boarders. In my case, my parents lived overseas so I hardly saw them from the age of 8 to 18. Everything else you owned could be scrutinized by the teachers or taken by anyone else. Only the tuck box was private. I had a lock on the outside, and only I kept the key. Every time I open the lid I can still smell my old school inside and it takes me back there."

I then gently opened the lid a crack.

"Does anyone want to smell inside?"

"Sure," said Josh at the back of the room.

He swaggered up to my desk and when I raised the lid, he gingerly lowered his nose and sniffed inside. Josh jokingly said, "It smells like something has died in there, Mr. Thomas."

I then turned to the students very solemnly and said, "Here's my message to you all today: You are tuck boxes yourselves; whereby you keep everything inside of you. Many of you have emotional walls you have created to keep the outside world out. Sometimes I see pain concealed within you, and I see it in class in the way you act out. I encourage you not to live in the box provided, which is the Eastern Shore. Break out and explore who you are; find out what you like doing. Your own security will come from understanding yourself.

"Don't depend on others for your income and don't feel trapped by others who want to keep you here. Also, don't depend on family to be there for you and give you praise. Just because you share chromosomes doesn't mean they will always be there for you. Your friends might be the best thing in your life and praise you more.

"Remember that video I showed you at the beginning of the year "Knock Knock?" It discussed that you are not your mums' and dads' choices. You have to live your own life and not one dictated by someone else. I know you feel pressured to stay here on the Eastern Shore, but you owe it to yourselves to leave and explore what is out there.

This show-and-tell brought me full circle and allowed me to confront my own demons from my former school days. My worries about becoming a hypochondriac and my homesickness were nothing compared to what these students had to endure, as I fortunately never grew up in poverty. These kids' very lives were turned upside down. They had far more to cope with than I had ever had. They also had very few people to provide support for them and very few role models.

Two things happened before the class finished on that last day. I asked Jaquan to sign my stool, not one of the A students sitting in the front. Jaquan had shown me the most improvement in class and passed the course. He had changed from a disrespectful, belligerent annoyance into a student who didn't shout out as much, used appropriate language at least to me, and was far more respectful. He was my project, and it had worked.

Curiously, the battery in my classroom wall clock died after he signed the stool. I guessed it knew it was time for the crazy school year to finish. It had been a year with insufficient to no disciplinary consequences from what happened in my class, poor school communication, and constant classroom interruptions. It was a wonder I had been able to accomplish anything, but I had found a few diamonds in the rough, students I had liked and been able to help. That is what made it all worthwhile.

On two occasions, I had students come to me asking for personal advice on words they had written to someone special. One student shared his love letter with me and asked if it read well. Another shared a poem he had written about his relationship with his mother. I was touched that these students chose me with whom to share their personal words. Somehow they knew I cared. Maybe I appeared to be curious about their lives. If I could change a few lives, then my efforts made me feel valued.

The students asked me if I was coming back. I guessed they saw many teachers not return or leave during the year, as we had seen this school year. The students got used to the upheavals, which was a shame. I asked them if they wanted me to return, and they said yes.

When the final bell sounded at the end of the day, the teachers had to escort their students out to the buses or "yellow limos," as some referred to them. Rumours of a fight brought a heavy police presence. The principal and Ms. Williams waved to each bus as it left. Ms. Williams, I was told later, used a few choice words under her breath as she waved. In my head, I was singing the words to a well-known British naval song, "Spanish Ladies." It was a song about bidding farewell and not seeing someone again. I thought of the last moments that Robert Shaw sang that tune on his doomed boat Orca in the class movie "Jaws".

For me, it was my "goodbye to the students" song. As we teachers strolled back into the building afterwards, the only words I could hear around me from other teachers were, "Thank God!" I felt the same and was very glad to drive away at the end of the day. According to English speakers, Arcadian can mean "idyllically pastoral" or "idyllically innocent, simple, or untroubled." O the irony ...

I closed the school year and jumped out of the fire to paint and enjoy my summer on the island.

EPILOGUE

I have accepted that the many painful things that happened to me were for a reason. Losing my rifle on Salisbury Plain and losing my teaching job in New Jersey each pointed me in new directions. Had I pursued a career in the army I would have led a very prescribed life and never explored my creative talents.

How I faced up to my setbacks has made me a better person. My insecurities as a growing boy have allowed me to recognize those same weaknesses in some of my high school students. I wish more people believed in them. I share their pain, having experienced similar loss of family and relationship issues. My students' lack of confidence reminds me of myself and how important it was for me to know that one teacher, Mr. Tideswell, saw something in me when I was young. Maybe some of these students will remember me as someone who helped them along the way.

Unbeknownst to me, I have been trying to solve a puzzle for sixty years. The puzzle pieces I have explored are the army, art, boats, birds, and teaching. I have examined each piece closely to see if it fit into who I was becoming. All along I didn't know what my final picture looked like. The army piece never fitted in, even though it was the first piece I was born into and started with. The art, birds, and boat pieces I always carried with me, but I didn't know in what landscape they belonged. My move to Chincoteague has brought clarity of vision whereby the pieces all finally fit.

This Come'ere has become more accepted and more comfortable in his American phase of life. I have joined a community, gained some recognition, and have a sense of belonging. I am very lucky to have Debbie in my life, and now we have a real home together, not simply a place that I live in, like so many times before. I am no longer torn from school to school, and from army posting to army posting. I live on an island that offers many activities I enjoy.

I don't yearn for the busy city life from my past, as I can always dip in when I wish and travel back to Europe. Sometimes we need to take a drive off the island to Norfolk or New Jersey, to experience more sophistication in a more cosmopolitan atmosphere. When Debbie and I leave the island, it reminds us that there is an enormous world out there, with a lot more going on, some great stuff, and some not so wonderful. It's very noisy and busy though, so after a while, it's a joy to come back to the slower pace of life on the island.

I belong on Chincoteague but I will always remember with nostalgia the culture I came from. Around the winter holidays, I miss the rugby, the Welsh mountains, and a great-tasting cup of tea. I suffer what Welsh people call a bit of '*hiraeth*,' which means "longing" in Welsh, longing for the places and people of the past, like taking a scenic ride on the Ffestiniog railway for which my grandmother gave me a life membership. Despite its dreary cold and damp weather, there is a pull from North Wales. It's primeval, raw, and barren, where life is more evenly paced. When there, I am bathed in the simple comforts that surround me, the friendly banter of ladies at the Copper Kettle restaurant, the warmth from the radiator in the spare room, a good pint, and the cosy atmosphere sitting by the fire in the Queens Head pub.

I also miss the British sense of humour and a more orderly way of doing things. There is a quirky thing about our sense of humour. We seem to connect with each other on another level instantly when we talk. We all grew up on comedy with the "Carry on Movies," "Only Fools and Horses," and "Benny Hill," so maybe that's why we all connect so quickly. It's our therapy for enduring such lousy weather and imperfect health-care. Perhaps it helped us get through two world wars as well, but one thing I know for sure, a back-breaking laugh makes all the difference to the day.

Chincoteague is another shore far removed from the shore I know as Borth-y-Gest back in Wales, yet they are similar in many ways. Both places have the constant rhythm of life played out by the daily tides and setting sun and are in constant touch with nature and the changing seasons.

I think back to my very early days when I first saw the boats down in the compact cove of Borth-y-Gest. Maybe something inside of me knew I was going to live by the sea one day.

Opting out of a stressful life takes courage. One has to believe in oneself and take a risk. I advise people not to wait until it's too late.

Debbie and I laughed at a recent obituary in the paper, which read: "Charlie died from complications from a life well-lived." It sums up all that is important about living. As Hunter S. Thompson wrote, *"Remember, life's journey is not to quietly go to the grave in a well-preserved body, but to skid in sideways screaming "holy shit, what a ride".*

My father used to say his version of the traditional blessing at the end of every church service. The times I heard it were so numerous that I can't forget it. There was one word in it that meant a lot to me, and that was courage. He said this to his parishioners:

"Go out into the world in peace and be of good courage, be of good cheer and hold onto everything that is good in life."

This is the 60th year of my journey and this year I finally took a trip to Malta to visit Big Dan's grave. I have always wanted to do this. On the way back I visited my father's grave in Sherfield-on-Loddon. I said a few words to each of them and told them about this book. I asked them if they had met each other and what do they think of me now. The process of writing my book has helped me understand both dads even though I have mostly been "dadless" throughout my journey. It is my wish that others in similar circumstances find the courage to work through life and make the best of life's curve balls.

The need to summon courage is often unpredicted in our daily lives. It tests our ability to cope and have self-belief. It is a shame that neither of my parents is around to see what I have achieved. If my father were alive today he would see that I have heeded his words and have taken plenty of risks and faced plenty of challenges to lead a more complete and contented life. Somehow I sense both my parents and Big Dan know that I have done okay.

WORDS OF GRATITUDE

I would like to thank the following people who gave so generously of their time in helping me create this memoir: Jon and Jane Richstein, Gwyn English Nielsen, Diane Minor, Graham & Wendy Argent-Belcher, Ennis Barbery, Jacki Reich, Hilary Ward Dorer, Hallie Moore.

Also to my wonderful editor, Donna Mosher, who worked tirelessly with me to craft and shape my story for publication. I can't thank you enough for your caring, well-considered critiques and suggestions for improvement.

Most of all I would like to acknowledge the incredible patience and support given to me by Deborah Hennel, without which this memoir would not have been possible.

BRITISH GLOSSARY

A Frame: A basic structure designed to bear the load of raising a mast using a pulley system.

Ballpoint Pen: A pen that dispenses ink over a metal ball at its point, i.e. over a "ballpoint". Also known as a biro, *ball pen*.

Bedstick: A wooden flat stick used to measure blankets so they are folded to the same width.

Bed block: A stack of blankets and sheets organized in an orderly manner so they are all the same height and width.

Bedsit: A one-room apartment typically consisting of a combined bedroom and sitting room with cooking facilities.

Bin: A garbage holder.

Binmen: A service that comes to people's houses to collect their garbage.

Birdcage Walk: A street in the City of Westminster in *London*.

Bonnet: The hinged cover over the engine of motor vehicles that allows access to the engine compartment.

Brogues: A style of low-heeled shoe characterised by multiple-piece, sturdy leather uppers with decorative perforations or "broguing."

Car Boot Sale: The selling of items from a car's boot. A form of market in which private individuals come together to sell household and garden goods.

Capacitor: Capacitors are widely used as parts of electrical circuits in many common electrical devices.

Caravan: A vehicle equipped for living in, typically towed by a car and used for vacations.

Char: Arctic char is a cold-water fish in the family Salmonidae, native to alpine lakes and arctic and subarctic coastal waters.

Chicken à la King: A dish consisting of diced chicken in a cream sauce, and often with sherry, mushrooms, and vegetables, served over rice, pasta, or bread.

Chips: Fries

Crass: Lacking sensitivity, refinement, or intelligence.

Cross: You are angry or upset with someone.

Currywurst: A dish of German origin consisting of steamed, then fried pork sausage typically cut into slices and seasoned with curry ketchup, a sauce based on spiced ketchup or tomato paste.

Divot: A piece of turf cut out of the ground by a polo club in making a stroke.

Exeat: The Latin word *exeat* ("he/she may leave") used to describe a period of absence from a boarding school.

Fag: Younger students in boarding schools were required to act as personal servants to the most senior boys.

Fete: These are usually outdoor shows held on village greens or recreation grounds with a variety of activities.

Flat: Apartment

Flashers: Hazard lights activated when a driver pushes the hazard light button/switch. The lights warn other drivers of an emergency situation.

Forfeit: A penalty for the breach of the rules in a club or game.

Genoa: A type of large jib or staysail that overlaps the mainsail.

Giclée: A fine art digital printing process combining pigment based inks with high-quality archival quality paper to achieve giclée prints.

Gobsmacked: Utterly astonished; astounded.

Goose winged: The position of sails in a rigged sailboat, in which the mainsail is set to the leeward and the jib to the windward.

Gutted: cause (someone) to feel extremely upset or disappointed.

Gyratory: A road junction or traffic system requiring the circular movement of traffic.

High Street: The main street of a town, especially as the traditional site for most stores, banks, and other businesses.

Household Division: This comprises seven regiments, five foot guards, and two mounted cavalry.

Housing estate: A group of homes and other buildings built together as a single development.

Husky: A padded sleeveless lightweight jacket

Jodhpurs: full-length trousers, worn for horseback riding, that are close fitting below the knee and have reinforced patches on the inside of the leg.

Jumper: Sweater

Kissing Gate: A type of gate, which allows people to pass through, but not livestock.

Kook: A crazy or eccentric person (US)

Lackey: Someone who does menial tasks or runs errands for another like a servant

Main Sail: *A mainsail* is a sail located behind the main mast of a sailing vessel.

MOT: The US DMV inspection sticker equivalent test.

Naff: British slang *meaning* uncool, tacky, unfashionable, worthless.

Nutters: A crazy or eccentric person (UK)

Officer's Mess: A place where military personnel socialize, eat, and (in some cases) live.

Plaid: A chequered or tartan twilled cloth, typically made of wool worn over the shoulder as part of Scottish Highland dress.

Pickfords: One of the UK's oldest functioning moving companies.

Pintles: One of the pins (on the forward edge of a rudder) that fit into the gudgeons and so suspend the rudder on a sailboat.

Plein Air: The act of painting outdoors, where a painter reproduces the actual visual conditions seen at the time of the painting.

Public school: An older, student selective and expensive fee-paying independent secondary school, which caters primarily to children aged between 11 and 18.

Prefect: Prefects have various responsibilities, which essentially involve them in assisting in the smooth running of the school. School prefects are responsible at all times for the good conduct of all members of the student body.

Prep: Study time at boarding school.

Ring road: A road or a series of connected roads encircling a town or city.

Rubber: Eraser

Rupert: An Officer that is upper-middle class or above, and may have a total lack of skill or common sense.

Sellotape: Scotch tape (US)

Skiff: A shallow, flat-bottomed open boat with sharp bow and square stern.

Snog: An act or spell of amorous kissing and caressing.

Soppy: Lacking spirit and common sense; feeble.

Stick: To give someone some stick is to criticise or punish.

Stickleback: The first small 'tiddler' fish caught by many school children. It is a tiny, beautifully streamlined, torpedo-shaped fish, with a broad tail fin.

Stile: An arrangement of steps that allows people but not animals to climb over a fence or wall.

Ta-ra: Means Goodbye.

Tab: A loaded march (a relatively fast march over distance carrying a load) known as a forced foot march in the US Army. Less formally, it is a ruck march in the US Army or a tab in the British Army.

Torch: Flashlight

Tuck: Candy or sweets in Britain

Turnovers: Socks folded over at the top.

Tube: Otherwise known as the London Underground system. A public rapid transit system serving Greater London.

Windscreen: Windshield

NOTES

For the love of roundabouts, caravans, and trainspotting

Remembering the lovely final roundabout on my third test, it might interest the reader to know that only in Britain can one find a roundabout appreciation society. The society states that roundabouts counteract a road's unsightliness. They state, "due to infinite variety, colour, and creativeness, these bitumen babes lift our sagging spirits on long tiresome trips. The roundabout is truly an oasis on a sea of tarmac." Indeed, on road systems anywhere in the world, there is nothing more expressive than the one-way gyratory which is another word for a roundabout.

You can put anything on a gyratory, the public have seen – statues, fountains, monuments, war memorials, gardens, topiaries, sculptures, laser & light shows, ship's anchors, canal locks, winged horses, pubs, cinemas, clocks, churches, shrines, duck ponds, and many other objects. You name it, anything goes on a roundabout, and this is what makes them so special.

Indeed, the notion that we supposedly have an English "driving decorum" doesn't seem correct, as most places are clogged with frustrated drivers these days, and one more round-about is yet another interruption on our way somewhere. We are so quintessentially English in the manner in which we all navigate and sail around these verdant islands.

The A5 road where one crossed the border from England into Wales was notorious for multiple roundabouts. Unlike robotic traffic lights that tell us to stop and go, the roundabout allows us to show one another our very own English driving decorum. We are supposed to approach the island at our own chosen speed, in the lane of our choice. We are then supposed to cooperate and queue accordingly with our fellow drivers. We wait for a gap and join the gentle flow in our own time, signalling our intentions and leaving at our chosen exit. The Appreciation Society states, "Never is a road system better suited to the English consciousness than one that involves a set of rules and guidelines."

The Society explains what these days seems very rare to me: an orderly queue of well-mannered motorists all cooperating together with etiquette and protocol to get around the system. Most times, manic drivers beeping at you from all sides to get on with it shunt us onto a roundabout.

When I lived in the UK, being stuck behind a caravan on a meager Welsh road occurred to me several times. Why do the British love caravans so much? Bart Day, head of marketing for Bailey of Bristol, which is one of Europe's biggest *caravan* manufacturers, sums it up pretty well:

> "It is partly the British belief that we're all explorers; being able to do what we want, when we want", as well as a fondness for owning our "castle", even if it is on wheels.

> "It is the freedom to move on that has proved to be the main attraction. You can park it wherever you want, and wherever you wake up, it is somewhere completely different. In addition, if you do not like it you can move on. It's all about the adventure."

Percy, Dad's friend who died at the train station, was a train spotter, a hobby enjoyed by a minority whose interest is the recording of locomotives. The number of train spotters has declined markedly from its heyday, when it peaked at around 100,000, with the most popular locations in the country being in Clapham, London, and York stations; this number is miniscule compared to the number of rail buffs in America. Train-spotters have a reputation as "geeks." Some refer to them as "Anoraks," people who have a very strong interest, perhaps obsessive, in niche subjects. One often gets an instant look of disgust on the majority of people´s faces when you proudly admit that you are a train spotter.

Source: http://www.tripbase.com/c/trainspotting/

CPSIA information can be obtained
at www.ICGtesting.com
Printed in the USA
FSHW020004140719
59843FS